PERSONAL RELIGION AND SPIRITUAL HEALING

SUNY series in Western Esoteric Traditions
David Appelbaum, editor

Personal Religion and Spiritual Healing

The Panacea Society in the Twentieth Century

Alastair Lockhart

Cover art: Leonora Simpson, "Weave VII," photographic image of linen with water stain.

Published by State University of New York Press, Albany

© 2019 Alastair Lockhart

All rights reserved

No part of this book may be used or reproduced in any manner whatsoever without written permission. No part of this book may be stored in a retrieval system or transmitted in any form or by any means including electronic, electrostatic, magnetic tape, mechanical, photocopying, recording, or otherwise without the prior permission in writing of the publisher.

For information, contact State University of New York Press, Albany, NY
www.sunypress.edu

Library of Congress Cataloging-in-Publication Data

Names: Lockhart, Alastair, author.
Title: Personal religion and spiritual healing : the Panacea Society in the twentieth century / Alastair Lockhart.
Description: Albany : State University of New York, 2019. | Series: SUNY series in western esoteric traditions | Includes bibliographical references and index.
Identifiers: LCCN 2018012737| ISBN 9781438472850 (hardcover) |
  ISBN 9781438472867 (pbk.) | ISBN 9781438472874 (e-book)
Subjects: LCSH: Bedford (England) —Church history —20th century. | Panacea Society. | Women and religion —England —Bedford —History —20th century. | Christian communities —England —Bedford —History —20th century.
Classification: LCC BR763.B38 L63 2019 | DDC 267/.43 —dc23 LC record available at https://lccn.loc.gov/2018012737

10 9 8 7 6 5 4 3 2 1

To the memory of
RUTH KLEIN (1932–2012)
The "last" Panacean

CONTENTS

List of Illustrations, ix

Acknowledgments, xi

Introduction. The Panacea Society and the Study of Religion, xv

Chapter One. The Panacea Society's Healing, 1

Chapter Two. Sources of the Healing, 15

Chapter Three. Understanding Religion, 31

Chapter Four. The Healing and Other Movements I: Great Britain, 51

Chapter Five. The Healing and Other Movements II: The United States, Jamaica, and Finland, 63

Chapter Six. War and Anxiety, 83

Chapter Seven. Religious Language and Metaphysics, 99

Chapter Eight. Theories of Transcendence, 121

Postscript. The End of the Healing, 133

Appendices, 135

Notes, 141

Bibliography, 171

Index, 185

ILLUSTRATIONS

Table 1.1. Ten largest countries by number of applicants to the Panacea Society Healing (1924–1998),   12

Chart 3.1. Panacea Society Healing, global application numbers over time,   45

Table 3.1. Average duration of contact, number of letters written, and letters per year for index card sample of Panacea Society Healing users, analyzed by decade of initial application, for all countries. (Excludes applicants writing no letters after initial contact),   46

Table 3.2. Average duration of contact, number of letters written, and letters per year for index card sample of Panacea Society Healing users applying from England, analyzed by decade of initial application. (Excludes applicants writing no letters after initial contact),   46

Table 3.3. Average duration of contact, number of letters written, and letters per year for index card sample of Panacea Society Healing users applying from Jamaica, analyzed by decade of initial application. (No records for 1924–1933. Excludes applicants writing no letters after initial contact),   47

Table 3.4. Average duration of contact, number of letters written, and letters per year for index card sample of Panacea Society Healing users, analyzed by gender. (Excludes applicants writing no letters after initial contact),   48

Table 6.1. Percentage of applicants writing no letters, one letter, or two or more letters for a sample of Panacea Society Healing users after applying from British addresses, analyzed by period (prewar, wartime, and postwar) of initial application,   88

Table 6.2. Average duration of contact, number of letters written, and letters per year for a sample of Panacea Society Healing users applying from British addresses, analyzed by period (prewar, wartime, and postwar) of initial application. (Excludes applicants writing no letters after initial contact), 89

Chart 6.1. Annual number of British Isles, Jamaica, and USA Panacea Society Healing applications, 1924–1978, 90

Table A.1. Alphabetical list of countries/territories showing year of first registered application received in Bedford and total number of known applications, 135

Table A.2. Total number of applications by year, 1924–1998, 140

ACKNOWLEDGMENTS

The funding for this research was provided by the Panacea Charitable Trust. I am incredibly grateful to the Trust for its support and generosity in providing access to its unique archive. As a postdoctoral researcher in the Faculty of Divinity at the University of Cambridge in 2010, I had the good fortune to be included as a member of a project entitled Spiritual Healing in Modern Context, led by Dr. Fraser Watts. The Modern Context Project was designed to examine the Panacea Society's archive of twentieth-century documents related to its healing and to develop our understanding of the nature of modern religion using the sources available there. I had the privilege then of spending several years studying the Society's healing letters—many of which were seeing the light of day for the first time since they had been neatly packed away nearly a hundred years earlier. Dr. Watts had been my Ph.D. supervisor at Cambridge, and, as a member of his team on the Modern Context Project, I continued to have the benefit of his enormous experience and insight. Many others contributed to the project as it progressed. I would like to record my gratitude to Samuli Siikavirta and Anna Porko, who provided working translations of a number of passages of Finnish prose on which my English quotations are based; to Kelly Stock and Nicola Swinburn for their assistance in the archive; and to Hazel Bird at Wordstich Editorial for her help proofing the manuscript.

    A book of this nature depends to a very large extent on the archival sources on which it is able to draw. In having access to the Panacea Society's archives, I have been able to work from a remarkable and unique collection of materials. The credit for uncovering the Panacea Society's archive and making it available to academic study goes to Dr. Jane Shaw at the University of Oxford. Following her discovery of the archive in 2001, Dr. Shaw convened the Oxford Prophecy Project with Professor Christopher Rowland—also based at Oxford—in 2003. The Prophecy Project initiated the process of opening up the Panacea Society and its extraordinary archive. Thanks to the archival work of Dr. Philip Lockley[1] and Dr. Shaw's *Octavia, Daughter of*

God: The Story of a Female Messiah and Her Followers (2011), which emerged from Dr. Shaw's own work on the Society, the project that formed the basis of this book could build on a firm base in getting to grips with the archive—and with the Society's healing in particular. On a day-to-day basis, much of the Trust's activities are overseen by Mr. David McLynn. I am most grateful for his help and support as the project developed.

This book brings together a number of strands of research centered on the Panacea Society archive's Healing Collection. Some elements have been previously presented, including in the following publications: "Heterodox Healing and Alternative Religion in the 20th Century: An English Spiritual Healing Practice in Finland," published in the *Yearbook of the Finnish Society of Church History for 2013 (Suomen kirkkohistoriallisen seuran vuosikirja 2013)*—especially for the discussion of Finland in chapter 5. "Religious and Spiritual Mobility in Britain: The Panacea Society and Other Movements in the Twentieth Century," in *Contemporary British History* 29 no. 2, published in 2015 by Taylor and Francis—especially for parts of the discussion in chapters 4 and 7. "A Southcottian Healing Panacea, 1924–2012," in *The History of a Modern Millennial Movement: The Southcottians*, edited by J. Shaw and P. Lockley and published by I. B. Tauris in 2017—especially for parts of the discussion in chapters 1, 5, and 7.

In addition, I have presented elements of this research at several conferences, which have been helpful in testing and refining my approach to the project. I am grateful to have had the opportunity to present papers at the "Healing and Curing Medieval to Modern" conference at the University of Glasgow in August 2012; the Modern British History "Society, Culture, Politics and Religion" conference at the University of Edinburgh in June 2013; the Annual Meeting of the American Academy of Religion in November 2014 (two papers); and the International Network for the Study of War and Religion at the Modern World Annual Conference in July 2015.

Within the University of Cambridge, the Faculty of Divinity, Hughes Hall, and the University Library—not to mention the multitude of smaller libraries in Cambridge and elsewhere—have provided me with resources and contexts for an infinity of small and large interactions with students and academics across disciplines. These have been immensely valuable to me throughout this research, and I am most grateful to these institutions.

In the midst of years of research, my wife has been a constant source of support and encouragement. She holds all the important things together, and without her I doubt this book would have reached publication. Thank you, Emma.

Finally, the last member of the Society's religious membership, and the last overseer of the healing, Mrs. Ruth Klein, passed away in 2012 while this project was in process. While my presence in the archive must have represented something of an intrusion into her daily life, in her kindness and willingness to help me understand the archive she was unfailingly considerate. Her dignity, thoughtfulness, and sense of duty remain present to me—it is only appropriate that this book is dedicated to her memory.

INTRODUCTION

The Panacea Society and the Study of Religion

In 1924, a group of women living as a religious community in the town of Bedford in the south of England began a public campaign to promote what they believed was a method of spiritual healing discovered under divine inspiration. For ninety years, the group, which called itself the Panacea Society, advertised its healing system and attracted inquiries and applications from all over the world. While the Society continues to exist as a secular institution with charitable and educational purposes (and the funding for the research on which this book is based was provided by that charity), the healing closed in 2012 when the last member of the Bedford leadership passed away. While the healing was available, nearly 130,000 people from more than one hundred countries submitted applications; all of those wrote to the Society at least once (when they applied), many wrote several times, and a few wrote a great many letters during their periods of contact. With a striking level of efficiency, the Society's workers in Bedford took great pains to catalogue the letters they received from the users of the healing, and for thousands of users the Society retained complete runs of original correspondence. As such, the Society's archives contain many thousands of letters on spiritual and religious matters, across nearly a hundred years of recent history, from people who are normally lost to the historical record. The purpose of this book is to present the outcome of a close study of the materials in that archive—to provide insight into the spiritual and metaphysical thinking of people whose ideas about such things are otherwise almost invisible in the historical study of religion.

The method of healing offered by the Society was a simple one; an applicant who wrote to the Society asking for healing was sent a small piece of linen to which the Society's leader had imparted healing power. The linen came with an instruction paper that detailed how the linen should be dipped in water, and how the water should be either drunk or applied to the body in special ways with the intention of healing specified ailments.² In addition to using the water as prescribed, users were required to write regularly to update the Society about their progress in recovering from their ailments. Those letters provided the occasion for many users of the healing to communicate about their experience of the healing, and to go beyond that to discuss their personal and spiritual concerns in their own ways and on their own terms. In this way, the letters of the users of the healing are samples of a conversation about religious matters that is carried on, to varying extents, in all societies and at all times. Whatever the historical trajectory of religious belief and practice across the twentieth century and into the twenty-first, the Panacea Society's healing letters have a unique capacity to show the nature of individual grappling with the transcendent (or its absence) through that recent history and across a range of countries and societies. The approach taken in this book turns to these noncanonical and highly individual sources and pieces of evidence as valid accounts of the theological views of people we would not normally treat as theologians. This provides the material for the central purpose of the book: an attempt to understand something of what religion *is* in people's lives, how people experience it, and how they understand it.

Scholarly discussion about religious change has frequently centered on a distinction between two forms of religion: large, mainstream, organized movements of allegiance to what is thought to lie beyond the mundane on the one hand, and small-scale, personal experience of whatever is experienced as beyond each individual's earthly existence on the other. Of course, both "forms" of religion are invariably blended together, and the distinction is a useful if somewhat artificial convenience of contemporary understandings. Nonetheless, the processes affecting these two forms of religious activity, the relationship between them, and their destinies (whether each is growing or shrinking so as to eventually either flourish or fade away) has been a central interest of historians and social scientists of religion for some time. It is a core claim of this book that scholarly debate has inadequately accessed something of fundamental importance but hard to see when attempting to understand religious change from an overview position: complex and dynamic individual thinking in all types of religious activity. Based on the evidence of the Panacea Society healing letters, this book seeks to excavate the signs of complexity and dynamism in the religious lives of people without access to publication outlets or conventional religious authority. In essence, it seeks to understand people's experience of religion and spirituality by acknowledging that they can all be metaphysicians, and by treating them all as such. Following an appraisal of how theories of secularization have been assessed (in chapter 3), this book argues that classics in the secularization literature have been underestimated for the extent to which they propose complexity and dynamism rather than outright decline. The method in this book pays special attention to that complexity and dynamism and uses the archives of the Panacea Society's healing department to generate a deeper understanding of the meaning of religion in people's lives in recent history. It ultimately suggests that, for many people, the transcendent is not an object distinct from their everyday lives that they try to relate to, but something caught up in the everyday conundrum of understanding life in the world.

THE ARCHIVE

In the early days of the healing in the 1920s, all letters making inquiries about the healing were reviewed by the Society's leadership and replied to. As time went by, and as the number of healing users grew, only the most difficult cases were formally assessed by the leadership; nonetheless, letters were regularly replied to, especially in special or difficult cases. The settled daily routine seems to have been that the head of the Healing Department would deal with new applications and letters from overseas, while a subdepartment dealt with update reports from ongoing "water-takers."[3] As the healing work grew, the Healing Department evolved a sophisticated and extensive filing and referencing system ("simple but efficient methods, so concise, complete, orderly, and up to date"[4]) to manage the enormous numbers of applicants and complexity of information it received. For every applicant, an index card was made with the patient's details, and a record was kept of every letter and ailment reported on. The Society also appointed an officer "in charge of the search for duplicate applications."[5] Each card includes the applicant's postal address, name, application date, and information about letters received at the Society and the progression of ailments as reported. For many longstanding healing users, there are a number of closely handwritten cards stored together. Although some are now missing from the archive, and there may be entire cabinets missing (for example, there are only a very few cards remaining for U.S. applicants), a substantial number remain in their original drawers. Cards are stored in drawers in alphabetical order by surname, so the contents are effectively randomly arranged as far as gender, geographical location, date of application, and other metrics are concerned. For the purposes of this research, a sample of the index cards of approximately the first fifty applicants stored in each of the eighty-one drawers were studied for information about their applications and careers as users of the healing. A process of eliminating blank or evidently erroneous data, and removing cards with inadequate or incomplete information (for example, those without a stated country or with missing application dates), resulted in a sample of 3,894 applicants from thirty-five countries or territories and with application dates from January 1924 to July 1990. Applicants with addresses in Jamaica and England made up the majority of those in the sample (with 1,893 from Jamaica and 1,206 from England).[6]

To reduce the workload at the headquarters in Bedford, a number of agents, called Towers,[7] were set up to manage affairs in specific countries and regions. Countries without Towers were all managed from Bedford, and over time the Healing Department developed a sophisticated network of translators both in house and outside.[8] Tower offices were organized in a similar way to the head office ("they have Index Cards, Reference numbers, Case-Papers, Registers, &c., just as we have"), and on a monthly basis they were expected to send full details of every applicant and ongoing patient to the Society's central registers—though some Towers, notably the one in the United States, were overwhelmed on a regular basis.[9]

In addition to the index cards in the Society archive's Healing Collection, its general holdings include numerous volumes of manuscript register books alongside a great array of personal, institutional, and administrative papers. The registers are sometimes inconsistent and discontinuous, though there are long runs of integrated information for some countries in some time periods, and it is possible to assemble an overview sketch of the rise and fall of subscriptions to the Society's healing method over the course of time. The appendices include summary data based on these materials, giving an overview sketch of national patterns of interest in the healing. However, the nature of the source material is such that these data should not be treated as more than approximate.

The final major archival source of information about the healing is hundreds of packets of letters stored in dozens of large archival boxes held in the Panacea Society archive's Healing Collection. Periodically, the Society's members in Bedford seemed to have gathered runs of letters from individual users, carried out sorting and disposal, and wrapped them into packets for long-term storage. While these letters were apparently stored in various places at the Society's headquarters over the years, when the last two members of the Society at the headquarters sought to modernize and regularize the Society's activities amid fading membership at the end of the twentieth century, a process of reorganization took place in the archives. Under the oversight of academic researchers and archivists, letters and registers were gathered together from cellars and cupboards, the process of cataloguing began, and suitable archival storage was introduced. That process was initiated by members of the Oxford Prophecy Project, led by Dr. Jane Shaw and Professor Christopher Rowland, one outcome of which was the cataloguing of the Healing Collection and the wider Panacea Society archives. In 2010, when just one Panacean, Mrs. Ruth Klein, remained active at the headquarters, this project began to attempt to penetrate and understand the contents and significance of the materials in the Society's Healing Collection.

While in recent years the letter bundles have undergone a process of archival reorganization and rescue from sometimes precarious storage conditions, they reflect a long history with their own processes of sorting, triage, and, no doubt, occasional accidents. As such, while there are many thousands of letters from thousands of correspondents, runs of letters are not always consistent or complete, and the individual items are yet to be fully catalogued. The samples examined in this book are based on a detailed analysis of letters uncovered during a long process of reading and searching through the Healing Collection. While there has been some systematic sampling, the selection of letters for inclusion in the analysis carried out for this book had the intention of encompassing a wide and deep range of expressed religious and spiritual thinking, so letters were included opportunistically as they were identified. The intention in the letter analysis has been to subject correspondents to close analysis in order to understand the nature, function, and experience of religion and transcendence in people's lives.

In presenting these themes, the importance of preserving the anonymity of those whose letters and records were studied for this research has been kept constantly in mind. This reflects the established practice of the Panacea Society's periodical, *The Panacea*, which regularly published anonymized testimony from water takers. In this book, the names of users of the healing are included only in the very few cases where people wrote publicly about their use of the healing. Other than those few individuals, healing users are referred to in the text by randomly allocated identification numbers; the corresponding archive codes and locations for these are held by the archivist at the Panacea Charitable Trust. As an additional precaution, potentially identifying information, such as specific geographical references and definite ages, have been omitted or changed.

THE STRUCTURE OF THE BOOK

The book is divided into eight chapters. The first chapter provides an introduction to the personal stories that the letters make available to us and illustrates how the Panacea Society's healing was experienced in people's lives. It also introduces the Society and its early formation and discusses how letters from users of the healing provide insight into the underlying metaphysical and theological ideas of people not normally regarded as metaphysicians or theologians. While the healing and the Society were very much products of their time and era, the Society's leaders and central administrators believed themselves to be the expression and fulfilment of an ancient spiritual impulse dating back to a line of esoteric prophets in England including Joanna Southcott and Jane Lead. Chapter 2 provides detail on the sources of the Panacea Society's theology. It describes the lineage of the English prophecy tradition the Society believed itself to be a continuation of, and it presents an account of the two core elements of the Society's theology: a physical form of salvation and the fundamental role of the female in eschatology. This is framed against contemporary scholarship examining the continuities between ancient nonmainstream religious traditions and newer forms of alternative and New Age religion.

The third chapter presents an account of the ways in which processes of religious change during the period of the Panacea Society's religious function have been described and explained in historiography and sociology. It discusses how the Panacea Society's healing and those who used it can inform us about the nature of those descriptions and explanations. The chapter develops an account of the secularization thesis that extracts the essential insight that recent times have seen a religious and spiritual dynamism that is unpredictable and highly energetic. Deemphasizing the need to use a grand historical trajectory to make predictions about a future state of religious culture, the chapter proposes that dynamism and religious persistence are inherent in a range of classic accounts of secularization, and it suggests a way of using the core insight of the idea of secularization—not that religion is in decline, but that it is in flux—as a methodology in the study of recent religious history, using the letters in the Society's Healing Collection in particular. The chapter also examines the information that Collection records can provide about the patterns of use of the healing.

With the broad framework thus established, chapters 4 and 5 begin with the deep historical, spiritual, and theological sources that the Society understood itself to be part of and the analysis of scholarship seeking to understand the nature of religious change in recent history. The chapters move on to the more immediate social and cultural history of religion that makes up the ecosystem within which the Society came to be formed. Chapter 4 provides a detailed case study of how the healing in Britain was interlaced with new spiritual movements and the response of the Anglican Church. Chapter 5 extends that discussion to the national contexts of the United States, Jamaica, and Finland. Those countries each had very distinct religious histories, and the chapter examines the ways that the Panacea Society's healing was articulated and how it can inform us about those distinctive landscapes and the personal stories enacted in them. Commencing the process of assessing how the letters allow us to see and understand ordinary people's religious and spiritual ideas and experiences, chapters 4 and 5 discuss the range of religious forces that are represented in the letters of the users—and the ways the water-takers encountered, understood, and engaged with those forces.

The great wars of the twentieth century were fundamental social and cultural crises in the history of Europe and the world, and the evidence from the rates of application to the healing and from the personal testimony of the letters shows how the Second World War caused a significant fluctuation in the way the healing was taken up. Building on theoretical and empirical research in the relationship between existential anxiety and religiosity, chapter 6 discusses war and geopolitical anxiety as themes in the letters of the water-takers.

Chapter 7 tracks the variety of ways that individual users of the healing understood it, expressed their religious ideas, and grappled with the metaphysics they were practically engaged with. The chapter develops the core theme of seeking to understand the meaning and function of religion in the lives of ordinary people and excavates how they engaged with and enacted transcendent and metaphysical concerns. Developing the theoretical themes discussed in chapter 3 and emerging from the examination of personal modes of engaging with transcendent and metaphysical concerns in subsequent chapters, the concluding chapter, chapter 8, develops the notion of vernacular religion to formulate an understanding of the complexity of religious and spiritual thought in terms of vernacular or quotidian engagement with the transcendent.

The Panacea Society's healing came to an end in 2012, when the Healing Department was closed after the death of the last active member. A postscript presents an account of the healing membership in the final decade and reflects briefly on the end of the Panacea Society's healing.

CHAPTER ONE

The Panacea Society's Healing

SEEKING A SPIRITUAL CURE

Personal Stories

In the late 1930s, in a coastal town in southwest England, a dental surgeon was seeking a cure for digestive and breathing troubles (98356). He wrote to a religious group, which advertised a special form of spiritual healing in newspapers and magazines, and asked for more information—and in August 1939 he asked to subscribe to its system of healing. The religious group, which called itself the Panacea Society,[1] issued him a membership number and sent him a piece of linen—that, it was explained, carried a spiritual power of healing—and a detailed instruction sheet explaining how to use it.[2] The basis of the healing was drinking and washing the body in water to which the healing power of the linen had been imparted. This was done by putting the piece of linen into a bottle or jug and filling the container with drinking water while saying a prayer ("I ask for Divine Healing by Water and Spirit, and for other benefits)—this made "Water A." The preparation was to be drunk four times a day.[3] A second version of the water—a dilution of the first, called "Water B"—was for "external use" and was to be applied to the body from time to time in bathwater or on sponges, or in other ways. The particular instructions sent to the dentist have been lost; however, copies of similar instructions are available, and these are explicit about the use of different treatments for different complaints. As the dentist was suffering from breathing troubles, he was probably advised to add Water B to a cup of boiling water and to inhale the vapour under a towel—as well as to drink Water A, which was expected of all subscribers to the system.[4]

At around the same time, in a town in the English Midlands, a woman wrote to the Panacea Society looking for a cure for a varicose ulcer on her left foot (16746). She said she had suffered from the complaint for many years and

"God has answered my prayer and healed it in the past, but this time it is worse than before."[5] She was issued a membership number and, like all who subscribed to the healing, was advised to drink Water A four times a day. In addition, the treatment for skin troubles and ulcers was a dilution of Water B applied to the wound with a dressing.[6]

Although the Panacea Society's healing system was popular in England—the West Country dentist and the Midlands woman were two of many thousands who applied for the healing in England—and had some circulation in other countries of the British Isles, in time it found an international following. An American woman, who was one of the Society's earliest adherents, applied in 1924, when she would have been in her early fifties, from a city in Ohio (44871). She complained about a number of ailments, including trouble with her eyesight, tooth decay, catarrh and bronchitis, and constipation.[7] She was required to drink Water A as usual, and like the dentist she would have been advised to inhale the water's vapour to treat her lung complaints. "Constipation," the instructions said, "is not so serious when the Water is being taken, as sometimes the food is required for the building-up process"—but it could nonetheless be treated with extra Water A in liquid food, or the water could be used as an enema.[8] Another American correspondent wrote from a small town in southwest Arkansas in the middle of the Second World War (42811). She was suffering from gallbladder problems and high blood pressure. She saw herself and her context in a highly spiritualized way and believed she had been mystically directed to seek the cure provided by the Panacea Society. "My doctors told me that I was suffering with gall bladder troubles, I prayed over it, in the spirit I was told to go to the universal doctors."[9] She would have been directed to drink Water A like all subscribers, with the additional treatment for problems with vision, gallbladder, and blood pressure complaints by "hot dry sponging"[10] with Water B.

The healing found its way to all corners of the globe, especially to countries with a strong British influence. In the mid-1930s, a woman wrote from the southeast of Jamaica, on the recommendation of her brother (40371). She wanted treatment for constipation, kidney trouble, and bladder weakness.[11] As we have seen, the treatment for constipation was extra Water A to drink, and in severe cases an enema. The kidney trouble was treated by hot dry sponging,[12] and the bladder weakness was probably treated by the usual consumption of Water A. In the 1950s, a female teacher wrote to the group from the northeast coast of Jamaica (17930). Her small child had a problem with his neck, and she had diabetes and problems with her vision and hearing.[13] The nature of the child's neck complaint is unclear, though no doubt it was recommended that he bathe in a bath with two tablespoons of Water B added, which was advised for "Rickety or Weakly children," and that he use the hot compress method "for acute pains in any part of the body."[14] Drinking Water A in the normal way was the main treatment for diabetes, though the teacher would also have been recommended the hot dry sponging method for her ears and eyes. Children were not permitted to correspond with the Society until they were at least age sixteen. The Society detected significant benefits for children in taking the water,[15] as evident in an article on Africa in *The Panacea*, the Society's journal, in about 1928.

> One great joy attached to the Water is the way children keep strong and healthy and are able to do their lessons more easily, and are free from those attacks of listlessness and mental strain so common with growing boys and girls in a semi-tropical climate. Such diseases as typhoid fever and dysentery, common in Africa, do not attack our patients so readily, yet the Water quickly destroys and drives out the germ from the system, should they have it, and they recover more quickly than one who has not had the water.[16]

The Society even speculated on the possibility of one day forming "some Panacea Establishments" where "children, whose mothers get tired, can be treated professionally."[17]

The healing was also picked up in non-Anglophone countries. In Finland, a burgeoning association of Theosophists and of folk and alternative healers began to translate and distribute the healing method from the 1920s. Shortly before the Second World War, a woman in Helsinki, for example, wrote for help (44613). As she could not speak English, she asked a friend to translate on her behalf. Her troubles were broad—she was "struggling with illness, worries, economic difficulties and many sorrows"—but she believed it her duty to "raise one's head and try again, believing in a change for the better, to manage to get on even a day at a time."[18] She had breathing problems and found even a small exertion would tire her out, so she would have been directed to inhale the water, in addition to the usual consumption of Water A. She also suspected some spiritual forces at play: "It seemed as if something of the spirit world would have attacked me."[19] Another Finn, who probably applied in the 1930s, became an enthusiastic and long-term user of the healing (19880). Her complaints in the 1950s included being overweight (after overeating at Christmas), a blocked tear duct, and smoking. She also administered the water to her children to treat their poor behavior— she reported that they variously swore, exaggerated, deceived, and were unkind ("otherwise they are very affectionate and agreeable").[20] Although she drank the water enthusiastically, she had trouble using it to bathe, as she and her family washed at a bathhouse. Nonetheless, she sewed the blessed linen into her family's clothes, added the water to their food, and sometimes persuaded them to drink it directly.[21] The smoking was treated with a special piece of linen supplied by the Society called a "tobacco section"; she reported that she "used it among cigarettes and gradually they begin to taste foul."[22]

Wider Benefits

The Panacea Society had its origins around the time of the First World War and emerged under the impulse of communications transmitted through a group of women—including Mabel Barltrop (1866–1934), who would become the group's leader—who were believed to be divinely inspired. The kernel of the Society's formation was the belief that an eschatological conclusion to human history, predicted by the eighteenth-century English prophet Joanna Southcott (1750–1814), was about to occur.[23] Barltrop had a fairly conventional upbringing as "a middle-class girl born into a family with literary connections and the usual Church of England attachments and sensibilities of the time."[24] She had married a curate, Arthur Barltrop, who died in 1906, leaving her with four children.[25] Barltrop was something of a religious quester all her life, and in 1914 she discovered and began to follow the teachings of Southcott.[26] Barltrop made a close study of Southcott and campaigned for the Church of England bishops to recognize the authenticity of her teachings; through this study and campaigning, she became part of a network of women interested in the prophet.[27] An early impetus to the group's formation was the work of Alice Seymour (1857–1947), who had published several volumes of Southcott's works and distributed numerous leaflets about Southcott during the early twentieth century.[28] It was one of Seymour's leaflets that had first interested Barltrop in Southcott's teachings,[29] and she subsequently made contact with another founding figure, Rachel Fox (1858–1939), who was already a follower of Southcott and promoting her teachings.[30] In time, Fox would emerge as a great support to Barltrop, and she became the official chronicler of the Society, publishing a series of books on its history.[31] Along with some other correspondents, these women formed the center of a network of interest in Southcott and her legacy, and they began to look for the fulfilment of her eschatological promises.[32]

As the group developed in confidence and came to recognize Mabel Barltrop as a prophetical heir to Southcott and even as a divine being in her own right, the healing was discovered and distributed as a practical deployment of the end of history. While the healing was believed to cure individuals of their day-to-day ills, because of its cosmic significance they believed that it also had almost limitless powers in other domains. The Society believed that "there really is no trial or trouble to which the help of the Water cannot be applied" and observed that many people "look to Headquarters for guidance in every problem physical, domestic and spiritual."[33] The Society informed users of the healing that they could employ it to protect their homes in times of "Civil or Social Strife or in Warfare"; the method was to "sprinkle a wineglass of Water B outside each of your street doors and gates (back and front and side)" and say Psalm 91 shortly afterwards.[34] Another benefit was making up for nutritional deficiencies in times of food shortage during strikes, war, or flood: "Should food-shortage loom in sight, a teaspoon of Water A for each person added to the liquid food of the family will make up for deficiencies," and "in actual famine, a wine-glass of Water A at each meal will support all persons taking it."[35] The water could also be used to protect and heal animals; a special animal section could be requested and the water added to their drinking water, applied to injuries, or even poured into streams and pools where animals gathered to drink.[36] It was found that water-takers were helped with money troubles while they took the water,[37] and special pieces of linen could be supplied to keep in a purse or pocketbook to help pecuniary affairs. The water could even be sprinkled on letters concerning "serious business or monetary affairs, before posting them" or sprinkled onto a handkerchief to be carried into important interviews.[38] Furthermore, as long as "reasonable precautions" were taken and "traffic rules obeyed," a "Car Section" could be put in motor cars to provide protection to drivers and vehicles.[39]

An editorial in *The Panacea*, written in the context of preparations for war in Europe in the 1930s, expressed the Society's belief that the positive power of the panacea extended beyond the needs of individuals. The article noted the "grave danger for America and other countries" but observed that Britain was safer than other countries because "what we are not prepared with in the way of anti-aircraft and munitions generally, we shall easily make up for by the use of the Blessed Water."[40] The editorial was echoing a similar notion in a periodical written a few years before, which had suggested that "no weapons formed against England will prosper when she awakes to the power of the Panacea remedy. Our air-ships, carrying the blessed water . . . will be a wall of defence to Britain, a wall which no enemy will be able to pass nor to destroy."[41] The great power and range of the healing were made clear to the Society in the 1920s, when King George V was reported as suffering from a number of illnesses. Although they were not able to have direct contact with the king, the Panacea Society attempted to use the healing to come to his aid, and they discovered that the healing power could be communicated over a distance.

> Perhaps one of the greatest additions to our understanding of the Healing, through this national event, is that distance makes no difference whatever, and if the Divine Mother ordains it, persons, not even taking the Water, and knowing nothing whatever about it, can have the spirit conveyed to them by another vehicle than water.... The knowledge has come that we can reach a sick bed in palace or hovel, if the Divine Parents require it.[42]

The Society offered its healing method to the Church of England, which it believed to be the one true Church, but it was thoroughly ignored by almost every cleric it sought to persuade.[43]

The Panacea Effect

Although a great many of those who applied for the healing did not continue the treatment—so presumably did not find benefit from it—a considerable number found it to be highly effective. After reaching a certain level of involvement in the Society and subscribing to certain petitions, a person would be required to send a "confession" to the Confidential Department, a process that the Society believed could ultimately lead to spiritual transformation and enable full membership of the Society.[44] The Healing Department would from then onwards oversee only a person's physical wellbeing, awaiting the failure of death.[45] The dental surgeon from the West Country (98356) found the healing to be "little short of miraculous"; a month after starting the treatment, he reported that "the digestive and chest troubles have almost entirely disappeared" and related a positive side effect: a "gradual clearing up and marked dissolution of corns and callositis on the foot." He wrote to tell the group's Healing Department that he was "very, very grateful ... to be the privileged recipient of this wonderful work," and he reported a general improvement in his wellbeing: "apart from the actual healings I am experiencing, I can truly say that I never felt happier, healthier or more vigorous in all my life."[46] His counterpart in the Midlands (16746) also found great benefit from the water. She wrote in October 1939 that "I can feel myself getting better each day ... the broken ulcer on my left foot is healing up, it is now only half the size it was when I started the treatment 4 weeks ago, and the pain from it lessens each day."[47] The success of the treatment whetted her interest in the Society; she asked for literature and inquired about meetings. When she reported that two of her sons (aged eleven and thirteen) were "getting out of hand," the Society suggested she give them the water and advised, "Don't nag them but try to be firm and do what you have said you will."[48]

The woman who wrote from Ohio (44871) reported rapid improvement: "If it is not miraculous, then I do not know what miraculous means." She added, "I am forgetting my ills and ails so fast that I can make no special report of any of them. Suffice it to say that each and every one is better." Though the constipation was "the slowest to yield," she had found no need to take other remedies for it since starting with the Society's healing.[49] She became a devoted user of the healing and communicated with the Society into the 1950s, consistently reporting health and personal benefits from the healing.[50] Though preoccupied with spiritual matters, the woman who wrote from Arkansas (42811) reported improvement in her physical complaints; she said "I am doing nicely so far" and "I don't get tired out as quick as I have been."[51] When she informed the Society that she had been inspired to seek help from it by divine inspiration ("I prayed over it, in the spirit I was told to go to the universal doctors. It was 2 [sic] I asked which one the man or the woman, he told me to go to the woman"[52]), she was rebuked by the Society:

> We do not know what kind of Doctor you describe as the Universal Dr. It is best for you to go to a properly qualified medical Doctor ... either man or woman. Are these universal doctors qualified doctors? Do not have anything to do with any kind of spiritual or magnetic healing, nor place any belief in voices or visions. They are most deceiving and very dangerous, they mix seeming truth with errors and will do you harm not good. The power in the Water is Divine, but you cannot expect benefit from it if you rely on spiritualism, the water will help you if you rely on it.[53]

The woman explained that she had responded to newspaper advertisements for a man "saying he had power from god to heal[;] he was a minister in Washington DC." He had charged her $15 but "never did me any good." Understanding the healer in Washington to be the man of her vision and the Society to be the woman, she had written to the Society: "I am trying to obey the best I can. Please pray a special prayer for me. For sure I have been helped through your advice, may God be with you and continue to bless you."[54]

The woman who wrote from the southeast of Jamaica (40371) with constipation, kidney trouble, and bladder weakness seemed to have found gradual improvement. Writing six months after starting the healing, she said, "I am still taking the medicine I don't feel well yet, but it is working" (though she was talking about a cold in this case), and "I trust that I will be healed some day, nothing more."⁵⁵ She remained hopeful and nine months later wrote: "I trust that God will help me to be in good health again, and cleanse me from all my sins."⁵⁶ The teacher (17930) living on the other coast had some firmer signs of the efficacy of the healing: "I am awfully delight[ed] to report that the little boy's neck is perfectly well again. He is proud and you cannot get it from him that it is not the Healing Water or Magic Water did the job (as he calls it)." She said of herself, "I find changes in my life too, I can eat and drink any food and drinks and I am no more suffering from the dreadful Thirst or other discomforts."⁵⁷ She found her diabetes benefitted for a prolonged period, writing six years later to say, "I continue to feel better. In fact, sometimes I feel as though I am perfectly well. All [signs] of excess sugar almost gone and my former size seems to be gradually returning."⁵⁸

The help of the Society extended beyond physical healing; in December 1955, she wrote saying she was planning to borrow money to build a schoolhouse (and hinting that the Society could lend it to her).⁵⁹ A handwritten draft of a response was added by someone at the Society in the margins of her letter (which is still held in the Society's archives); it expressed surprise that she should borrow money for the venture, or attempt to beg it from friends, and suggested she start her school in a large room and build up from there.⁶⁰ The woman replied with gratitude for the Society's rebuke: "I thank you for your scolding letter of the 2nd Jan which I received with gratitude and firm affection for your great interest, and your protecting statements which you have excused and pointed out for my benefit."⁶¹ There was even some direct intervention by divine powers: "The Lord had some interview with me immediately after I posted yours [the letter requesting help]"; she had reportedly lost interest in the project.⁶² She also sought the advice of the Society about her dreams. As a Baptist who had married and raised children in the Anglican tradition, she appears to have taken Communion at the latter for some time. But she was uncertain: "I dreamt, some time ago, that someone was reprimanding me about the Communion I had started to take at the Church of England here. Accordingly, to my vague understanding, I should not partake"; the dream had apparently disconnected her from her commitment to the Church.⁶³

The two water-takers from Finland (44613 and 19880) wrote to the Society to report a number of benefits. The woman with breathing difficulties and other anxieties reported some improvement, for when an x-ray of her lungs discovered a "flaw," she had a significant dream about the Society's healing. "I dreamed that I was standing in a large room, and in the doorway of the next room stood a figure dressed in [a] pale blue dress, who asked: 'Have you used Panacea as directed?' to which I answered: 'Yes, as well as I have been able under the circumstances.' Then I awoke."⁶⁴ Working as a nurse in the 1930s, she used the water in her work.

"Last Saturday I gave some water to a little child who was dying, and had terrible pains. To my delight the end was much easier for him then. It was great to be able to help."[65] The Second World War broke the chain of communication, and it was not until 1946 that she made contact again and began sending letters via a friend in the United States. She wrote of the "long hard years of war" after her last letter on the day Denmark was invaded, and her sense of a "protecting hand of the Unseen" during the "many hostile experiences" of the war years—before asking to have the linen sent again, so she could take up the healing once more.[66] Another Finn reported very positive results from the healing. Early on she said, "I am the happiest person in the world because you care for me and my family" and "all my friends are astounded at the change in me."[67] Later on she wrote of her gratitude for the help of the Society, and her experience of tangible positive benefits in various areas of her life.

> My life would have no meaning without your help. There have been a number of indispositions in my family, but they have all been healed with the Blessed Water. My sincere thanks. My life feels so secure and good now. It is wonderful that I seem to succeed in all I do now. Even when I set to make a dress and pray and take water A, it turns out beautifully.... My hair too looks beautiful, and everything I attempt turns out right. My son too passed his examinations after I had written to you. I give you all the credit and my thanks, also to God.[68]

Although the benefit lasted a short period, as the behavior of her family members became extremely unpleasant, for a time she detected the help of the water in their behavior. "My son ... who was so nasty has become a good boy and my husband is now kind to me—he even prays now! My life has undergone a great change for which many thanks."[69] Within a year, however, she reported that the behavior of her family members was again becoming severe and unkind. The letters in the Society's archive from this water-taker end with some pathos; she reported that her bruises were healed by the water and that the water gave her "a remarkable inner feeling of peace"; "nothing hurts me when I take the Water."[70]

THE PANACEA SOCIETY

Though it believed its mission was cosmic in significance and that its spiritual power could penetrate from "palace to hovel," the Panacea Society itself was a small and outwardly rather domestic religious group based in Bedford, a large town around fifty miles north of London. In the 1920s, it had begun to advertise and distribute its healing method, sending out the small pieces of linen[71] that had been blessed by Mabel Barltrop—who was believed to have the power to channel divine communications and spiritual healing. Barltrop had attracted a group of women (and a few men), disenchanted with the established religious institutions of society, to follow her and prepare for the perfection of humanity and the dawn of a new spiritual age. Although she was the inspired leader, Barltrop assembled a capable team. In the interwar heyday of the healing, the volunteers at Bedford were overseen by administrators such as trained nurse Mildred Hollingsworth, who helped to compile the instruction paper and went on to manage the group's Healing Department,[72] and Barltrop's enforcer and second in command (also at one time a nurse), Emily Goodwin, who helped to maintain order and momentum at the headquarters. Despite the increasingly complex and effective institution, at the core of the healing was the divine power of Barltrop. The pieces of linen and the group's bureaucracy were part of a sacred mission designed to efficiently and systematically distribute her healing breath to all who might need it anywhere in the world.

The chapter focused on the healing in Jane Shaw's *Octavia: Daughter of God*, the only major study of the Society presently available, highlights the significance of the healing for the Society's leadership in Bedford and for its impact in extending the reach of the Society's ideas, and so the enlargement of its membership.[73] The two core effects of the healing for the Society's leadership were the ways the growth of the healing "led to an increased codification of its structures and greater bureaucracy" as it developed an extended international network, and the fact that it secured the authority of Emily Goodwin, Barltrop's second in command.[74] In broad terms, Shaw associates the growth of the healing with a general expansion of interest in religious forms of healing in the period. She cites the absence of the British National Health Service, the limited capacities of contemporary medicine, and the impact of the 1918–1919 influenza epidemic among the motivators for this growing interest and the emergence of new movements engaged in spiritual healing.[75] While Shaw argues that by the early 1920s the Society had attracted as many recruits from other Southcottian groups as it was able (in part by alienating many of them),[76] the healing extended its range of potential recruits worldwide, and its advertising attracted the interest of a number of members of theosophical groups from the British Isles and around the world.[77] The Society's interest in other groups as a source of membership, and the individual interest of some members of those groups in the Society's healing, indicates a set of cultural and personal interactions that have the potential to be highly instructive about how people were "working" with religious and spiritual ideas in this period. There are hundreds of thousands of letters in the Society's archive, and many of these came from people who were engaging with religious ideas at these points of interaction. By giving these letters detailed attention as theological documents, we gain access to information about the personal and individual ways people were interrogating spiritual ideas and living in a mobile religious space.

Starting in February 1924, the Society carried out an advertising campaign for the healing that would continue for decades. The advertisements did not use explicitly religious language and employed a dry, medical tone; the healing was referred to as a "treatment," and the wording referred to "complaints" and listed physical ailments. Religious ideas were indicated only in allusion; for example, the word "deliverance" was prominent.[78] It was suggested that any ailment could be cured, with things like cancer, consumption, and paralysis listed.[79] In the mid-1930s, the advertisements became less medical and more religious in tone—quoting from the Bible and making the spiritual associations more overt. (The advertising is discussed in greater detail in chapter 6.)

On occasion, the Society employed what might now be regarded as guerrilla marketing tactics; it features in an eye-catching report in the *British Medical Journal* about the 1924 Church Congress.

> That much troubled and very troublesome lady, Joanna Southcott, whose followers at the Church Congress last year at Plymouth were heaping maledictions on the heads of the bishops because the bishops would not take her cult with sufficient seriousness, reappeared in the spirit last week at [the Church Congress at] Oxford.... The streets were invaded by numerous sandwichmen, who carried placards declaring in startling red letters, a "Great discovery by the Panacea Society of the healing of disease through Joanna Southcott." That is about all that can be got on a placard, and for further particulars the curious were referred to smaller bills which were pressed by ardent ladies into the hands of those attending the twenty meetings of the Congress.[80]

The publicity work of the Society was not unsuccessful. A combing of the archive registers has identified more than 122,000 applications from 102 separate countries or territories from the Society's inception in 1924 up to its closure in 2012.[81] The great majority (75 percent) of countries from which applicants wrote to the Society saw their first application in the fifteen years between the beginning of the healing and the outbreak of the Second World War, at an average rate of just under five countries added to the tally per year in this period. There was a significant surge in the lead up to the Second World War; of the 62,261 applications received from around the world during the fifteen years up to and including 1939, nearly half (27,733) arrived during the four years between 1936 to 1939. A sharp decline during the war years (which may have owed as much to disruption in international postal services as any other causes) was followed by a steady average of around 1,450 applications a year up to 1978. And the rate at which countries generated their first application also slowed dramatically, to less than one new country added per year after 1945.

The largest sources of applications by a considerable margin were the United States (32 percent of all applicants) and Jamaica[82] (27 percent), which together made up more than half of all applicants to the Society's healing. The British Isles is significant by volume (19 percent, mainly from England[83]), but the next nearest country (Finland) accounts for less than 3 percent of applicants overall.[84]

TABLE 1.1. Ten largest countries by number of applicants to the Panacea Society Healing (1924–1998). See appendix A.

Country/Territory	Number of applications
US	39,055
Jamaica	33,074
British Isles	23,385
Finland	3,186
France	3,030
Ghana/Gold Coast/British Togo	2,863
Norway	2,494
Poland	2,302
Germany	1,766
Australia	1,597

From some countries there were, of course, fewer applications. To pick some of these arbitrarily, Nigeria was the source of around 1,500 applications, 865 have been found from the Netherlands (with the last recorded in the 1980s), and 289 from South Africa (with the last recorded in 1957). Other countries showed just a handful of applications; there were three applicants from Malaysia (in 1930, 1931, and 1988), two from Chile (1931 and 1941), and one from Rwanda (1982).[85]

As a general pattern, the main period of interest in the Society's healing seems to have been in the years leading up to 1939, when application numbers for the three most important countries in terms of numbers of applications overall (United States, Jamaica, and the British Isles) reached significant peaks. They all also then showed notable declines before reaching relatively low but steady application numbers after the Second World War. The archive record becomes less reliable after the end of the 1970s, perhaps reflecting a decline in interest and the breakdown of recordkeeping systems at the Society. Nonetheless, it is evident that letters related to the healing came in from about eighty people in Jamaica, about fifty in the United States, and about forty in the British Isles in the ten years leading up to 2012, when the healing closed. There is also evidence in the archive that in those later years letters arrived from Nigeria and Ghana, and a few from other countries. Those who were in contact with the Society about the healing in the final decade were not just the legacy of the success of earlier years; about half of them were new applicants who signed up to the healing during that decade.[86]

As well as having an extraordinarily wide distribution, the Panacea Society's healing is unique as a historical resource because the Society required the users of the healing to write to the headquarters with an update on the progress of their ailments three or four times a year. While a great many users did not keep to the regimen, a large number did write regularly and some did so over several years, so the Society has retained an archive of letters dating from the 1920s to the present for tens of thousands of applicants and users covering the complete span of time from the commencement of the healing in 1924 to its closure in 2012. The research presented in this book is based on a sample of the letters and records of hundreds of users of the healing; it covers a wide geographical range and the full time period of the Society's activity. The archive and this research therefore provide a rich and intimate window into the personal and inner religious lives of a diverse selection of people throughout the twentieth century and into the twenty-first. In particular, study of the archive permits an insight into the personal religious and spiritual processes of ordinary people caught up in the great social, political, and cultural shifts described by historians.

The great majority of those who wrote to the Society for healing were not trained clergy, theologians, or metaphysicians—rather, they were ordinary individuals, sometimes quite educated and sometimes barely literate. The applicants whose letters remain available in the archive were not preoccupied with questions of theological or metaphysical magnitude; rather, they were intent on dealing with the everyday demands of life and living—sometimes in extraordinary and demanding circumstances, and sometimes amid the settled security of the prosperous and well-to-do. The letters are therefore extraordinary in the way they provide an insight into underlying metaphysical or theological ideas—sometimes half-realized or only shown implicitly—of ordinary folk from dozens of countries across nearly a hundred years of recent history. Understanding those ideas and the role and function of religious and spiritual ways of being in those people's lives is the purpose of this book.

CHAPTER TWO

Sources of the Healing

THE PANACEA SOCIETY AND THE PROPHETS

The English Prophets

The earliest evidence of a notion of a spiritual healing practice in Barltrop's mind dates to January 1916 when, during a period in a psychiatric hospital, she wrote: "The conditions under which I have suffered would have touched a heart of stone. I wish the primitive church had retained the ideas of healing and the need to fight disease as it fought sin."[1] In February 1921, a strange event occurred, and the wish began to become a reality. Barltrop recorded in a notebook:

> At 10-15 p.m. my Aunt asked me to sing "Jesus calls us o'er the tumult." I did so and I said to her new Nurse ... "This hymn mostly means a fresh call for me." When I went to my room, I got some tabloids which I was taking at the time, poured out the water and said as usual, "O Lord bless this medicine to me," when the tabloid was as it were, flicked out of my hand. I was exceedingly surprised and said to myself "I am not to take it." Then I recalled the words "Cease from every means," and I took the water only, saying "O Thou who didst make water wine at Cana of Galilee, cause this water to be made effectual in the place of medicine." In the night I have been thinking that this was a call to overcome sickness by relying on the Lord alone, and I have remembered that yesterday I had seen the blue St. Andrew's Cross of the Scottish Command, which was sent to me one Christmas. I can only say "Give me strength to obey, if it be a fresh call and may it be shewn me plainly." God grant that it may mean that sin has been overcome here and sickness is to be the second step to be overcome.[2]

Shortly afterwards, on 23 March 1921, Barltrop received what she believed was a divine communication on the matter.

> I will encourage you, My children, to put forth your hands unto the Healing Leaves, yet will I be very patient, dealing with you as the Mother deals with the child who is full of fears in the darkness of the night. Ye shall strengthen yourselves with the Scriptures upon My Healings of old time and with My Word . . . ye shall gradually expect healing at My hands without any medicine of healing and ye shall cease to voice accounts of illness and of fatigue all that is possible.[3]

When a medical doctor became a full member of the Society, the leadership seemed to have felt they had reached an important turning point, as his involvement symbolized medicine submitting to the divine healing. The doctor was affected by "blood pressure and memory loss" and reportedly quickly improved after treatment.[4]

While Barltrop derived her special position from recognition by her peers of her status as the incarnation of something divine linked to Joanna Southcott and by her capacity to receive and pass on communications from the godhead, she was also thought to be heir to an older esoteric and prophetic tradition that was unrecognized by the more mainstream and traditional religious institutions. The origins of that esoteric strand were traced by the Society to the sixteenth-century philosopher Jakob Böhme (1575–1624), and especially an English stream of Behmenist thought found in the seventeenth-century mystic Jane Lead (1624–1704).

Julie Hirst has identified Lead as "probably the most important female religious leader and prolific woman author in late seventeenth-century England."[5] Lead's writings had some important links to groups of followers of Joanna Southcott in Britain and America that persisted for a considerable period and continue to some extent today,[6] and the Panacea Society was amongst those detecting resonances between their beliefs and Lead's mystical vision. One of the Panacea Society's books, from 1927, gives an account of Jane Lead.

> We must explain here that Jane Lead arose as a Prophetess in England at a very critical moment (1666 to 1704,) when men's minds had been profoundly exercised by the Plague and the Great Fire of London. She undoubtedly received from the hand of the Lord . . . "a cosmic ball of truth" upon what was to come. That ball of truth has been either overlooked completely, or has been too battered about by [theologians;] they reduced it to a mere mystical rhapsody.[7]

Lead was a visionary and a prophet in the tradition of Böhme, and she developed a mystical theology that emphasized the female and the feminine. She understood the Millennium to be due, but she understood it in gendered terms—not simply as the return of Christ and the judgement of God, but also as the awakening of the feminine principle of wisdom, Sophia, and the inner transformation of humanity. Willi Temme proposes that Lead "established a new dynamic association among the terms Sophia, mother, womb, and rebirth" and coined the notion of "God as the eternal father and of wisdom as the true natural mother.... Through Jane Leade we meet a divine creative pair."[8] Hirst observes that in Lead the female principle becomes a counterpart to God or Christ acting in history. "Sophia was often depicted as one of God's attributes, yet Jane took the concept of Sophia further ... with Sophia almost becoming a fourth aspect of the godhead."[9]

While Lead was claimed as an important source for the Society, their links to her and their activation of her theology were limited. More important in practical terms was the English prophet Joanna Southcott (1750–1814). Southcott was born into a working-class family in the southwest of England and labored for most of her life in domestic service of one form or another.[10] From around 1792, she began to experience voices and visions, and in that year "the whole Bible broke in upon" her as if "Angels that were ministering Spirits were sounding" in her ears.[11] She became known as a prophet locally and was launched to a national profile when she published *The Strange Effects of Faith* in 1801.[12] In 1802, with her publications continuing to appear (Southcott would publish sixty-five pamphlets and generate an enormous amount of unpublished material in her lifetime[13]), she moved to London.[14] Southcott quickly attracted a significant following, and the movement showed "spectacular growth in the first months and years of its existence as her following climbed from a handful of supporters to thousands."[15] Although numbers fell away between about 1805 and 1813, the year 1814 saw another surge in membership when "the movement regained and, indeed, surpassed the extraordinary recruitment of the first years."[16] James Hopkins suggests there were more than seven thousand members in total, though this is based on incomplete data.[17]

Southcott's prophecies have been summarily dismissed by some writers; Susan Juster summarizes "contemporary and historical verdicts on Joanna Southcott" as "converg[ing] on one score: that her writings are tedious, and maddeningly opaque."[18] E. P. Thompson called *The Strange Effects of Faith* "mystic doggerel" and said it was Southcott's "first cranky prophetic book."[19] Hopkins refers to Southcott's theology as "an unexceptional restatement of usual millenarian beliefs" and comments on the fact that she made "little significant alteration in liturgy" and "offered virtually no doctrinal innovation."[20] Others have been less abjuring. Gordon Allan notes that Southcott's "well-developed theology"—which he suggests might qualify her as "an early biblical feminist"—"is sometimes overlooked."[21] Matthew Niblett comments that "we need to take her seriously as a theological figure if we are to comprehend her mission and extraordinary appeal," concluding that "she had a more coherent and developed theological outlook than is commonly believed."[22]

Amid the great breadth of Southcott's writings, there are two fundamental tenets that stand out and that were of vital importance to the Panacea Society: (1) that the Millennium foretold in Revelation was imminent, and (2) that the "female" had a special role to play in its advent. The first tenet had been laid out from the beginning; Southcott's 1801 pamphlet included the message that:

> By types, shadows, dreams and visions, I have been led on from 1792 to the present day; whereby the mysteries of the Bible, with the future destinies of nations have been revealed to me, which will all terminate in the Second Coming of Christ, and the Day of Judgement, when the seven thousand years are ended.[23]

The second tenet emerged more slowly. J. F. C. Harrison dates the "doctrine of the woman" to 1796, when it was revealed to Southcott that "I'll tell thee what thou art—The true and faithful Bride."[24] Southcott identified herself with the "woman clothed with the sun" of Revelation 12 and the "Bride of the Lamb" of Revelation 19. The eschatological significance of Southcott's theological feminism is perhaps best summed up in a verse of a Southcottian hymn quoted by Harrison:

> A woman Satan chose at first, to bring on man the fall;
> A woman God has chose at last, for to restore us all.
> As by a woman death did come, so life must come the same,
> And they that eat the fruit she gives, may bless God's holy name.[25]

The denouement of Southcott's career as a prophet came at the end of her life, in 1814, when she was in her mid-sixties. As Hopkins expresses it, "everything became prologue to the moment in 1814 when Joanna stunned her following by announcing that she was pregnant by her divine spouse."[26] The announcement generated a new notoriety for the prophet, as well as a surge in members.[27] In time, she did indeed show signs of pregnancy, and a number of medical practitioners confirmed that this was the case.[28] Given the verse following the mention of "a woman clothed with the sun" in Revelation 12:1, ("And she being with child cried, travailing in birth, and pained to be delivered"), the pregnancy was the culmination of Southcott's identity and mission. She identified the unborn child with the "Shiloh" of Genesis 49:10 ("The sceptre shall not depart from Judah, nor a lawgiver from between his feet, until Shiloh come; and unto him shall the gathering of the people be"[29]) and awaited the arrival of the baby and the eschaton.

Despite the opinions of the doctors, a child was not delivered. Southcott died on December 27, 1814, and the autopsy found no fetus and no "disease sufficient to have occasioned death."[30] The disappointment surrounding the pregnancy did not lead to the complete collapse of the movement, and many retained the hope that the eschatological promise would be fulfilled in some way. Some believed, for example, that Shiloh *had* been born (physically or spiritually) but that the infant had been taken up to heaven until it would return, or that Southcott would in due course return to life, or that the birth was "spiritual, not temporal," and that a follower would emerge to take on the mantle of leadership.[31] For members of the Panacea Society, the problem of what had happened to Southcott's child was resolved in the person of their leader, Mabel Barltrop: they came to see Barltrop as Shiloh.

Although Southcott was the primary prophet of the Panacea Society, seven further prophets (known as the Visitation) were recognized as providing true witness of the eschaton. These were Richard Brothers, George Turner, William Shaw, John Wroe, James White, Helen Exeter, and finally, of course, the Panacea Society's leader, Mabel Barltrop. The Society believed that each of the subsequent prophets elucidated "a salient feature of Jane Lead's prophecies, as that feature began to take shape and form. These persons knew nothing of Jane Lead, yet her work and their work make a perfect whole."[32]

Born in Newfoundland, and at one time a naval lieutenant (though biographical information is scarce), Brothers (1757–1824) was contemporary with Southcott (and active in prophecy before she was), and his main period of activity occurred in the early 1790s—after which he was confined to an asylum.[33] J. F. C. Harrison links Brothers's interest in millennial and prophetical religion to his wife's infidelity and notes his interest in mystical writings, including Jane Lead's *A Fountain of Gardens* (1696–1701).[34] As they have for Southcott, scholars have commented on the lack of originality in Brothers's writings. Harrison says that Brothers offers "the usual millennial mixture from the scriptures . . . Nor was the interpretation out of line with the accepted Protestant teachings of the day."[35] The distinctive aspect of Brothers's teaching was his revelation of

> the secret that Britain is part of Israel . . . that the ten tribes—who, unlike Judah and Benjamin, never returned to Palestine—found their way from the cities of the Medes to Northern Europe, and, under the names of Saxons (Isaacsons), Danes and Normans, arrived in these Isles, which had been prepared for their advent by the Romans.[36]

Brothers proclaimed himself "Prince of the Hebrews" and believed he would lead the tribes back to Israel.[37] Although, in the view of the Panacea Society, Brothers subsequently fell away from true prophecy, this core revelation of Britain as Israel was adopted as a central tenet of the Society's doctrines.

With Southcott standing as the second prophet in the chronology of the tradition, another of her contemporaries, and indeed one of her followers (as well as an erstwhile follower of Brothers), George Turner (d. 1821) was recognized as the third prophet of the lineage and, by many, as Southcott's successor as head of the movement.[38] Turner's pronouncements became increasingly contentious as time went by, and he subscribed to Brothers's notion of British Israelism.[39] Nonetheless, his importance for the Society stemmed from his succession to Southcott and his theology of the child of Southcott; that Shiloh had been removed from Southcott's womb and taken to heaven in readiness to return incarnate to earth.[40] About the fourth prophet, William Shaw (d. 1822), there is little extant information.[41] He was contemporary with Southcott and was "recognized as a true Southcottian prophet"; however, his writings were never published and were circulated only in manuscript form (including correspondence with Turner).[42] The elements of his pronouncements that seem to have been of interest to the Panacea Society were associated with an emphasis on the significance of Britain and London in the Millennium.[43]

John Wroe (1782–1863), the fifth prophet, was the first of the Southcottian prophets who did not know Southcott in person, though he was a follower of Turner. Wroe had visions rivalling Turner's; when Turner died, Wroe found himself inspired to lead the movement, and, in time, he was recognized as the leader by a significant number of Southcottians.[44] At the center of Wroe's teaching was Christian Israelism, of "the observance of the whole of the Mosaic law together with additional rules commanded by the Lord through Wroe."[45] He imposed heavy demands on his followers in the form of a code controlling diet, sexual and family relationships, dress, Sabbath observance, and the treatment of animals.[46] Ultimately, Wroe lost his standing among the Southcottians following a community trial for sexual impropriety.[47] Despite the range of the Mosaic regulations in Wroe's teaching, it was the detail of one aspect of his theology that gave him importance to the Society, and in one place they identified his Visitation as "of the greatest moment to the world" "next to Joanna's."[48] Of particular importance for the Society was Wroe's doctrine of woman, including the idea that "Woman has the cleansing period, being purified every fourteen days, and remaining so for fourteen or sixteen days ... but unhappily man, who was inoculated with evil after the Fall has no means of purification. Therefore, as things are at present, *no perfect child* can be born."[49] With the Millennium, the Panacea Society believed humanity would be purified and a *physical* redemption would take place; thus, the redemption that the Society believed it carried to the world was a "redemption of soul *and body.*"[50] Fundamental to the importance of Wroe was that, according to the Society, he foresaw the incarnation of Southcott's spiritual child in Mabel Barltrop and in the healing.[51]

James White (c. 1848–1885) used the name James Jezreel in his prophetic career and took over the leadership of a group of Wroe followers in the 1870s.[52] His *Flying Roll* was regarded by the Panacea Society as "an epitome of the whole of the works of the foregoing prophets for the public."[53] White was an effective proselytizer and found recruits around the world, eventually setting up a community base in Gillingham in southeast England.[54] Among White's teachings was the idea, shared by Wroe, that believers would be saved not only in their souls (as everyone could ultimately be) but also in their bodies.[55] The Panacea Society subscribed to an understanding, taken from White, that a human person is composed of a body and a soul, both of which are constituted by an individual's parents' nature—so a soul is compounded of parents' souls just as the body is widely understood to be. To this is added the spirit, which is derived from God: "When the body dies the spirit returns to God who gave it, the body turns to dust, and the soul sleeps in the dust of the body, in the chambers of the grave, until the resurrection."[56] Furthermore, White developed the feminine theology adopted by the Panacea Society, urging that "the Deity, Jehovah Elohim, is of both masculine and feminine essence, and humanity, bi-sexual, is made in this image and likeness." He suggested that, though Jesus healed, his healing was only intermediate: "those whom he healed at his first coming ... again sickened and died" and a greater healing would come with the second coming.[57]

The final prophet recognized by the Panacea Society was Helen Exeter, the name the inner membership of the Society gave to Helen Shepstone (c. 1853–1918), an associate of Rachel Fox and Mabel Barltrop. Before her death in 1918, Shepstone had been instrumental in the elevation of Barltrop. Shepstone's importance stemmed from her role in supporting Barltrop in the period before Barltrop realized her own significance. "Helen's messages sustained Mabel and gave her directions: that she should go home, that she would be healed and sheltered, and that she herself should listen for God."[58] After Helen's early death, she was identified as the seventh prophet by Barltrop and Fox.[59]

Octavia

One hundred years after Southcott's death, Mabel Barltrop's group initially subscribed to the notion that the child Shiloh had been spiritually born and would appear on earth in due course ("Of course, the 100,000 believers melted away, but a percentage remained firm, having realised through the next instrument of prophecy... that it was a spiritual Child, and that it would come again to do its work"[60]). The turning point in Barltrop's religious career came in February 1919, when an associate came to the conclusion that Barltrop herself was in fact the spiritual child of Southcott made flesh.

> The Child was born in 1866 [the year of Barltrop's birth], but all was secret. She lived an ordinary life, but one full of the needed and varied experiences which enabled her to deal with every side of human life. In 1914, exactly 100 years after the soul-birth, she was introduced to Joanna's Writings and in a moment realised and accepted them as the Message the world is waiting for. Little by little persons gathered around her, but it was not until 1923 that a prophecy was fulfilled that 77 years would be taken off Satan's power over Believers in the Visitation and that the method of healing by Water and the Spirit was revealed.[61]

Barltrop's eschatological significance was confirmed in a communication the Society believed it had received from God in March 1919.

> Behold I am with thee always, I am knit unto thee, My child. Dost thou know who thou art, even *My* Child sown in the womb of thy Mother Joanna, and caught away unto the heavenly places until I found a body likely to suffer, into which, after sufferings great and terrible, My child Shiloh should enter and dwell there.[62]

Barltrop came therefore to be recognized by her associates as the instantiation of Southcott's promised child—and she became known as Octavia (derived from her position as the eighth prophet recognized by the group).[63] With this identification, Octavia emerged as the leader of the group, and her home in Bedford became the physical center of the emerging religious society.[64]

Key among the beliefs of the Society was the notion, derived from Southcott's teachings, that the Millennium of Christ foretold in the Book of Revelation was imminent, and that a Church on earth must prepare the way for it. The Society campaigned assiduously for the bishops of the Church of England to take up this role and to open a box said to contain further writings by Southcott.[65] (Southcott had left instructions that the box could only be opened by twenty-four bishops of the Church of England.[66])

Between April 1915 and October 1916, Octavia had been a resident at a psychiatric hospital, where she began to develop a skill in automatic writing.[67] By the middle of 1919, she was taking daily messages from God, and these writings formed the basis of worship services that she led in the Society's chapel.[68] Over time, various followers joined the Society and bought houses in Bedford to be near Octavia, so that her home and other houses nearby came to form a campus headquarters for the sect.[69] The group in Bedford had sixty-six resident members at its peak in 1939.[70] Along with the members in Bedford, followers were allowed to join the Society as "sealed" members once they had achieved certain spiritual and ritual tasks;[71] sealed members numbered almost thirteen hundred in 1934 and reached a high of nearly two thousand by 1943.[72]

The end of the nineteenth century and the transition into the twentieth has been identified as a phase in which the perceived role of women in society was modernized and developed. Alex Owen has commented on the concept of "New Woman" as "a journalistic and literary invention that nevertheless spoke to the social realities of a changing climate for women at the end of the century," despite the controversial nature of the idea from more conventional vantage points.[73] Although the idea of the New Woman was somewhat restricted in its extent and an essentially middle-class phenomenon, the period did see new opportunities in work and education for women.[74] This nineteenth- and twentieth-century development has been identified as part of a much older tradition, dating back to the medieval period, in which religious literature served as an outlet and means of empowerment for those outside traditional and institutional structures "who did not identify as 'male' or 'heterosexual' in their relationship to a divine."[75] New movements in religion and spirituality at the end of the nineteenth century were intrinsically linked to the changing conception and social role of women. "Feminists were attracted to groups like the Theosophical Society because the occult offered a 'Transcendental View of Social Life' that spoke directly to feminist aspirations for change."[76] Indeed, and more than that, spiritual and occult learning and activities represented a distinct outlet for women who did not otherwise have access to modes and roles for intellectual and group activity like those that were available to men.[77] Speaking about "the occult," Alex Owen says:

> It permitted women the exercise of a "masculine temperament" and provided an intellectual and spiritual outreach that were difficult to find elsewhere. Occultism appealed to an aspiring, questing nature regardless

of sex, and additionally presented a viable context in which women could explore that nature while enjoying the felicities of like-minded companionship.[78]

Owen says that women found occult organizations to be "unique sociospiritual environment[s] offering personal validation and an intellectual rapport that was not easily duplicated" and that they "were attracted by the prospect of the kind of dedicated advanced study that practical magic required" at a time when women's access to higher education was restricted.[79]

As middle-class women coming of age in Britain at the close of the nineteenth century, the founders of the Panacea Society can be understood as a late flowering of the long tradition of nonofficial spirituality encountered as a counterweight to the hegemonic and mainstream institutional forms consistently led and interpreted by men. Jane Shaw's discussion of the ways the Panacea Society membership in Bedford "refracted [their theology] through a domestic lens" and "took up household and domestic images" links their theology to their fulfilment of "the domestic expectations of middle-class spinsterhood and widowhood."[80] While Shaw associates this with the Society's instinct for "carefully preserved hierarchies" and a rather nostalgic patriotism,[81] she also links it to women's suffrage, suggesting a parallel between the impact of legislation granting property rights to married women and the ways the Society invested domestic objects with significance.[82]

A number of theorists have commented on the long and ancient pedigree of an alternative stream of spiritual thought and practice in western culture, and they consistently recognize a dynamic relationship between the old persisting strand and personal individualized innovation. Steven Sutcliffe and Marion Bowman have suggested that, aside from some exceptions (flying saucers and Wicca), "there is in fact very little in contemporary spirituality that was not already present and available in the 1920s and 1930s, in the Edwardian era, at the *fin-de-siècle* or *even earlier*."[83] Robert Ellwood goes somewhat further and suggests that New Age religion or "what may be called the alternative spirituality of the West" is a "contemporary manifestation of a western alternative spirituality tradition going back at least to the Greco-Roman world."[84] Ellwood represents the process as "like an underground river through the Christian centuries, breaking into high visibility in the Renaissance occultism of the so-called 'Rosicrucian Enlightenment,' eighteenth-century Freemasonry, and nineteenth-century Spiritualism and Theosophy."[85]

Even a stronger form of the argument for the novelty of recent religious forms, such as Alex Owen's, recognizes an old and ancient pedigree (though Owen's emphasis is somewhat different): "occultism cannot be written off as a retrogressive throwback or fringe aberration, a reworked 'shadow of the Enlightenment,' but instead must be understood as integral to the shaping of the new at the turn of the century."[86] Wouter Hanegraaff has argued that "the New Age movement can be regarded as a contemporary manifestation and transformation of" a set of esoteric beliefs and practices that "originated in the early Renaissance."[87] While Hanegraaff identifies a deep continuity between modern and older forms of western esotericism, he also argues that the radical changes effected by secularization generated a new phenomenon, "secularized esotericism," which he refers to as "occultism."[88] In the Panacea Society's doctrines and formation, the long tradition it understood itself to be part of, going back to Böhme and through the Southcottian prophets, was explicit. A similar process is evident in local adaptations and interpretations of the healing—for example, in the Finnish association between the healing and the nation's foundation myth, and the Jamaican integration of the healing with the matrix of spirituality in that context (both discussed in chapter 5). Alongside this linking to old and ancient traditions, the Society's negotiation with intermediary strands of religious thought, evident in its relationship with contemporary movements such as Theosophy and Christian Science, is evident in the lives of core members in the interwar period and in the experiences of some healing users.

THE THEOLOGY OF THE HEALING

New Salvation

At the center of the theology of the Panacea Society was the observation that the fundamental condition of humanity is a wretched one. In the preface to a 1922 pamphlet, Octavia described "the insecurity and the misery of human life."

> Strong and healthy to-day, one may find oneself prey to an insidious disease, or the victim of some accident tomorrow, and even if well oneself, are not thousands wretchedly ill? If one is well off at the moment, the wheel of circumstance may easily turn us and our families into abject poverty, and even if we are permitted to be in affluence, are not millions barely able to keep body and soul together?[89]

The insecurity and misery of life are ultimately punctuated by "the crowning point … that well or sick, rich or poor, happy or miserable, death is bound to come to haul us to the grave" and an uncertain and unknown afterlife.[90] Octavia objected that while the contemporary churches minister to this longstanding state of affairs, they do nothing to repair it. The church is "merely a guardian and teacher of the 'common salvation'—the salvation of the soul alone"; it supports "a priesthood which serves only to aid people to die," and people "see naught but a life in heaven reached by way of the grave."[91]

The Panacea Society, however, believed that, thanks to its prophetic knowledge derived from Lead and those who came after her, it proclaimed a new priesthood and a new salvation.[92] There is, Octavia argued, a fundamental error in Christian teaching that directs people towards the salvation of the soul and accepts the concomitant destruction of the body—because this is "the very body … which the Lord came to redeem from the power of death."[93]

> A man is no longer a man when he is dead, the Bible says plainly, "the *spirit* returns to God who gave it." A life in Heaven lived in spirit, has nothing to do with the Hope of the ages—all who go to Heaven have missed the Hope of the ages, which is the Restoration of MAN, body and soul to his primeval condition of health, of sinlessness and of immunity to death. "These all died **not having received the promise**," what could be plainer.[94]

The Panacea Society, on the other hand, promised "the 'so great salvation' of body, soul and spirit"[95] and offered "LIFE ON EARTH in a redeemed restored body."[96]

The Society believed that, despite appearances, humanity had been in continuous decline since the time of Adam and Eve. "Progress in learning, in inventions, in multiplying of goods and chattels, is not progress in the race! To prove that MAN has progressed, you must show a steady decline in disease and a growth in longevity."[97] Yet "Adam and his immediate successors" lived longer than modern humans: "Compare their 900 odd years with our three-score years and ten."[98] The decline in human vitality would continue until ultimate dissolution, but for the dawn of a "new age" ordained by God.[99] The Church's error, the Society believed, had been such that not all could now be saved; those who did not realize the Church's error and failed to accept the truth of the Panacea Society's teaching would continue to bodily death and the grave (though their souls might go on). Only an elect and predestined few, the "remnant" of the human race, would achieve full bodily salvation.[100] The process of the new salvation is obscure; Octavia said it involves a "grafting" or a "cross-breeding" between humans and God: "God would impregnate man with His Own Life and thus would make his body Immortal."[101] Humans, who have been "grafted into Christ" by Christ's act of redemption,[102] must graft Christ into themselves to become, as Jesus Christ became, "a God-man."[103]

The mechanism of the new salvation was indicated, in an incomplete way, in the experiences of the mystics of the past. Octavia taught that "the joyful experiences of a saved soul, leads persons to suppose that the spirit which is upon them, is in them, and Jacob Böhme, Jane Lead, William Law and hundreds of mystics, mistook the 'overshadowing' for an 'In-dwelling.' "[104] According to the Society, this was the fundamental error of all mystics up to the prophecy tradition appropriated by the Panacea Society: "Jacob Boehme can be as wrong as anyone else if his primary thesis or point of departure be wrong."[105] Others may have declared it earlier;[106] however, after a six-thousand-year process beginning with Adam, Octavia could announce in 1922 that "the time is come for the 'In-dwelling' and such as receive the graft must come under the immediate tutelage of the Great Husbandman, in a prepared place, where they will be saved from the general cataclysm, in order to be 'changed.' "[107] The secret of how to achieve the new salvation was transmitted by the string of seven prophets "of whom Jane Lead is the forerunner or precursor"[108] and of which Octavia, the eighth, was the culmination.

The error of in-dwelling was to think that the divine perfection was in some sense already ensconced in each individual and that it was only necessary to release it. By the Panacea Society's account, the divine element needed to be introduced to the body—a physical process mediated by water. So there was no psychospiritual process to undergo, and those who practiced the healing were not expected to subscribe to any particular doctrines for the healing to be effective.[109] The point was emphasized in the instructions sent out to applicants:

> Remember that you need not "have faith in," nor "understanding of," nor "be in harmony with," the treatment, nor "demonstrate," nor do anything at all, except what you are told. You are sure to gain advantage if you obey and persevere.[110]

and

> Faith in the prophecies is not demanded, the Will is not worked upon, Psychology and Auto-Suggestion, Higher and New Thought are useless, while Spiritualism plays no part in our work. The only acts required are those of drinking and of using the Water, and of reporting obediently.[111]

There was no personal mechanism to release the divine and no need for faith, just the attentive use of the water and its physical introduction—in effect, a kind of faith healing for those without faith.

The Female and the Fall

When the Panacea Society initially developed the healing in 1923, a document formally announcing its commencement was issued. The document is striking not least for the fact that one of Octavia's followers, Emily Goodwin, who had come to Bedford as a nurse to Octavia's aunt, spoke as the mouthpiece of a female aspect of the godhead, as the "instrument" of "Me, the great I AM, the Spouse of God." The proclamation calls Octavia "My beloved Daughter, Shiloh Jerusalem, the Queen, who alone in the whole world has power to heal," and it presents her as the fulfilment of a unity with Jesus Christ. "They are never to be separated again—the Twin Saviours—Jesus for the Soul, Jerusalem for the Body, a complete whole, Father and Son, Mother and Daughter, that Soul and Body may be redeemed, making a complete whole."[112] In effect, Octavia was understood to be a fourth person of a divine quaternity comprising Father, Mother, Brother, and Sister.[113] The Mother, counterpart of (and spouse to) God the Father in the conventional Christian trinity, was personified by Goodwin (as the Mother's "instrument"). The Society thus expressed the culmination of Lead's theology of transition from masculine to feminine cosmological authority: "The Great Father and His Son have done all that they could do, from the Masculine point of view, for the human family and therefore, 'in the fullness of time,' the Motherhood is revealed as essential to any further development of the race."[114] Christ had achieved the special "masculine" role, which was the salvation of souls, and this had been continued, albeit inadequately, by the church. The Society's healing, they believed, would implement the special "feminine" role of saving the body.

The capacity for a "female" divine element to carry out the salvation was regarded by the Panacea Society as more than a new phase in cosmological history; it represented a repair of the initial cosmological disruption of creation contained in the Fall. Within Joanna Southcott's theology, because of Eve's part in the Fall of humanity, a healing of the "fall of the woman" is necessary as the preliminary step before a general "Redemption of Mankind" can take place.[115] The individual healing offered by the Society was seen as an outworking of the eschatological healing necessary to repair the Fall, for "as the woman innocently brought about the Fall, the woman shall be given the power to bring in the Redemption."[116] Thus, the Society's May 1923 proclamation of the healing identified Octavia as the one with "healing in *her* wings" and associated this healing with physical and spiritual repair.[117]

The Society believed that in order to prepare for an immortal soul, a spiritual cleansing must first take place.[118] That cleansing was initiated by the healing water, and the Society was explicit that the instructions had to be scrupulously followed.[119] The Society regarded healing as an effect of the elimination of mortality from the body—a side effect, as it were, of physical salvation. Under this scheme, obedience to the instructions was not just a practical matter; it reflected a vital link to the world before the Fall. In the view of the Panacea Society, obeying the instructions of the Society in taking the healing water was engaging in a restoration of the human state before the Fall; it was thus counterpart to Adam and Eve's disobeying of God's injunctions in the Fall.[120] The instruction papers received by applicants with their pieces of linen were explicit about this:

> The 6,000 years of the misery caused by the Fall, which was brought about by disobedience to the Laws of Lev. 15, are just ending. During the shortening of the days, the Lord, as the Good Physician, will heal as the Physician heals, namely, by Treatment; and all who are willing to reverse the Disobedience of the Fall by obedience to this Treatment by Water and the Spirit will obtain health, or deliverance, or cure.[121]

In offering the healing water, the Society was offering the world something that went far beyond mere physical healing: it was offering to reverse the Fall.[122]

CHAPTER THREE

Understanding Religion

The classic historiographical and sociological claim about the nature of religious change amid the modernization of societies has been understood as a claim about the decline of religion—the secularization thesis. In line with recent ideas about this thesis, which query the validity of the inherent teleology of the notion and seek instead to understand religious change as being made up of lived social and spiritual processes, this chapter analyzes and assesses a range of formulations of the theory. It suggests that while classic theorists may have been presented as predicting and describing the ultimate demise of religion, an attentive reading of many of these authors' texts identifies how religion is explicitly presented as persisting in some way. After establishing the core point, that theses of secularization have not inherently excluded the continuation of religion into the future, the chapter proposes a framework for employing a revised secularization thesis as a method in the study of contemporary religiosity, and especially those forms that are generally understood to be characteristically recent developments: flexible and individual forms in dynamic and noninstitutional contexts. In the framework of the Society's extraordinary global reach, its accessibility to people of all faiths and across all backgrounds, and its chronological spread across the twentieth century, the letters of the Panacea Society's healing users are a valuable resource for a study using the methodology proposed.

THEORIES OF RELIGIOUS CHANGE

There is a longstanding tradition of sociological analysis and conventional wisdom that has perceived a more or less inevitable process of religious decline in modern cultures, especially in those where Christianity has been the dominant mainstream religion. The historian Hugh McLeod, for example, lists a canon of sociologists who "shared a commitment to the 'secularization thesis' ... that the dwindling social significance of religion is an inevitable consequence of the process of social development in modern societies."[1] Anthony Carroll has observed that "secularization has been, until recently, an uncontested motif of accounts of modernity" and that "for much of the twentieth century, the theory of secularization was a cultural *a priori* that informed all thought about the modern world and its emergence from the medieval past."[2] Classic accounts of the dynamics implicated in secularization theory, such as Peter Berger's *Social Reality of Religion*, describe "the process by which sectors of society and culture are removed from the domination of religious institutions and symbols" with a concomitant process for individual consciousnesses so that "the modern West has produced an increasing number of individuals who look upon the world and their own lives without the benefit of religious interpretations."[3] A number of contemporary scholars have found evidence to confirm the paradigm. Perhaps the strongest protagonist for secularization as a fundamental theoretical tool for the understanding of religious change presently is Steve Bruce. Bruce notes an ebb and flow of religious influence in Europe over a long period but detects decline overall and finds no historical case where there has been a "reversal of decline."[4]

Despite a longstanding consensus, there is, nonetheless, evidence for Philip Gorski and Ateş Altinordu's assertion that at present "secularization qua sociological theory" finds itself "in an increasingly defensive and even beleaguered posture."[5] While a decline in traditional religion is generally accepted as being evident, especially in western Europe, the attack on the thesis has come from a perception of vitality in new and alternative forms of religion and spirituality generally, and in more traditional forms of religion outside western Europe. In essence, a perception of the persistence of religion despite the decline of some longstanding dominant traditional forms of it has undermined the apparent validity of the secularization thesis. This can be exemplified in academics' conclusions about religious change in three countries on the margins of or outside western Europe that form a significant part of this study: the United States, Jamaica, and Finland. Thus, R. Stephen Warner has argued that a paradigm shift has taken place in sociological ideas about secularization, and he has identified the "older paradigm" as "fac[ing] increasing interpretive difficulties and decreasing rhetorical confidence" with "inconclusive results ... chronic in the field" in the face of "resurgent traditionalism, creative innovation, and all-round vitality in American religion."[6]

In his study of religion amid cultural postmodernity in the United States and elsewhere, David Lyon says "religious life is not shrinking, collapsing, or evaporating, as predicted," and he draws attention to the ways religious groups "negotiate new conduits for commitment, fresh breakwaters for belief."[7] The essence of his objection is that "much secularization theory produced earlier in the twentieth century mistook the deregulation of religion for the decline of religion."[8] In Finland, a country with a longstanding and widely affiliated national church, Jeffrey Kaplan has noted an underlying "vibrant current of mysticism, [and] a willingness to borrow foreign religious ideas."[9] And a study published by the Church Research Institute in Finland identifies that "firm attachment to Christian beliefs has declined" along with a decline in institutional religion. However, "belief 'in some form' of God has not declined," and there has not been a decline "of religion *per se*."[10] The study suggests that "from the point of view of religious beliefs, the thesis of the decline of religion does not have full support."[11]

Jamaica suggests a similar process to that evident in Finland, but with a more highly diversified ecosystem of religious forms. Thus, while Jamaica was among Caribbean countries showing "most notable declines in the dominant religion" between 1900 and 1980, indigenous groups "grew strongly" in the same time period, and the country has flourishing adherence to Rastafarianism, spiritism, and Seventh-day Adventism, alongside a plethora of new religious movements.[12] Claire Taylor's doctoral thesis on the ways Jamaican migration to Britain affected British churches observes that "the process of secularization noted in Europe in the twentieth century, has never been part of life in Jamaica."[13] Taylor also suggests that Jamaican migrants may in fact have helped to sustain religion in Britain.[14] In a global perspective, and with a definition of religion wider than traditional and mainstream churches, there are numerous instances cited as counterexamples to a standard model of secularization.

Jane Shaw's history of the Panacea Society indicates a similarly complex process of religious change within the Society itself. Shaw describes a decline in religiosity in Britain after the 1940s when "with the change in values in post-war Britain and the emergence of a different, less religiously inclined culture, the Society gradually went into decline."[15] This decline, however, is mainly associated with the Society's members at the Bedford headquarters and with the sealed members (who seem never to have numbered many more than two thousand).[16] This internal decline notwithstanding, Shaw observes that the healing, at least, continued to grow for a considerable time after the death of the original inspired leadership (Octavia died in 1934 and Emily Goodwin in 1943), and it is clear that applications continued to arrive at Bedford throughout the rest of the century. To that extent, Shaw's book captures the multiple strands of the processes of religious change in the twentieth century identified by many scholars: a decline in the structured and hierarchical institution at the center (though, of course, rather unconventional in the Panacea Society's case) and a continued vitality among ordinary users in its devolved and individualized locations.

In formulations of the secularization thesis, the majority of writers (whether for or against the idea of overall religious decline) agree that there are, in effect, three identifiable consumers in the economy: (1) those affiliated with institutional religion, (2) those subscribing to new or alternative religious forms, and (3) a large and indistinct atheistic or nonreligious population.[17] Moreover, they consistently recognize a decline in traditional religion and the growth of new religions. For example, Harvey Cox's account of the link between religious change and urban life describes a complex dynamic between all three groups. He refers to modern people "shedding the lifeless cuticles of the mythical and ontological periods" and in fact becoming attuned to "hear[ing] certain notes in the biblical message that [they] missed before."[18] Paul Heelas and Linda Woodhead assess the range of spiritual and religious activities people engage in within a provincial English town and find a relative shift from traditional forms of religious expression to novel forms of spirituality. They predict a potential "spiritual revolution" where the latter overtakes the former at some point in the future.[19] A similar double process, of flourishing new spiritualities alongside declining traditional religion, is noted in Dick Houtman and Peter Mascini's study of religious change in the Netherlands.[20] They examine the extent to which new religious forms can be thought of as compensating (or failing to compensate) for declining affiliation with traditional religion.[21] They conclude that there is an undermining of "the moral basis of the Christian tradition" but that "the growth of posttraditional types of religion" and non-religion has been stimulated.[22]

In a similar way, Christopher Partridge comments that the reality of the decline of institutional Christianity (at least in Europe) "cannot seriously be questioned"; in fact, "the popular Christian milieu ... has collapsed" but "that collapse does not mean that the West has become fundamentally secular. Another religio-cultural milieu has taken its place."[23] The new milieu has, Partridge suggests, the potential to form the basis for a spiritual renewal built on "a confluence of secularization and sacralization."[24] Egil Asprem's work has a similar leitmotif to Partridge's, though he goes further by explicitly "moving away from the dichotomous positions of disenchantment and re-enchantment theories," instead seeing "these issues rather as a negotiation in which spokespersons adopt various strategies and come up with various solutions to perceived problems."[25] Among the strongest statements of the significance of the persistence of religion is Wouter

Hanegraaff's assertion that "the weight of evidence demonstrates quite clearly that, regardless of how one defines 'religion,' it remains fully alive and shows no signs of vanishing.... It is not vanishing, but is being transformed under the impact of new circumstances."[26]

While these writers emphasize the renewal effect of the new forms, others place the emphasis on the decline of the traditional. David Voas and Mark Chaves critique the notion that the United States defies the secularization thesis, as evidenced in a persisting religious landscape. They argue instead that high levels of religious affiliation and a slow rate of religious decline there have masked an underlying trend of decline.[27] Nonetheless, to the extent that they propose the United States may simply match European patterns, and given that they do not exclude the growth of "diffuse spirituality," their argument endorses the idea that generative processes remain present in the wider religious culture. Recognizing a flourishing of individualized forms of alternative religion (identifying them as "'really' religious"), Steve Bruce concludes that these forms of religion are more fragile, "harder to maintain," and "more difficult to pass on intact to the next generation."[28] Although in Bruce's account the ways that alternative forms of religion sustain religion-in-general are transitory and limited, in a similar vein to Voas and Chaves, his account reinforces the impression of dynamic processes linking conventional religious practices in decline with the exuberance of non-traditional and new forms.

Contrasted with the views of those suspicious of the secularization thesis, the interpretations of Voas and Chaves and of Bruce highlight the two intangibles at the center of the thesis: (1) that it is about a *future* state of human culture, and (2) that it depends on the definition of religion employed. Jeremy Morris's discussion of secularization in Britain brings the two together.[29] Morris calls for a "secularization" thesis with "the teleological assumptions ... taken out," permitting an analysis that "would register variations in religious practice over time, but seek to include these into a broader account of the development of British religion than is conventionally assumed."[30] In essence, Morris highlights the prejudgment of the classic secularization thesis that religious change (at least in "modern" societies) was inexorably headed towards decline, and he draws attention to the variation and dynamism inherent in all and any religious culture. All scholars discussed here—whether proponents or opponents of the view that religious change is tending to the elimination of religion—agree that religious culture is dynamic and energetic. The debate, though putatively about the destiny of religion in contemporary culture, pivots on the ways religion as a personal and social aspect of human culture is interpreted and understood. The endpoint of the changes under examination—religion's demise or a spiritual renewal—is less important than its dynamism and energy.

Alongside the contemporary accounts of religious change that recognize the complexity and dynamism of the process, reassessments of classic secularization theses have suggested that these are not unequivocal in their assertion of religion's decline. Warren Goldstein responded to R. Stephen Warner's account of secularization (cited earlier) to suggest that Warner's viewpoint "misunderstands and misinterprets the theory of secularization as articulated by the old paradigm" by seeing it as a relatively simple linear movement "from the religious to the secular, from the sacred to the profane." Goldstein argues instead that a review of exemplars of the old paradigm suggests that their models contain a "dialectical" account of secularization that is an oscillation between periods of high religion and low religion, which can even paradoxically occur at the same time.[31] He interprets classic proponents of secularization as indicating it is a "two-party system" where "neither side will be able to dominate over the other."[32]

The central figure in Goldstein's assessment is Peter Berger, whose work Goldstein characterizes as a classic expression of the old paradigm.[33] The dialectic between the religious and the secular identified by Goldstein is somewhat hidden or implicit in Berger;[34] nonetheless, Goldstein highlights that Berger laments secularization and concedes that "the supernatural survives 'in hidden nooks and crannies of the culture.' "[35] Furthermore, Berger has, in any case, "recently reversed himself" and implicitly conceded the dialectic; Goldstein says that "the early Berger argued that secularization was occurring, while the later Berger argued that a process of desecularization was occurring. He does not seem to acknowledge that secularization is a two-way process."[36] Thomas Luckmann shares much with Berger's account; as Goldstein says, he "picks up where Berger left off."[37] While known as an advocate of secularization theory, Goldstein observes that Luckmann's theory suggests that "religion has not disappeared from modern society, but instead has become "invisible" because "the individual has become sacralized."[38] The conclusion of Goldstein's account is that

> The paradox of secularization can be solved through a dialectical understanding of it as a two-way process.... Religious movements in the direction of rationalization, and social movements in the direction of secularization, spawn religious countermovements in the direction of sacralization and dedifferentiation.[39]

Though offering a somewhat different account of how religion is retained in the writings of these thinkers, Oliver Tschannen makes a similar observation that religion *is* nonetheless retained. He says Berger "stresses that religion survives in the most private and in the most public spheres"[40] and that "Luckmann's whole aim is to demonstrate that religion has not disappeared . . . but has merely become 'invisible.' "[41] Tschannen quotes Bryan Wilson with approval: "Religion is not eliminated by the process of secularization, and only the crudest of secularist interpretations could ever have reached the conclusion that it would be."[42]

Building on the lead set by Goldstein and Tschannen, it is instructive to return to classic approaches to religious change with the presumption of secularization suspended. In Luckmann's account of religious change, there is an important difference between churches as institutions and religions as elements of social worlds.[43] Religion, Luckmann suggests, performs a social function: it is the expression of individual values that are shared in societies, and as such it is the expression of the unifying agent of a group of people (i.e., a society).[44] Religious institutions have evolved by codifying and preserving these shared values, and they obtained their preeminence in society in relation to the extent to which they cogently carried out that function.[45] However, there is nothing in the institution *per se* that is required for society to exist; only the underlying "world view"— the kernel of religion, able to exist without an institution—is required.[46] In the natural course of events, religions come and go, and a particular religion may take its turn as the preeminent expression of a society's worldview, but it may lose its place too and be replaced by another.[47] There is, then, an oscillation in societies during this process. Over time, traditional church religion has become increasingly specialized and detached from the underlying unifying worldview of society and faded in importance.[48] This having happened, and no "counter-church" or new "official" religion having emerged to replace the retreating old one, there has arisen a diverse and irregular economy of religions (including the old "official" religions in lesser garb) appealing to individuals in different ways and at different times.[49] This has been compounded by a growing "consumer" approach to religion where the individual is the ultimate arbiter.[50] So, Luckmann says, "we are not merely describing an interregnum between the extinction of one 'official' model and the appearance of a new one, but, rather . . . we are observing the emergence of a new social form of religion."[51] The new form is an " 'ultimate' significance market" browsed by private individuals.[52]

In a more recent work, Luckmann develops his account of contemporary religion. He describes three grades of transcendent encounter in people's lives:

(1) "the '*little*', spatial and temporal, transcendences of everyday life" that occur "whenever anything that transcends that which at the moment is concretely given in actual, direct experience can be itself experienced"; (2) "the '*intermediate*' transcendences of everyday life" in encounters with referents to things that cannot be experienced directly (such as experiencing another's body as referring to "the 'inner' life of the fellow being"); and (3) "the '*great*' transcendences"—experiences that point to "something that not only cannot be experienced directly ... but in addition is definitively not a part of the reality in which things can be seen, touched, handled."[53] According to Luckmann, experience of transcendence in its various flavors is universal, and the process of interpretation, systematization, teaching, and so on tends to the institutionalization of these experiences; "they become quasi-objective social realities"—i.e., institutional religions.[54] However, Luckmann says that at a certain level of complexity, societies can no longer "maintain the social universality of an essentially religious world view oriented to the supremacy of a salvational articulation of the 'great' transcendences."[55] The consequences of this process, for religion, have "been customarily interpreted as a process of secularization, of the shrinking and eventual disappearance of religion from the modern world."[56] However, rather than seeing this as religion shrinking, he suggests it is better described as leading to a "change in the 'location' of religion in society ... as *privatization* of religion."[57]

Luckmann has been clear that religion in society is an institutional articulation of individual and continuing "experience on various levels of transcendence";[58] what he shows to be shrinkable is not the range of the transcendence in experiences (indeed, comments elsewhere in his article suggest that the range persists[59]), but instead the universalizability of *references* to transcendence (to little, great, or intermediate). It may be the case that "intersubjective reconstructions and social constructions shifted away from the 'great' other-worldly transcendences to the 'intermediate' and, more and more, also to the minimal transcendences of modern solipsism";[60] however, by Luckmann's own account, intersubjective reconstructions and social constructions are not the same things as "wild" experiences of transcendence—they are merely the shared articulations and formulations of experiences of transcendence. Individual experiences of transcendence persist.

In the 1960s, Peter Berger argued that "today, it would seem, it is industrial society in itself that is secularizing" and "modern industrial society has produced a centrally 'located' sector that is something like 'liberated territory' with respect to religion. Secularization has moved 'outwards' from this sector into other areas of society."[61] The thrust is that social institutions come progressively less under the sway of overarching religious institutions and that a concomitant "secularization of consciousness" also takes place: "Put simply, this means that the modern West has produced an increasing number of individuals who look upon the world and their own lives without the benefit of religious interpretations."[62] While it is clear that Berger's work of the 1960s and 1970s represented religion as in overall decline, he has famously changed his mind in recent times:

> The assumption that we live in a secularized world is false. The world today, with some exceptions ... is as furiously religious as it ever was, and in some places more so than ever. This means that a whole body of literature by historians and social scientists loosely labelled "secularization theory" is essentially mistaken.[63]

Secularization linked to modernization has, Berger says, "turned out to be wrong," and "secularization on the societal level is not necessarily linked to secularization on the level of individual consciousness."[64]

Notwithstanding his recent retraction, Berger's earlier writings were suggestive of some persisting role for religion. His *Social Reality of Religion* referred to religion as "the audacious attempt to conceive of the entire universe as being humanly significant."[65] Because the endpoint for all humans is death, societies can be seen as "in the last resort, men banded together in the face of death," and the power of religion depends "upon the credibility of the banners it puts in the hands of men as they stand before death."[66] Furthermore, while institutional religion was shown to have declined, people were instead "confronted with a wide variety of religious and other reality-defining agencies that compete for [their] allegiance"; thus, a kind of "religious market" or a system of "religious free-enterprise" has emerged.[67] This presages Berger's reassessment at the turn of the millennium that although "certain religious institutions have lost power and influence in many societies, ... both old and new religious beliefs and practices have nonetheless continued in the lives of individuals, sometimes taking new institutional forms and sometimes leading to great explosions of religious fervor."[68] While the old pattern of secularization seems evident in western Europe, Berger says that "a body of data indicates strong survivals of religion, most of it generally Christian in nature, despite the widespread alienation from organized churches. A shift in the institutional location of religion, then, rather than secularization, would be a more accurate description of the European situation."[69]

Both Luckmann and Berger have a considerable theoretical debt to Émile Durkheim. The central claim of Durkheim's theory of religion is that it is an expression of society. For Durkheim, religion is "something eminently social" and collective that is expressed in shared rites and beliefs, and in individuals' senses that they are part of something greater and that something greater inheres in them.[70] Thus, common metaphysical ideas are expressions of the social superstructure that individuals participate in. While Durkheim's account of religion is plainly less supernatural than conventional religious self-understandings (society in general provides the ultimate referent, rather than any conventionally transcendent power), religion in his scheme is unlikely to evaporate completely:

> There is something eternal in religion which is destined to survive all the particular symbols in which religious thought has successively enveloped itself. There can be no society which does not feel the need of upholding and re-affirming at regular intervals the collective sentiments and the collective ideas which make its unity and its personality.[71]

In effect, according to Durkheim, unified social groups need unifying ideals to integrate them—those ideals are the elements of religion.

Durkheim says that religion "is nothing other than a system of collective beliefs and practices that have a special authority" through the adherence of a whole society and thus performs a special unifying and integrating function in society.[72] As society changes, it is natural that old religions must fade and new ones arise.[73] In Durkheim's account, the replacement for religion, the supplanter of church religion, is qualitatively the same as what it has replaced (aside from the paraphernalia of "symbols and rites" or "temples and priests"[74]). Whether Durkheim is right that the religion of individualism is the natural replacement of traditional church religion, what is important here is his observation that there is an essential continuity (in Durkheim's case, understood in strongly—if not unalloyed—sociological terms) between the old religion and the new spirituality. From the point of view of the secularization thesis, religion as social function will persist even if its object changes.

Durkheim's representation, and that of Luckmann and Berger, has striking parallels with the nature of much contemporary spirituality. For example, Meredith McGuire writes that the new form of religiosity

> turns pluralism, individualism, and freedom of choice, characteristic of the modern world, into religious virtues and advantages.... A meditation center or healing circle might attract a number of participants who individually are pursuing many different paths for their physical-emotional-social-spiritual well-being. They may be unified only by their common value of spiritual approaches to well-being.[75]

And Hanegraaff has highlighted the striking parallels between his account of New Age spirituality, in which "religion becomes solely a matter of individual choice and detaches itself from religious institutions," and Durkheim's expectations of religious evolution, which "sound like a veritable prophecy of the New Age movement."[76] Of course, the diversity of communities in which the Panacea Society's healing found a following is perhaps not the unified social group Durkheim had in mind. Nonetheless, insofar as the Society did not demand adherence to doctrine, presented its healing as a kind of exultation of human perfectibility, and was plastic and unstable and subject to individual reformulation, it met the core criteria of Durkheim's future religion and exemplified McGuire's ecosystem of physical-emotional-social-spiritual searchers.

In his study of the 1960s as a turning point in popular spirituality, Hugh McLeod takes pains to use (unpublished) personal testimony to avoid relying solely on "celebrities or activists, whose experiences may be quite unrepresentative of the wider population."[77] Using a variety of written sources of evidence of religious understanding,[78] Jeremy Morris sketches a historical approach to personal and interior spiritual lives that focuses on the internal element.[79] Recognizing the problem of sources, Morris observes that "most of the accounts [he cites] come, naturally, from the highly educated"; however, "there is no intrinsic reason to believe that the spiritual world of the poor was any less complex ... than was that of the rich and educated."[80] David Lyon enjoins researchers to "listen sympathetically to the accounts of believers," as "taking seriously insider accounts ... helps us avoid the elitism of some secularization dominated stories" and "chart the actual 'meaning routes' that individuals take in everyday life."[81]

In turning to these kinds of sources, if considered within the bounds of conventional sociological practice that might divide religion into the public and the private, approaches such as these putatively seek to access the "private"; however, they might be better understood as entering a third realm between the two: the transcendent expressed in interactions between people (inside or outside churches). Kelly Besecke has identified this as "the noninstitutional-but-public kind of religion" in a "third sphere of society, neither institutional nor individual, but cultural."[82] Besecke says: "If private religion is located primarily inside people's psyches, and public religion is that which engages politics or economics, or else takes place in the churches, then we lack a category for everything else."[83] Within this understanding, it is explicit that "religion is a meaning system and not a social institution."[84] Shaw's account of the "domestic feel" of the theology of the Panacea Society is perhaps an example of the kind of interactive theology that expresses the interaction between spiritual seekers, although the Society's reference points may be more conventional than those Besecke has in mind. Shaw shows how in the Panacea Society "ideas about God and what was happening in their midst were repeatedly refracted through a domestic lens," and the core members "took up household and domestic images that are a key part of the Bible—though often missed—with alacrity," reflecting their sense of female duty.[85] Nonetheless, the Society's core membership exemplifies a dynamic negotiation in spirituality and religion spanning the personal and the public realms, as well as conventional and innovative social and cultural movements. (This example is perhaps blunted by the fact that the Society attempted to establish itself as an institution along the lines of the Church of England its leadership knew so well.)

The idea of this kind of intermediary and dynamic religious space is coming to prominence, but it has long origins. It can be found, for example, in Don Yoder's work on western folk religion in the 1970s.[86] This is the region that Leonard Primiano calls "vernacular religion."[87] It is described by Bowman and Valk as "religion in everyday life, practical religion, religion as it is lived," which is not studied with an emphasis on "artificial expectations of theological homogeneity or 'orthodoxy' " but examines "what people do in relation to extra-liturgical praxis.... The overriding interest, is on what people in a variety of cultural, religious and geographical landscapes, think and say in relation to what they believe about the way the world is constituted."[88] This is one framework within which to interpret the various approaches of those who see the decline of mainstream religion as the decline of religion-in-general, and those who see it as part of a dynamic and broader economy. As Primiano has observed in the field of folklore studies, "the two-tiered model employed by historians, anthropologists, sociologists, and religious studies scholars ... residualizes the religious lives of believers and at the same time reifies the authenticity of religious institutions as the exemplar of human religiosity."[89]

In his discussion of vernacular religion, and in a bid "to redress a heritage of scholarly misrepresentation" and do "justice to the variety of manifestations and perspectives found within past and present human religiosity,"[90] Primiano coins a new approach pertinent to the study of religion in all its forms. Vernacular has a range of meanings, and Primiano settles on two or three important senses of the term: "the indigenous language or dialect of a speech community"[91]; "simply 'personal, private' "; and "of arts, or features of these: native or peculiar to a particular country or locality."[92] In his usage, Primiano refers to "the omnipresent action of personal religious interpretation[, which] involves various negotiations of belief and practice including, but not limited to, original invention, unintentional innovation, and intentional adaptation."[93] Thus, vernacular religion

> takes into consideration the individual convictions of "official" religious membership among common believers, as well as the vernacular religious ideas at the root of the institution itself. Individuals feel their personal belief system as believers to be "official," and they also at the same time feel the belief system disseminated by the agencies of the institutional hierarchy to be "official religion."[94]

The significance of Primiano's discussion of the scholarly approach to folk religion is pertinent in the study of the dynamics of modern religious change more broadly; it challenges religious studies to examine "the religious individual and the significance of religion as it is lived in the contemporary context."[95]

The study of vernacular religion "understands religion as the continuous art of individual interpretation and negotiation of any number of influential sources" and recognizes that "all religion is both subtly and vibrantly marked by continuous interpretation even after it has been reified in expressive or structured forms." The study of vernacular religion thus "shifts the way one studies religion with the people becoming the focus of study and not 'religion' or 'belief' as abstractions."[96] This is an attempt to grasp the "stubbornly ambiguous" "lived religion," for all its inaccessibility, that lies at the base of all forms of religious expression.[97]

These analyses indicate a particular challenge to the study of religion in modern times. Previously, a historian of religion might validly engage with authorized and shared (normally published) accounts of experience of transcendence, thereby capturing something of a society's consensus about the realm beyond immediate experience. In more recent times, in societies where accounts of transcendence are less susceptible to shared forms of expression, there is no convenient window into any general religious worldview. Indeed, the only source of this kind of information would lie in individual testimonies—such as those in which the Panacea Society's Healing Archive is so rich. In societies where it is not assumed that there are individuals who can convey a shared metaphysics, the historian of religion must potentially treat everyone as a metaphysician and be prepared to study them as such. At root this is a problem of sources, because we are interested in the personal views of people who did not normally record their thinking in published form, or whose papers were not generally preserved for posterity or in other ways. The letters of the Panacea Society's healing users provide a window into those views; they allow us to sample a multitude of people's thoughts about transcendent matters across the twentieth century and across national and cultural boundaries. The method employed here uses these highly individual sources as valid and authentic expressions of the theological and metaphysical ideas of people who were not normally trained as theologians or metaphysicians.

PATTERNS OF PANACEA HEALING AFFILIATION

The main part of the task outlined in this chapter will be carried out in the body of the book through an analysis of the letters of the Panacea Society's water-takers. Prior to that, it is useful to examine some of the general trends and patterns of people's correspondence with the Society's Healing Department. While the overall pattern shows an early peak followed by decline and stagnation in application rates, indications of the gender breakdown of water-takers, and the stable intensity of people's contact, are suggestive of some important themes in the nature of religious change in the twentieth century.

As we have seen, between its launch in 1924 and its closure in 2012, the Panacea Society's healing received more than 122,000 applications from people in 102 countries or territories. The United States, Jamaica, and the British Isles were the main sources of applications, with the USA generating nearly 40,000 applications and Jamaica over 30,000. The British Isles, the third-largest source of applications, generated around 23,000 (overwhelmingly from England[98]). After the British Isles, there was a considerable drop in numbers to Finland, the fourth most significant national source of applications, which produced more than 3,000 applications overall.[99]

After an early peak followed by a second high point in 1939 (the relationship between the application data and war is discussed in chapter 6) with some recovery after a postwar collapse in numbers, the number of applications received each year steadily declined. The pattern is similar for many of the countries for which data is available in the archive.

Based on the sample of 3,894 applicants' index cards (using the sample of the first 50 applicants stored in each of the 81 index card drawers),[100] the average number of letters written by each applicant in the sample to the Society (excluding their application letter) was 5.3 during individuals' careers as communicating users of the healing. If all those who applied and never wrote again are discounted from the sample (leaving 2,354), the average number of letters is 8.8 per applicant. The most voluminous correspondence identified in the sample amounted to 209 letters from a man (16017) who applied from New York in

December 1927 and remained in contact until November 1989. A woman (16902) from Norfolk, England applied in March 1936 and went on to write 203 letters up to June 1986.[101] The average duration of contact (excluding those identified as writing no letters after their application) was about three years and nine months (1,379 days).

There were steady declines in the duration of contact and in the overall number of letters written by each applicant to the Society over the course of the century (excluding those who did not write again after applying), with each applicant maintaining contact for an average of just over five years (1,864 days) and writing an average of fourteen letters to the Society if they applied in 1924–1933, and these numbers dropping steadily to 551 days of contact and 3.8 letters among those applying after 1983. Healing users were enjoined to write to the Society on a quarterly basis, and the average number of letters per year written by each applicant remained very steady; its low was the 1944–1953 intake (4.1) and its high was the 1924–1933 intake (4.8).[102] Overall, the number of letters written each year by applicants ended the century at an average of 4.7 (for those who applied from

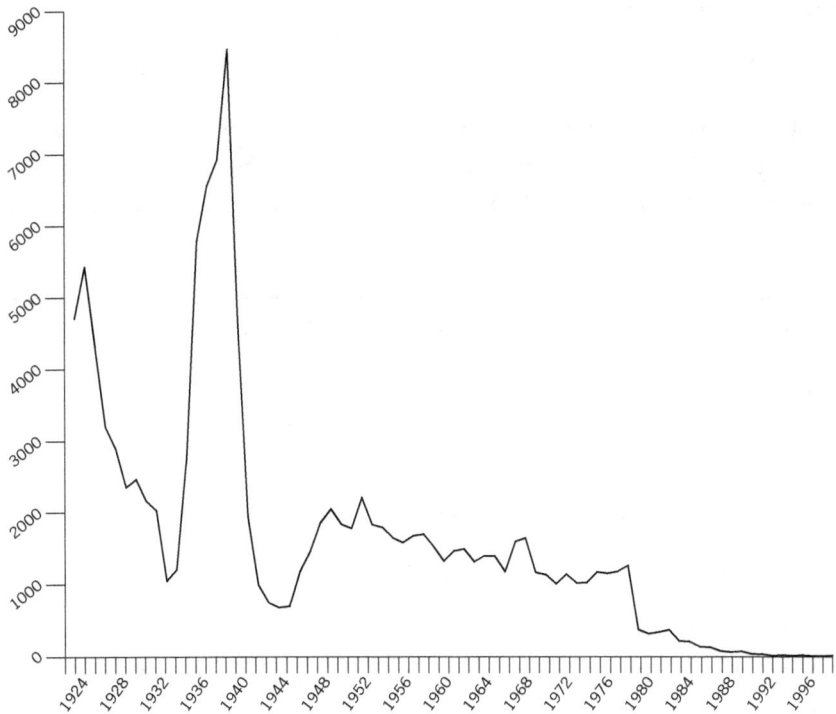

CHART 3.1. Panacea Society Healing, global application numbers over time.

TABLE 3.1. Average duration of contact, number of letters written, and letters per year for index card sample of Panacea Society Healing users, analysed by decade of initial application, for all countries. (Excludes applicants writing no letters after initial contact.)

Application decade	Duration (days)	Number of letters	Letters per year	Number in sample
1924–33	1,864	14.0	4.8	547
1934–43	1,447	9.9	4.6	695
1944–53	1,619	7.1	4.1	291
1954–63	1,197	6.4	4.3	225
1964–73	1,009	4.7	4.2	263
1974–83	684	3.6	4.7	242
>1983	551	3.8	4.7	91

TABLE 3.2. Average duration of contact, number of letters written, and letters per year for index card sample of Panacea Society Healing users applying from England, analysed by decade of initial application. (Excludes applicants writing no letters after initial contact.)

Application decade	Duration (days)	Number of letters	Letters per year	Number in sample
1924–33	1,509	11.7	5.1	361
1934–43	1,248	11.3	5.7	199
1944–53	1,235	8.2	6.7	46
1954–63	1,613	11.2	5.7	40
1964–73	781	4.1	6.6	37
1974–83	752	4.8	6.3	53
>1983	262	3.3	7.1	20

1974 onwards), almost precisely the same average number of letters written each year by applicants who applied in 1924–1933 (4.8). Thus, while the century saw people corresponding for less and less time and writing fewer and fewer letters, they continued to communicate at similar rates—that is, the intensity of contact remained the same, even if its duration fell.

The pattern holds for the two largest countries in the index cards sample: Jamaica and England. Indeed, each of these countries saw an overall increase in this intensity at the end of the century compared to the earlier period of healing. The intensity of correspondence (i.e., the number of letters per year) indicates the rate at which the decline in the number of letters written by applicants during their periods as users of the healing kept up with the decline in the duration of contact. An increasing intensity suggests that the number of letters written did not decrease as rapidly as did duration. (The prominent pattern is the overall consistency of the rate.)

The place of a female messiah was fundamental to the theology of the Panacea Society, and the group's leadership and managers were predominantly women. The majority of applicants to the healing (more than two-thirds) were women. The levels of interest of women compared to men and the importance of

TABLE 3.3. Average duration of contact, number of letters written, and letters per year for index card sample of Panacea Society Healing users applying from Jamaica, analysed by decade of initial application. (No records for 1924–33. Excludes applicants writing no letters after initial contact.)

Application decade	Duration (days)	Number of letters	Letters per year	Number in sample
1924–33	–	–	–	–
1934–43	1,016	3.4	3.8	407
1944–53	1,844	5.4	3	185
1954–63	868	3.6	3.8	145
1964–73	975	4.3	3.8	203
1974–83	652	3.1	4.4	156
>1983	651	4	4	67

the female in the Panacea Society's theology may be reflections of wider trends in late nineteenth-century and early twentieth-century religious innovation. The Panacea Society is, for example, among the groups mentioned in Marta Trzebiatowska and Steve Bruce's study of the relationship between religious innovation and women.[103] The ratio of women and men who applied to the healing seems in line with research indicative of gender ratios in other alternative spiritual practices. For example, Liselotte Frisk's study of New Age participants in Sweden suggests that 83 percent were women; 80 percent of those involved in alternative healing groups in New Jersey, USA, in research by Meredith McGuire were women; and Paul Heelas and Linda Woodhead concluded that females made up "80 percent of those active in the holistic milieu" in their area of study in northern England.[104]

Of the 3,802 applicants in the index card sample whose index card records give an indication of gender, 2,598 (68 percent) are identifiable as female. Among the countries making up the larger proportion of the index card sample, females make up a larger proportion of the applicants, and the proportions are in striking agreement with the studies here cited. For example, the index cards from applicants with Jamaican addresses include 1,853 applicants with identifiable gender, and of these, 68 percent (1,264) are female. And 1,192 people with identifiable gender applied for the healing from English addresses, with 73 percent (866) women.

Women were also more likely to persist with the healing after their initial application; 37 percent (962) of the female applicants applied and made no further contact, whereas the equivalent figure for the 1,204 men in the sample was 43 percent (522). While, on average, men maintained a relationship with the Society

TABLE 3.4. Average duration of contact, number of letters written, and letters per year for index card sample of Panacea Society Healing users, analysed by gender. (Excludes applicants writing no letters after initial contact.)

Female/male	Duration (days)	Number of letters	Letters per year	Number in sample
Female	1,420	8.9	4.48	1,636
Male	1,305	8.5	4.53	682

for a shorter period of time and wrote fewer letters overall, on average the intensity of their contact with the Society (4.53 letters per year) was almost precisely the same as that for female water-takers (4.48).

The evidence of the sustained levels of intensity of contact with the Society (letters per year) is striking from the point of view of a classically conceived secularization thesis, though the steady declines in duration and number of letters might be expected. While the Society's request that users of the water communicate on their progress quarterly no doubt contributed to intensity rates, from a traditional secularization viewpoint, it might be expected that this intensity would also decline as other metrics declined. Instead, the findings suggest that there is something consistent that underlies changing patterns of spiritual practice. Furthermore, as the level of intensity among the applicants after 1983 was about the same as it was for those who applied during 1924–1933 in the global sample and is consistent between genders, this aspect of spiritual engagement would seem to be less susceptible to outside factors than might be expected. Similarly, the broad pattern of a sustained intensity of contact in both Jamaican and English applicants suggests some continued and sustained interest somewhat independent of local conditions. While the overall decline in numbers applying to the Society may be evidence of the declining attractiveness of the Society's offering (or of a general decline in the "volume" of religious affiliation in the wider society), the sustained intensity of contact is suggestive of a pattern of declining quantity but steady and somewhat universal quality of engagement as the twentieth century went on.

CHAPTER FOUR

The Healing and Other Movements I

Great Britain

Before the outbreak of the Second World War, the numbers of applications for the healing from the British Isles[1] show some significant rises and falls, but they stabilized after the war. A careful search of the register books retained in the Society's archives shows British Isles applications for healing reached in excess of twenty thousand overall between 1924 and 2012.[2] In the first year of the official availability of the healing (1924), about 2,700 people applied, and this jumped to about 4,000 in 1925. After the early peak, applications declined steadily to about 320 in 1936.[3] From there, and perhaps associated with global instability and the buildup of pressure towards war (discussed in chapter 6), applications increased substantially to about 2,000 in 1939, though this number declined precipitously to 550 in 1940 and then to 101 by 1945. After 1945 until 1978, the annual number of applications averaged 141, with lows in 1959 and 1960 (71 and 81, respectively) and highs of 221 and 215 (in 1978 and 1976, respectively).[4] After 1978 recordkeeping at the Society seems to have been more disordered, so it is difficult to identify clear numbers. Applications continued to come in from the 1980s to the 2000s, and in the last ten years of the healing up to 2012, about forty British healing users contacted the Society, though most of those had applied for the healing in earlier decades.

Analysis of the index card sample[5] indicates that 38 percent of individuals who applied for the healing from Great Britain did not write again after applying. About 14 percent wrote one additional letter and so can be surmised to have experimented with the healing, albeit to a limited extent.[6] The remainder (48 percent) wrote two or more letters to the Society after applying, so they can be seen as having had a more sustained relationship with the healing. On average, water-takers in this latter group wrote slightly more than thirteen letters during the time they were in communication with the Society, and they kept in contact on average for about four and a half years (1,678 days). It is evident in the index card sample that women made up 72 percent of applicants from Great Britain. The sample of index cards for Great Britain indicates that about 96 percent made their applications from England.

For the purposes of this research, the letters of 187 water-takers who were filed as applicants from Great Britain were subjected to detailed analysis.[7] The Panacea Society did not collect age data from applicants on a consistent basis, and only limited information about the ages of water-takers can be gleaned from letters. For forty-six of the British water-takers analyzed in this study, the average age at the time of the writing of their first known letter appears to have been fifty-six years.[8] One applicant as young as nineteen at application (94199) can be identified (though children also applied through their parents), and the oldest applicant was aged seventy-six (84676). The oldest correspondent was a man who wrote his final letter in 1957 when he was ninety-six; his application had been received in 1928 (73698). The oldest female correspondent identified maintained contact until 1977, when she was aged eighty-eight; she had applied some time before November 1950 (35296).

The majority of users of the healing do not refer to their working lives in their letters, though occupations can be identified for some of them. Where this is possible, healing users can normally be identified in working and middle socioeconomic categories, including teachers (14562, 54577, and 53601) and farmers (24684, 45913); domestic and care personnel and factory workers (43635, 15974, 75084, 35123, and 65762); and laborers and their wives (86153, 94199, and 71480). It is also possible to identify an electrician (55485) and a furniture maker (35772), as well as a dental surgeon (98356), a civil servant (59407), and a dress designer (60957).[9] It should be noted that a great many users of the healing were married women, many of whom may not have had work outside their support of their families. Many are likely to have been retired or wealthy, so perhaps without definitive occupations.

The Panacea Society as an institution, and the water-takers as individuals, were interlaced with a wide range of the religious innovations prevalent in Britain at the time of the Society's formation in the 1920s and earlier. Octavia and other founding members had practiced spiritualism and automatic writing, and they were conversant with a number of the new, nonmainstream, and occult forms of spiritual practice prevalent at the time. And the letters from the water-takers include regular references to a wide range of growing nonmainstream spiritual and religious movements and practices—with mentions of Christian Science, Spiritualism, and Theosophy, with other varieties of spiritual healing peppering the letters, especially during the interwar period. Though the Panacea Society did not have the profile of many of these types of movements, it inhabited the same ecosystem, had a membership that overlapped, and was tied to similar intellectual and doctrinal leitmotifs.

NEW MOVEMENTS AND THE PANACEA SOCIETY

The main spiritual and religious organizations discussed in this chapter are part of the "vast spectrum of beliefs and practices" providing the sources of ideas and practices making up what Christopher Partridge calls western "occulture"—the broad and diverse variety of spiritual ideas embedded in nontraditional spiritual thought in the West.[10] Jane Shaw discusses how the earliest members of the Panacea Society "were attracted to the vogue-ish movements of the early twentieth century—vegetarianism ... Theosophy, Higher Thought and spiritualism"—and the same might be said of many of the users of the healing.[11] Perhaps the most significant movement in this respect is Theosophy. Joy Dixon has commented that an important impact of the Theosophical Society was to "produce a kind of generic 'eastern mysticism,' one that has had a significant impact on modern New Age movements, many of which have borrowed their terminology and basic concepts from theosophical teachings."[12] Wouter Hanegraaff makes a similar case for the importance of Theosophy (and Anthroposophy), especially in England, as the seedbed for a distinctive strand of the later flourishing of New Age ideas that are widely evident in nontraditional popular metaphysical thinking today.[13] Similarly, James R. Lewis has drawn attention to the difficulty of making any theoretical distinction between predecessor movements (such as Theosophy) and the later New Age movement.[14]

Theosophy had come to Britain in 1878, when its Russian–American founder, Helena Petrovna Blavatsky (1831–1891), and some of her associates stopped in Britain for a few days (and founded the British Theosophical Society) on their way to India to establish a new headquarters for the movement in what they regarded as its spiritual homeland.[15] Blavatsky and her followers had formed the Theosophical Society in New York in 1875 with the purpose of bringing about "a Universal Brotherhood based upon the essential divinity of man."[16] They believed themselves to be in communication with "superhuman spiritual realities," a "group of Superhuman Men, Teachers, Masters, [and] Adepts" from whom guidance and spiritual knowledge could be obtained in the journey of the human species to "Universal Brotherhood; the realisation of the Unity of the Eternal Self in all things; and the unfolding of the divine qualities in human nature."[17] At the end of the nineteenth century, Annie Besant (1847–1933), a spiritual seeker who had taken up Theosophy in the late 1880s, was appointed president of the London Blavatsky Lodge.[18] Membership grew steadily in the British Isles, to a peak of around 5,000 members in the 1920s, before a period of steady decline to the 1960s.[19]

In her preface to a leaflet of extracts from the works of Jane Lead, Octavia quotes Blavatsky in some detail and recognizes a parallelism between aspects of Blavatsky's ideas and some Panacean doctrines.[20] Although she makes clear that "Theosophy is wrong,"[21] Octavia does concede that the movement has greater awareness of bodily salvation than the Christian churches (though poorer in its understanding of salvation of the soul).[22] Although the "results" of Theosophy "are nil," she acknowledges the movement has the benefit of providing "much data useful to those who are 'the wise' and understand the old mysteries."[23] At one time, Octavia wrote to the Theosophical Society's leader, Annie Besant, proposing a distribution agreement for the Panacea Society's healing through the Theosophical Society.[24] In 1924, the extent of affiliation with the Theosophical Society among Panacea Society members was perceived to be so large that Octavia attempted to define the relationship between the societies, and the Panacean antithesis to Theosophy. At the same time, she recognized the importance of Theosophy as a way into the Panacea Society for many, but she also asked rhetorically "need you cling to the ladder by which you climbed up."[25]

The form of Spiritualism that flourished in the nineteenth and twentieth centuries had its origins in New York State in the 1840s, when a farming family began to communicate with spirits. The incident garnered much interest, and "Spiritualist Circles" quickly spread across the United States, reaching the British Isles about five years later.[26] As in Theosophy, an important theoretical element of Spiritualism was the capacity of people to communicate with disembodied spirits. However, while embodied individuals such as Blavatsky and her cohort who had the capacity to communicate with the disembodied spirits were a privileged band in contact with a community of wise and spiritually superior masters, Spiritualism had a more democratic ethos. Theirs was a multitude of otherwise ordinary individuals able to mediate between living inquirers and a host of deceased spirits who retained their interest in the everyday concerns of the living. In its developed form, Spiritualism associated the idea of continued existence after death with the idea of moral and spiritual progression. The physicist Oliver Lodge (1851–1940), who was president of the Society for Psychical Research, was Spiritualism's chief advocate in Britain. His "Spiritualist's Creed," published in 1925, proposed that after release from the physical body, an individual spirit would live a "more unhampered, more real, more wakeful, more intelligent, more hopeful existence" on the other side of death.[27] The Creed asserts that after death, individuals "enter on the state for which [they] are fit, whether it be higher or lower," and might one day rise beyond to "regions far above our ken."[28]

There was a spiritualist undercurrent to much of the early beliefs and practices of the Panacea Society's founding members. Of all the spiritual and religious alternatives, Spiritualism, though ultimately regarded as useless in the doctrine of the Society, was perhaps rejected by the Society less fulsomely than the others. To the extent that it represents an interaction with another plane of existence, Spiritualism was recognized as authentic by the Society. However, as a transaction between living people with bodies (who therefore have the potential to achieve the highest human state and to attain an immortal body) and those who have died and lost their physical aspects (so would be unable to reach the highest level of physical immortality), Spiritualism represented a resort to a lower metaphysical class by a higher in the view of the Society.[29]

Christian Science was another vital and dynamic contributor to the interwar ferment in Britain in which the Panacea Society's healing emerged, and many of the letters from users of the Society's healing testify to the writers' affiliations with Christian Science as well as other movements. Octavia had made an extensive study of Christian Science—a process which had been valuable, she claimed, so that she was in a position to refute it.[30] Christian Science was initiated by the New Hampshire Congregationalist Mary Baker Eddy (1821–1910) in 1866, after she injured herself in a fall and became convinced that she had managed to heal herself when she read miracle healing stories in the Bible. A report on "Mental Healing in Boston, U.S.A.," published in *The Times* (London) on May 26, 1885, gave an account of a "religio-metaphysical *furore*" in New England that was "almost sure to spread beyond American limits."[31] The article reported the practice's core notion, that "there is no such thing as sickness. Disease ... is an error of the mind." About ten years later, recognized members of the Christian Science movement in the British Isles are recorded.[32] Membership records for Christian Science in the British Isles are not available. The number of practitioners recorded in the *Christian Science Journal* give some indication of changing rates of popularity: from 50 full practitioners in 1902 there was a steady increase to 1,104 in 1940, after which there was a fall to 581 in 1969.[33]

The Panacea Society was prepared to "recognize the success" of Christian Science insofar as it implemented the "common knowledge" that "thinking wisely and healthily and usefully will help both health and circumstances." The Society's observations on the methods of Christian Science (and other "Thought Cults") went so far as to note that "when people do things under the aegis of a society they do them with greater interest and perseverance, and consequently do them with more effect"—and perhaps the insight informed their own approach to their healing ministry.[34] However, the mark of the success of Christian Science (and similar forms of healing) was precisely the mark of its limitation: it operated on the level of thought's interaction with matter, and not at the level of the mind's interaction with the Divine.[35] Again, the Panacea Society perceived itself to have special knowledge of the cosmological constitution of humanity and of the physical process of the spiritual remediation of the weaknesses of the physical body.

NEW MOVEMENTS AND THE PANACEA SOCIETY'S HEALING USERS

Theosophy was a key source of applicants to the Society's healing. *The Herald of the Star*, an important Theosophy magazine in the early decades of the twentieth century, seems to have generated a number of applications after people read about the Society there. Jane Shaw's account of the healing highlights the importance of Theosophists as a source of membership for the Panacea Society and shows how factionalism within the Theosophical Society was a driver of membership of the Panacea Society.[36] This reached a crisis point for the Theosophical Society in 1924, the same year that the Panacea Society launched its healing.[37] An early user of the Panacea Society's healing (30941), who first applied from Birmingham in February 1924 after hearing of it reported in *The Herald of the Star*,[38] saw the healing as the fulfilment of a personal and spiritual journey. Later on, she wrote to the Society in the middle of the Second World War saying the healing was a "pearl of great price" she had been promised in a séance.[39] When she discovered the Panacea Society's teaching, she disengaged herself from other new forms of spiritual practice, having given up receiving "teachings from the Editor of The Pathway of the New Age" and restricted herself "from now on to the Panacea Teachings." She said the magazine sent by the Society and the inspired scripts left her "enraptured."[40]

The flexible attitude of many who engaged with these practices is evident in a letter from another reader of *The Herald of the Star*, who wrote from Brighton in 1924 (27312) that she was "not at all psychic" but "should like to hear from you about the cures which you say are taking place through spiritual agency. I am a Theosophist [and] very really interested in all such matters."[41] Another applicant (16377) wrote about plans to attend one of the Society's meetings after she "read with great interest in the *Herald of the Star* that the Joanna Southcott Movement is effecting cures by Faith Healing in cases of deafness."[42] Another user, a woman from Hertfordshire who applied in 1924 (57730), wrote to the Society to tell it she had "been listening to the beautiful and simple teaching of Krishnamurti," though in time she moved away from the Panacea Society and engaged instead with the Krishnamurti school of Theosophy.[43]

As the Panacea Society's healing was specifically geared to the resolution of ailments, it is perhaps unsurprising that the letters seem to refer to faith and spiritual healing, including Christian Science, more often than they do other categories of alternative religious practices. A number of applicants had engaged in a variety of alternative healing practices; for example, one woman (38978) wrote in 1934:

> I am still very deaf, I have been having Spiritual Healing from a Church near by but altho I feel better in myself for the treatment, my hearing does not improve, I am now fully resigned to being deaf. I accept it as being God's will, and altho I do not know the reason I am leaving it in God's hand.[44]

A man from Lincolnshire (19077) wrote seeking help with epilepsy, having been through various conventional and unconventional treatments: "I have suffered since childhood with this complaint. I might say that I have [studied] Christian Science, also Science of Thought, and have also had Medical treatment. But have not found healing yet."[45] For some, resort to the Panacea Society represented a step in an anxious search: "I have had Spiritual healing also Christian Science but to no avail. / Can you please help me obtain Healing [and] deliverance ... Shall anxiously wait your reply."[46] A man in the northeast of England (41680) came to the Panacea Society after developing his own method of spiritual healing to help his young son who was blind.

> My care is for my boy, he had an accident when playing football which necessitated a serious operation to the head which left him blind. Since the operation I have treated him myself, and, thanks be to God he is making wonderful progress, and his eyes are strengthening daily, but he is not able to attend school yet.[47]

He additionally wrote:

> My treatment of [son's name] is not magnetism but with the laying on of my hand virtue passes from me, but when you realize he was discharged from one of the best known hospitals in England and also by another private expert declared as permanently totally blind in the left eye and

now there is such wonderful progress to be seen. I fully understand that by myself and of myself I can do nothing, and it gives me great joy to know that Christ is working through me.[48]

A mother of five who had lived in India and who approached the Society for a cure for rheumatism and malaria applied from London in 1929 (20109). She also sought help for the challenges of her demanding family life, including a difficult relationship with her husband. Amid all of her everyday concerns, however, her letters suggest that her preoccupation was with matters of religion. In her first letter, she said she wanted to learn more about the Society, as "I have read many books written by Roman Catholics, Protestants, Theosophists & Christian Scientists, but no one seems to reach the root of the matter."[49]

A woman (54577) in her late thirties who worked in an elementary school and applied in October 1930 was among those showing the most complex engagement with the healing. She said in her application that she was a Theosophist and "though I recognize Divine working in your movement, and Divine power, I am not in sympathy with some of the ideas expressed in 'The Panacea.' "[50] When her letters seemed to peter out, the Society made contact with her by letter to inquire about her progress with the water. She replied in June 1932 offering a carefully thought out and sophisticated assessment of her engagement with the healing.

> I am better mentally since I first wrote, and for that I am really grateful. Yet I cannot continue the treatment, I am not in sympathy with the beliefs + outlook of the movement. I do believe in the Divine Power behind the Healing, and this belief is not inconsistent with an utter disbelief in the teachings of the society upon many things, because it seems evident that the Divine Healing Power like water, penetrates every channel which offers a course more or less unobstructed, Faith healing, mental healing, psychotherapy, spiritual healing, Christian science, New Thought, Coué, Unity, Nature Cure, Magnetic Healing, all these + others claim their cures, + also have their failures. When the cure is real, is it not the Divine Power? So I can believe in the Healing, + also that it is a convenient means, But the mistake I made, was in trying to be loyal to the movement + take the "Panacea" I tried hard to learn from the latter, but could not. And I felt "mean" at receiving benefits from people with whom I had so little sympathy. . . . I determined at any cost to health, to be true to the faith which means everything to me—Theosophy. + to trust to God the Father who allows pain to affect us only so long as there are lessons to be learned from it.

> I am glad that there is a Panacea Movement, and that many people are helped by it. I testify willingly to the serenity and nobility of the one Panacea member I know. But that way is not for me.... I look upon you as a worker for God in another field, + send you greetings, but I am afraid you will reckon me as a failure.⁵¹

A man who applied for the healing from Birmingham in the mid-1930s (51835) became a committed believer in Spiritualism and linked it to the activity of Jesus Christ: "I have studied it well and came to the conclusion that Christ Himself preached Spiritualism."⁵² In a subsequent letter, he said more about his views.

> I think that most people have a wrong idea about it and seem to think that it consists of solely speaking with the dead. But they are not dead only the Body has died and the Spirit never dies. Also I believe that there are evil Spirits as well as good ones and I don't think that God would allow the evil ones to have sway over us without some means of protecting ourselves, hence the good Spirits. The Reason I think the Lord preached, what for want of a better word I call Spiritualism, is that He preached of most things Spiritual and not so much earthly.⁵³

In fact, his interest in the Panacea Society was just the latest step on a spiritual journey from the Plymouth Brethren where he had been baptized "and was very sincere but of late years I am what I suppose would be called a backslider" to Spiritualism, though "of course that is against the [Plymouth Brethren] principles."⁵⁴

MAINSTREAM RELIGION

The Society believed the Anglican Church to be founded on an essential truth, namely the fact of the sacrifice of Jesus Christ for the forgiveness of sins, a doctrine necessary for salvation of *"those who die."*⁵⁵ As time had gone by, the Society believed, the churches had misunderstood and misapplied the implications of this religious teaching. While Christianity is the religion for the salvation of the soul, they argued, Panaceaism "is merely an advance" on Christianity; it is the religion for the salvation of the body—a more complete salvation.⁵⁶ The Society had a long-standing poor relationship with the institutional churches, and the Society's writings are peppered with criticisms of the Church of England (the only conventional "Church" in any sense meaningful to a Panacean, despite its imperfections—though the criticisms could equally apply to other Christian denominations *mutatis mutandis*).[57] The Panacea Society saw the primary error of the Church to be its ignorance of the Panacean anthropology, which the Society felt to be self-evident in the Bible. Primarily, the Society believed that although the Church recognized that animals might not have immortal souls, it failed to subscribe to the Panacea Society's doctrine that this was also true of some humans. Furthermore, the Church did not understand that there are "immortals" with incorruptible souls and bodies, and instead it ministered to the "incorruptibles" with mortal bodies and mortal souls, but also an additional immortal soul that would persist beyond the demise of the mortal aspects.[58]

Indeed, early on the Society had hoped that its healing method would be embraced by the Church of England; the Church's rejection of its offer served to entrench its alienation from the Church and gave the Society a renewed purpose.[59] Shaw comments that most of the early members of the Society were members of the Church of England, and indeed that many of them were related to clergy in some way,[60] but were frustrated with it because it "gave them so few opportunities to express their spirituality."[61] However, Shaw notes a certain paradox in the Society's attitude toward the Church of England: they were "like other contemporary heterodox groups . . . in their scepticism" but the Church held a special place for them simply because "it was the state Church, headed by the monarch, and they were royalists and patriots."[62]

Recent studies of popular religious beliefs after the Great War have suggested that the Church of England was involved in a process of accommodation of people's new spiritual needs resulting from the conflict. Georgina Byrne, for example, has proposed that the Church of England before the Second World War was "essentially syncretistic."[63] And although Rene Kollar argues that "a number of its [the Church of England's] leaders and theologians began to address the issues brought into relief by the war," he argues that traditional Anglicanism was losing its appeal to many.[64] The growing realization of the significance of heterodox and alternative spiritual and healing movements is evident among the Anglican bishops as early as the Lambeth Conference of 1908. There, the American bishops had requested a special discussion of spiritual healing to help them organize their reaction to the emergence of Christian Science,[65] and the topic arose again at the 1920 conference.[66] Excitement surrounding the start of James Moore Hickson's international healing tour in 1919 also contributed to making spiritual healing a topic for discussion at the 1920 Lambeth Conference.[67] The result of the bishops' deliberations in 1908 was two resolutions that referred to healing: Resolution 33 called for greater emphasis on spiritual ways to "gain a fuller control over temptation, pain, and disease," and Resolution 35 recommended "some additional prayers for the restoration of health more hopeful and direct" than those existing at the time for pastoral use.

These resolutions can be understood as the Church's attempt to incorporate the burgeoning interest in spiritual healing into its practices, and thus to channel the subjective instinct for personal healing into the external and institutional channels of the Church. The deliberations of the 252 Anglican bishops attending the Lambeth Conference of 1920 included extensive consideration of Christian Science, Spiritualism, and Theosophy. Formal resolutions included one recording the conference's finding that each movement "ignores or explains away or contradicts the unique and central fact of human history, namely, the Incarnation of our Lord and Saviour Jesus Christ."[68] Nonetheless, elsewhere it was noted that each movement provided something thought to be neglected in the Anglican Church, and that the Church had ground to make up if it were to regain the members it was losing. The Church's interpretation is thus in line with the notion that an apparent decline in affiliation to the Church of England is associated with a burgeoning of nontraditional forms of religion.

The conference's remedy is a diagnosis of the distinctive offering of each movement. Responding to Spiritualism, the bishops said that "a larger place should be given in the teaching of the Church to the explanation of the true grounds of Christian belief in eternal life, and in immortality."[69] They further stated that greater "regard should be given to the mystical elements of faith and life which underlie the historic belief of Christendom" in the Church's teaching, in order to respond to the perceived attractiveness of Theosophy's "presentation of Christian faith as a quest for knowledge."[70] In response to Christian Science, the bishops called for greater use of prayer so that "the power of Christ to heal may be released."[71] Furthermore, another resolution instigated the formation of a committee to investigate "the use with prayer of the laying on of hands, of the unction of the sick and other spiritual means of healing."[72] The committee's findings were skeptical; it found "no evidence of any cases of healing which cannot be paralleled by similar cures wrought by psychotherapy without religion, and by instances of spontaneous healing which often occur ... in ordinary medical practice."[73]

A few letters to the Society give some detail about how users of the healing felt connected to the Anglican Church and their perception of the relationship between the Church and the Panacea Society. For example, a water-taker from Bristol who had applied in 1929 (99009) wrote with an inquiry.

> As you no doubt know, I am a member of the Church of England, but since joining your Society & knowing it to be better, I certainly do not

take the same amount of interest in Church, but I have been in the habit of making my communion at least once a month, now I am taking the water ought I still continue?[74]

Another example is a water-taker who had applied some time before 1940 (58019); she wrote about how she had "lost faith in medicine + Drs [sic] I only believe in Christ.... I am of the Church of England—my one quarrel with them is—that they have not the healing."[75]

The number of users of the healing commenting on the nature of their relationship with the Anglican Church is not great; nonetheless, those who did make these kinds of observations were in line with the perception that they were in search of something the Church was failing to provide. They also indicated their personal and spiritual trajectories through various forms of alternative religious systems—including Anglicanism—and the well-known innovative and spiritual practices discussed here. As we have seen, association with the Church of England is rarely expressed unambiguously in the letters. Nonetheless, some level of familiarity with or exposure to mainstream forms of Christian faith is not unlikely for every applicant from the British Isles. The letters from the Society's membership support the impression held by the bishops at the Lambeth Conference in 1920 that many in their flocks were interested in and moving into rival and alternative movements.

These letters evidence, then, the ways that people were flexible and mobile in a diverse religious economy in which the Anglican Church competed alongside arrivals such as Christian Science, Spiritualism, Theosophy, and the Panacea Society. What is especially clear from the letters is the earnestness and authenticity of the search for a suitable religious form of affiliation for many. Though we may grant that some who applied for the healing and never made contact again presumably applied for frivolous reasons—out of curiosity, or under some misapprehension—equally, those that discussed religion and the Panacea Society's place in their broader spiritual trajectory did so with heartfelt and theological intent. In this light, the marketplace metaphor that has become something of a standard analogy for contemporary religion appears progressively less useful. The browsers in the market are not merely seeking some spiritual tidbit to consume but a theological and practical truth that works for them. Presumably those who remain affiliated to old and conventional churches such as the Church of England do so out of a realization that the formula meets a deep-felt spiritual need, or out of habit, convenience, or convention. Granting that neither criteria continue to hold for those who seek within the plethora of spiritual alternatives and outside the established Church, then their search is at least a genuine one.

CHAPTER FIVE

The Healing and Other Movements II

The United States, Jamaica, and Finland

As we have seen, although the center of the healing was in the British Isles and especially England, and that territory generated more than twenty thousand applications for the healing, in time the United States and Jamaica emerged as the two major sources of applications overall during the century. The size of the task presented by American and Jamaican applicants for the water necessitated the creation of subdepartments to administer them within the Healing Department. The British West Indies section was set up in June 1936, and the U.S. section in December 1938. Application rates from the fourth-most significant country in terms of application numbers overall, Finland, were substantially lower than those for the United States, Jamaica, and the British Isles. Nevertheless, Finland had a lively and thriving community of water-takers supported by a vibrant local theosophical network.

The Society's register books indicate about 39,000 applicants for the Panacea Society's healing from the United States between 1924 and the 1990s. With an initially fluctuating rate of applications (about 730 in 1924 and dropping to about 50 in 1929), the number shows a rise in the buildup to the war, increasing steadily to around 3,800 in 1939. Following a steady drop to a low of about 340 applications in 1945, they rose again and averaged about 500 a year until the end of the 1970s (with highs in 1949 and 1952, of 972 and 944, respectively) before dropping off to single figures each year by the mid-1990s. Around 50 correspondents have been discovered who wrote to the Society in the last decade of the healing (up to 2012), and about half of those had initially applied during that decade. The index card records on U.S. applicants held at the Panacea Society archives is notably scanty (relative to overall numbers and compared to Jamaica and the British Isles especially), so they are of little value for the purpose of comparison with other major countries.[1] Nonetheless, analysis of the 53 American records included in the index card sample analyzed for the British Isles shows 41 applications from women (77 percent). An additional sampling of 100 water-takers from across U.S. letters indicates a similar ratio, with 79 percent female.

American applicants have been found in every decade of adult life up to the eighties. Among the oldest correspondents were a man (81008) from Michigan State who was eighty-five when he applied in 1925 (and did not make contact again, though there are signs he may have been in touch with the Society before that date), and a woman who applied from Ohio aged 80, also in 1925, who went on to correspond with the Society for about a year (17684).

From Jamaica, there were more than thirty thousand applicants for the healing. Applications from Jamaica were very few until the mid-1930s, when in 1935 more than 800 were recorded—and this rose to more than 3,000 in the following year and nearly 4,000 in 1937. While applications quickly dropped to a low of fewer than 100 in 1943 (no doubt due in part to wartime disruption to postal services), they steadily rose to about 750 in 1949 and averaged about 575 a year up to 1978. Around 130 individuals are known to have made contact with the Society from Jamaica in the Society's last decade of operation—about a third of those had initially applied for the healing during that time.

The index card sample of Jamaican applications shows that about 38.5 percent did not write again after their application letter (the British Isles showed a similar figure), about 24 percent wrote just one letter (higher than the British Isles's 15 percent), and about 37.5 percent entered a more developed relationship with the Society and wrote two or more letters during their period of contact (the equivalent for the British Isles was nearer to 45 percent).[2] Jamaican applicants in this latter group (those who wrote two or more letters) each wrote just under six on average and were in contact for an average of four years and four months (1,585 days).

In the Jamaican index card sample, 68 percent of applicants were women (similar to the 70 percent in the British Isles sample). The addresses contained in the records suggest that Surrey county, at the eastern end of the island, was the largest source of applications from Jamaica, with the great majority (about 35 percent) coming from Kingston and the Saint Andrew parish area—and possibly two-thirds of all from Jamaica applying from addresses in Surrey.

The internal evidence of the letters from Jamaican correspondents includes individuals in every decade of adult life up to the eighties. In Jamaica, the oldest applicant (41178) was seventy-four years old when he applied from north of Kingston in 1938—though he died in 1939. The oldest Jamaican woman who applied (25356) was sixty-three and from the southwest of the island in 1959. The oldest identified user of the healing from Jamaica was a woman (94080) who applied from Kingston in 1949 and was still using the water in 1953 when she was about eighty-four years old.

A report on the Healing Department for 1937–1938 for the Society's internal consumption noted very high levels of illiteracy in American correspondents.[3] And in 1948 it was found that "our [American] patients are drawn from amongst the very poorest classes and the standard of education amongst a large section seems to be very low indeed."[4] The few correspondents from the United States who wrote about their work backgrounds tended to refer to low-paying jobs or unemployment. Correspondents reported working as a blacksmith (45518), a beauty salon "shampoo girl" (15826), a cleaner (58050), and in a "common auxiliary job in a hospital" (11441); some said they were simply unemployed (66519), "very poor" (72150), or "poor negro" (79712). In Jamaica, the job profiles in evidence are a closer match to those of the British water-takers (and many from Jamaica went on to migrate to the British Isles): a number of applicants worked in nursing or care settings (95159, 77835, 54383, 90243, 66380, 77567); as shopkeepers and dressmakers (73405, 67987, 83880, 64757); and a fisherman (15694), a laborer (57961), and unemployed people (21994, 75262).

Finnish applications came in at a slower rate than the other countries discussed. The numbers of applicants were low but continuous, with a first phase of interest in the mid-1920s and a second in the late 1950s. There was a rise from two applications in 1924 to nearly nine hundred applications in 1926, followed by a steady decline to zero during 1942–1944 (postal services to Britain were cut off during the occupation of Finland; nonetheless, applications had been dropping steadily after 1926). Following a low and fluctuating rate of applications after the war, a revival occurred in the mid-1950s, with highs of 106 applications in 1956 and 152 in 1959, which then tailed off to single digits each year in the 1970s. Indications are that people from Finland continued to use the healing as late as the 1990s.[5] Analysis of Finnish index cards in the sample used in the discussion of the British Isles and Jamaica, which includes records of 43 individuals, shows that around 44 percent of applicants did not make contact again, just five percent made contact once after submitting an initial request for healing, and the remainder (51 percent) wrote an average of just over eight letters after applying.[6]

The letters from Finnish users of the healing do not regularly provide information on their working lives. Where they do make these kinds of references, they tend to identify service or clerical occupations such as teaching, office work, and shop work. Of the 43 Finnish index cards contained in the sample, the largest geographical source of applications was Helsinki, which supplied 49 percent of applicants, followed by Turku, with 37 percent. Of the Finnish index cards contained in the sample that disclose the gender of the applicant, 76 percent were women.

While Finland has something of a reputation for having a religious culture dominated by a Lutheran Christian hegemony, a number of scholars of religion in the country have commented on a lively and variable interest in nontraditional religion and spirituality.[7] In the 1920s in particular, Finland had a very active and developing theosophical scene led by Pekka Ervast. While the letters from United States and Jamaica do not contain the same kinds of discussion of non-mainstream movements as the letters from Britain, in Finland they (especially Theosophy) are prominent.

THE UNITED STATES[8]

Many of the varieties of new and nontraditional religious systems (such as Christian Science, Spiritualism, and Theosophy) discussed in the previous chapter, in connection with the diversity and fluidity of religious affiliation in Great Britain, had their origins or recent invigorations in the United States. While they are relatively prominent in the letters of the British Isles users of the healing (and no doubt the explicit references cited in this book are a small proportion of those who had *some* experience with these movements but failed to mention it), the same prominence is not evident in the American and Jamaican users of the healing. However, in the case of both, letters illuminate the ways that the healing entered into a dynamic and mobile religious environment. Indeed, they show us how, in individual practice and understanding, there was a continuous and energetic process of re-understanding.

While there are references in American letters to new movements such as Spiritualism and Theosophy that are prevalent in the British Isles letters, these have not been found to any great extent in the archive. A rare example is a woman from a city in western Pennsylvania (64297) who wrote of reading of the Panacea Society's healing in *The Herald of the Star* and applied in March 1924.[9] A very early American applicant from Missouri (61458), who applied before October 1924 and may have had a British reference number before a separate American numbering system was introduced, observed that some of the Panacea Society's writings "sounds like Christian Science" and that she had given up Christian Science before joining the Panacea Society.[10] And another female water-taker (86317, who wrote from Canada, though she was allocated a U.S. identifier) wrote of a relation's interest in "occult science . . . [but] I will have none of it."[11]

In 1943, a problem arose in America with a Mr. Jesse Green, who promoted the Panacea Society's healing in advertisements in spiritualist and psychological magazines in Philadelphia in particular.[12] He was an active promoter of the Society, though an unsuccessful and even detrimental one.[13] The Society complained that it had repeatedly called on him to cease promoting its work, as his actions resulted in applications that were "quite unacceptable as no complaints were stated and the applicants appeared to expect that the Healing was based on Astrology."[14] To some extent, then, the Panacea Society's healing was connecting to and integrating with the currents of Spiritualism and New Thought that were prevalent in some sections of American society at the time.

Perhaps equally evident in the American letters are less structured ideas about and experiences with spirits and dangerous unseen forces. A woman who applied in February 1940 from Mississippi (98027) saw a "faith doctor" to treat "snakes in side of me some one taking my hair out my head and put snakes in me by my hair" and went on to subscribe to the Society's healing.[15] A woman who applied from Arkansas in 1964 (53443) wrote of "visible and invisible spirits about the place inside and out," and another woman (25630) wrote from California, saying "I am tormented by evil spirits."[16]

> They do it through people and cats + dogs every thang the Devil can enter in to torment he do it they are tormenting me this very minute I hear them hitting the side of the and it feal like fire sometime and I burn and I have hot spells and people watch me all time and one will influence another one to do the same thing I am yet buy evil [spirits] I fast and pray pray all time rebuke evil spirits plead the blood of Jesus that is the only way I [can] get peace they put old poison on walk way porches in my clothes if I try to live with some one I an't live with eny one they will kill me with poison witch craft they put something on me that will cause other that is evil to do the same thing to me and pretend to be my friends I cut ... ropes last fall and they put poison in my jar that I keep coffee in and it made me sick [*illegible*] my livers They have try to kill [me] so many days but God is keeping me alive it is witch-craft miss can you help me and said me of this evil vexing of spirits. I please let me know soon I can't walk on no job I do a little farm work people don't want me around that don't do me evil. I am as the 22 psalm David prayed in great distress will you read it to see what I mean read to the 22 verse and tell me if I have sin is because the Lord want heal me I [try] to live the best I can.[17]

The Society advised her to sprinkle Water B on her doorways and gates and in her yard, and they suggested she keep food well sealed to avoid attracting dogs and cats.[18]

More prevalent, however, in the American letters, are references to the two conventional religious poles so far as the Panacea Society perceived them. These were forms of Christianity—often in evangelical and charismatic Protestant variants—and groups subscribing to variants of the persisting Southcottian tradition. A number of applicants for the Panacea Society's healing wrote from the Southcottian House of David community at Benton Harbor in Michigan. The House of David community was founded in the first decade of the 1900s by Benjamin Purnell (1861–1927) and his wife Mary (d. 1953), followers of James Jezreel in the Midwest.[19] Benjamin was an effective preacher and orator, and his writings offered a synthesis of Southcottian prophecy, especially by Wroe and Jezreel, and biblical teaching.[20] Like the Panacea Society and other Southcottian groups, the Purnells focused on physical salvation, and they preached giving up all material possessions.[21] Benjamin described four levels of progression for his members: (1) the initial fallen state of Adam, (2) recognizing the chain of prophets and gradual purification through abstinence, (3) accepting the spirit of God, which "produced a cleansing and purification of the blood," ultimately so they would be "without blood," before (4) a personal, communal, and physical Millennium.[22] The community lived, therefore, by abstinence; they followed vegetarianism, teetotalism, and celibacy.[23]

The Purnells sent out missionaries and the community grew rapidly at the same time as it developed a successful range of business interests, including an amusement park, a lumber operation, a canning plant, and other entrepreneurial projects.[24] However, a series of scandals, complaints, and legal challenges dogged the couple in the 1920s,[25] and the community's assets were effectively broken up after a legal ruling in 1927.[26] Benjamin Purnell died a month later.[27] With Benjamin's death the colony became divided, and by 1930 the assets were formally split to form two religious communities, the "Israelite House of David," led by Harry Dewhirst, which retained the original buildings and farms, and the "City of David," led by Mary Purnell, which took control of smaller buildings and a large amount of cash.[28]

Those who wrote to the Panacea Society for healing from Benton Harbor generally expressed dissatisfaction with their situation. A woman (76110) applied from the colony in December 1934 expressing frustration with her community, which frowned upon her developing relationship with an outsider: "I am condemned for associating with a man of highest character just because he doesn't belong to the organization, still it'd be alrite if a member even if he was of low standing, thats what gets me!"²⁹ Her letters roundly condemn others in the community for unkindness and lacking Christian feeling for her and the man she was forming a connection with. She expressed her desire to leave the community in her first and only letter to the Panacea Society, though it is unclear whether she did so or whether the Society's response was intercepted and her communications cut off. An older couple (99276 and 43594) managed to arrange for a friend who was not a member of the colony to post their letters for them to evade the surveillance of the colony's authorities: "she is most anxious to take the water but could not send direct to you as they are members of Mary & Benjamin's Colony [and] all letters have to be sent to Headquarters where they are examined."³⁰ Having become disillusioned with the colony, the couple found the fulfilment of their expectations in the Panacea Society—though they kept their interest secret until they could make arrangements to escape. An undated letter (probably from the 1920s) said:

> I do not know how to express my thanks for seal and for all your Love in sending such bounty every day do I thank God for such benefits. It has quite lifted me up from the gloom ... lovely to read the Blessed words of The Book of Healing for all also I have read some Scripts, oh The joy it gave me to know that Loving Spirit is once more talking to His people as he did to Joanna and so much more at Home with these calling them His Little Children oh how grand to know God has found some worthy to come to fulfil his promises too.³¹

A later letter spoke of the female correspondent's conviction that Octavia was the authentic fulfilment of the millennial promise:

> I accepted our Beloved Octavia Before I had half read its [*Healing for All*] contents and I knew it and was certain she was The Chosen Bride of Jesus and my prayers for her has always been that He would be with her continually working in her to will and to do his holy will that he may be glorified in his Bride.³²

Eventually, the female correspondent escaped the colony (her husband had by then died) and went to live with her son. She identified the close of more than twenty years with the colony with the realization brought on by *Healing for All*:

> I have been in The House of David over 20 years and kept faithful until I received The Book Healing for all, last September then I lost all faith in them, But kept it secret until I came away knowing how hard it would

be for me if they found it out. But for a long time I felt The Spirit had left them.³³

One British-born male applicant (81193), who applied in 1925 from Seattle, Washington, when he was in his sixties, said he had joined Benjamin and Mary Purnell's group at Benton Harbor, and indeed that he had been part of the predecessor community in Detroit led by Michael Mills in 1892. He said that he became disillusioned after staying with them for about two years, "so left and started life in the world again." He was a believer in the seven prophets that followed Joanna Southcott, and when he found a picture of Southcott discarded in some woods he was led back to the Panacea Society.³⁴ Another male correspondent (45518) was a blacksmith in Benton Harbor. When he discovered the Society, he saw it as a divine resolution to his discontent with the House of David:

> I came to America about four years ago from New Zealand in connection with the House of David, Mary & Benjamin but did not go in on account of not seeing eye to eye as regards Benjamin being the younger brother. So I prayed for more light and thanks be to God I have been led to the Writings of the Holy Ghost which is indeed Divine Writing.³⁵

Living in Benton Harbor, he came into contact with members of the colony, and he wrote later observing that "The Divine Healing is now known to a lot of People in Benton Harbor."³⁶

JAMAICA

Jamaica was a constant source of interest to the Society, and the Healing Department continued to be impressed and sometimes amazed by the growth of interest in the healing from Jamaicans. A report for 1937–1938 makes observations on some difficulties facing Jamaicans:

> Certainly they do not all report but considering the fact that many cannot write for themselves and have sometimes to pay a small sum to get their letters written for them, and that these same patients cannot read our casepaper and letters when they get them . . . but have to wait until someone is found who <u>can</u> read them—the proportion of reporters is good.
>
> Another difficulty for patients in Jamaica is that in the country parts water is often far to seek. Many of the poor folk having to fetch all their supply in petrol tins carried on their head—sometimes a distance

of a mile or more. In rainy seasons they fill tins from the water that runs off the cocoa-nut trees. One can see that under such conditions, hot-dry-spongings take on the nature of a luxury.[37]

The Society's work developed at such a rate in Jamaica that for a period around 1937–1938 a regular meeting took place on Sundays at Yallahs Bay, led by local fisherman. The Society sent meeting members some useful items including a Bible, a prayer book, a form of service, *Laws Out of Zion*, a special linen section, a copy of *Hymns Ancient and Modern*, copies of the Lord's Prayer, and literature on Panacea beliefs.[38] In early 1945, however, the Society was disturbed by reports of meetings at which the water was dispensed and "the *Writings of the Holy Ghost* were made use of to excite a form of occult frenzy." Following this, the Society decided to restrict sales of *Writings* in the West Indies.[39]

It was noted in 1947 that there was a consistent problem with people "who try to make money by charging for giving the Water, or the address of The Society, and in other ways not always easy to trace."[40] One outcome of this was that in 1952 the Society—concerned about the misuse of the spiritual aspects of its theology and the levels of illiteracy among applicants from the United States, the West Indies, and West Africa—formulated a new shortened case paper "embodying the essential treatments ... [and] omitting references to the spiritual side of the work of which mis-use is often made; these references are printed separately for use where desirable."[41] While in Britain and Finland the fact was made known that adherence to doctrine was not required for the healing to be effective, it was tempered in effect by some clear metaphysical and theological statements about the cosmic anthropology of humans. In Jamaica and the United States the absence of required doctrine was enacted in full by withholding information about the theology of the Panacea Society.

A consistent theme in the historical and ethnographic study of religion in Jamaica has been the leitmotif that "enslaved Africans, transported to Jamaica to labor on the sugar plantations, brought with them a meaningful set of beliefs and cultural practices," but these were "profoundly modified by the experience of Jamaican slavery and by the cultural domination inherent in British colonialism, but was sufficiently vibrant to present a challenge to the Christian missionary movement."[42] Thus, the distinctive story of the island's colonial past, from "neglected outpost of the Spanish Empire" followed by three hundred years of British rule as a sugar plantation colony after its capture in 1655,[43] sets the terms of religious and spiritual negotiation in the country. Throughout its colonial history, the island had a majority black population made up of slaves transported from

West Africa with a minority white population of slaveowners. Slavery was abolished in the 1830s and political rights were formally extended to the wider population from that period.[44]

The religious culture of the island has reflected the origins of its population, with British forms of Christianity practiced by the minority white population and forms of African traditional religion and (from the nineteenth century) nonconformist Christianity practiced by the black population.[45] As population groups gradually became mixed over time, religious beliefs and practices also became mixed and dynamic. Claire Taylor describes a trajectory from Spanish Catholic missionizing among the indigenous Arawaks and incoming African slaves, followed by the arrival of Protestantism with the British and the establishment of the Church of England in the country in 1662—to serve the British population. It was, instead, American Baptist, Moravian, and Wesleyan traditions that disseminated Protestant Christianity on the island in the eighteenth century.[46]

Inherent in the idea of a remnant of African religion developing in relation to European Christianity in Jamaica is the notion that the two are in some sense in opposition to each other: an African ethic of eudemonism and magical rite on the one hand, and pietistic Protestantism of individualism and sin on the other.[47] As Raymond Smith summarizes Diane Austin-Broos' argument in *Jamaica Genesis*, "a Jamaican creole religious discourse was created out of the confrontation of radically distinct cosmologies through practices intimately related to the circumstances, the ecology, of the practitioners."[48] The emphasis in Austin-Broos' account is notably not on the engagement of European and African but on the engagement of something distinctive and Caribbean with those two.[49] Robert Stewart discusses how the failure of European churches to implant a religious system was an expression of a distinct Jamaican negotiation. "The other side of the coin of missionary frustration was the triumph of Afro-creole religious practices and social and personal norms," which

> constituted not a total rejection of missionary Christianity but an adaptation of it on the basis of customs, values, and perceptions that began in Africa and were modified in the blacks' experience of slavery and emancipation that largely preserved a system of class and color relationships forged during the nearly two hundred years of Jamaica's status as a British slave colony.[50]

In essence, there is a tension between interpreting the Jamaican religious matrix as a mixing of African and European and interpreting it as a distinct and self-sufficient redefinition of the two.

Perhaps the most notable expression of this was in manifestations of Myalism, "a *Jamaican* syncretism of African spirit belief and apocalyptic Christianity."[51] An example is given by Austin-Broos, who discusses water baptism, particularly complete immersion. "Rendered as a form of healing in early Jamaican Christianity, this rite had meanings more akin to an African tradition than to the intent of missionaries."[52] Indeed, the Jamaican religious matrix was infused with notions of healing. There was a long-standing conjunction of pastor and healer.[53] And the special circumstances of abolition led to a conjunction of healing with Myalism. One nineteenth-century account published in London expressed it thus:

> The Myalman, having most of them been employed in attendance on the sick in the hospitals of estates, and thereby acquired some knowledge of medicine, have, since the abolition of slavery, set up as medical men; and, in order to increase their influence, and consequently their gains, have called to their aid the mysteries of this abominable superstition.... The more effectually to delude the multitude, the priests of this deadly art, now that religion has become general, have incorporated with it a religious phraseology, together with some of the religious observances of the most popular denominations.[54]

One of the most striking Jamaican coinings, emerging from and articulated with these various strands of religious activity, is the healing institution of the curingyard or balmyard. Austin-Broos refers to the example of "Leader Wally" (reported by Joseph Long), who maintained a church and a balmyard outside Kingston. "His balm yard had one large deep pool with four changing booths close to it" and "his practice specialized in herbal libations for anyone prepared to wait and pay the fee," though he "constantly observed to his clients that a 'finish cure rest on repentance.'"[55] Another example is the Watt Town Revival seal church, which had pools next to the church where "believers could avail themselves of 'holy' baths in consecrated water" to cure major physical and psychological ailments. Herbal baths and other forms of spiritual cure were also offered there.[56] Leonard Barrett describes "one of the oldest balmyards in Jamaica" at Blakes Pen—the example indicates the deep continuity and spiritual fecundity of the site.

> The Blakes Pen balmyard is of special significance in this area because it has been in continuous operation for over one hundred years under the leadership of two women: Mammie Forbes and her daughter, Mother Rita.... The mother of Mammie Forbes was an African slave who is said

to have been an expert in bush remedies, but seems to have given up her practice when she was converted to Christianity in the 1860 Revival.[57]

Barrett goes on to describe Mammie Forbes's call to healing in 1871 after she had grown "dissatisfied with the coldness of its ritual" when "an angel appeared to her holding a bunch of herbs and commanded her to 'rise up and heal the people.'" In time, the angel instructed her in the digging of a pool in the balmyard "from which a healing fountain would rise." The water had not appeared when Barrett was writing a hundred years later—though Mother Rita had explained this was due to "the breaking of a taboo by her mother." Barrett reported in 1973 that Mammie Forbes had performed healing for fifty-nine years and had died in 1930; she had been succeeded by her daughter, Mother Rita Adams, who was continuing the healing.[58]

While, generally speaking, modern "gnostic movements" such as Christian Science have "found very little response at any level of Jamaican society,"[59] the Panacea Society's healing offering—thanks to distinctive attachment points for long-standing elements of Jamaican religion—found a developed and widespread audience. Barrett's summary of "some aspects of African retentions in Jamaica" is suggestive of the natural fit for the Panacea Society's healing—shorn to some extent of its theological shroud (deliberately, by the Society)—in the Jamaican religious context. The first three items are:

> As in Africa, the people in Jamaica believe that sickness is caused by spiritual forces, and they speak of sickness as the "thing." Many see sickness as the intrusion of outside forces brought on either by the breaking of God's will or the evil work of enemies. Except in the case of death by old age, every human tragedy is suspect.
>
> As in Africa, healing to be effective, must be both herbal and ritual. That is why the peasant is more interested in what the doctor does with his stethoscope than he is in the prescribed medicine. The balmyard is the place where herbs and rites are wed in the traditional African pattern.
>
> As in many areas of West Africa, water has important healing values. The balm in herbal juices and the promised fountain in the balmyard are examples of the power of water. In Jamaica, revelation of healing streams form a common part of the folk culture.[60]

Stewart also comments on the significance of water rites in West African religion (which have a natural fit with Christian baptismal practices) and on "the Asante belief in the divine origin of water"[61]—both of which have a natural fit with the prominence given to water rituals in the Panacea Society's healing.

The Jamaican form of Pentecostal theology indicates the distinctive features of the Jamaican version, which links "human malaise" with heritable sin and, Austin-Broos says, transforms West African notions of affliction and suffering.

> No accidental outcome of life's events, the evil that brings malaise is the product of a person's very being, as is every history of suffering. Benign and malign spiritual forces no longer reside beyond the person as inherent aspects of ambivalent life. Rather, they are stretched between the poles of God's transcendence and the immanence of man. In this Christian scheme, it is man's fallen state that confirms the inherent humanness of suffering. This "morality of being," as John Mbiti calls it, was first introduced to Jamaica by the missionaries of the slavery period. It has been brought to fruition through a politics of moral order that has shaped a creole religious discourse. This discourse now includes Jamaica's Pentecostalism.[62]

This is reflected in an interesting account of a blending process for the use of the Society's healing water in Jamaica, which appears in the Society's annual report for 1947.

> There exists a firm belief in devils and evil spirits. One patient complained that demons threw away her bottle and took the Section. Further enquiry elicited the information that there were in that district two sorts of "Spiritualists"—"Preaching Balmers" who profess to heal by ointments, and "Duppy Divers" who drive out evil spirits which their own spirit shows them. One of these lived next door to our patient and decided that there was a bad spirit in the Panacea Water. "But now," writes our patient, "we shun them all, for we say it must be demons that tell them such lies. And they don't get well like we do."[63]

For many of the Jamaican users of the healing, the Panacea Society's offering was integrated into their usual Christian perspective. A woman who applied in May 1954 (73405) wrote to the Society from Saint Andrew parish, near Kingston, in 1956, saying: "At times the way seems dark but there is always something however small provided for me. So I am asking you all to continue to pray for me that the Lord will continue to bless me & that I will continue to derive benefits from the Blessed Water."[64] Another female water-taker (12608), who applied in February

1936, wrote in September 1936 to say: "Please from I start my Divine Healing I can say thank God. I can say little by little I am [coming] on very well. because I believe that what my Healing has dones unto me no man on earth could ... do that unto me Praise God."[65] A man (47040) wrote from Spanish Town in 1935, saying "as a Christian man, I believe in the prophecies on Divine Healing," and he sought treatment for failing eyesight.[66] (He remained in contact until 1947 and was reported as having died in 1949.)

The letters of those who wrote about the details of their spiritual and religious experience regularly expressed an awareness of a visionary spiritual power redolent of the long tradition of Jamaican spirituality here expressed. For example, one woman (16880) reported dreaming of her sister telling her she was ill, and she experienced fits the next day; a man (98286) was compelled to continue using the Panacea healing when he was ordered to continue doing so in a dream; another woman (56842) wrote to say that her daughter "was growing [into] a lovely little girl" but "she keeps seeing visions, people who are not there"; and another woman (91921, writing from an address in north London) felt her daughter was "under the influence of evil and she is acting very strange."[67] A man (84805) writing from Saint Catherine parish found that the Panacea Society's instructions wonderfully fulfilled a prophetic vision experienced by his wife. He wrote that she

> got a vision one night that she is to consecrate water by prayers [and] used it daily [and] sprinkle some at her gates [and] doors [and] in the yard [and] drink a glass of same daily [and] bathe in it [and] read the 90 psalm [and] we carried on daily until your letter received with pamphlet that teaches us the very same lesson: with the exception of the Linen Section.[68]

He remained in contact until at least the early 1960s. Others referred to realistically conceived evil spirits and powers, in the forms of a "black bat which visit the home very often," and odd smells in various rooms of the house (53777)[69]— which one user identified with a demon (52353)[70]—or just "strange sounds" in the house (97655);[71] others (39408) experienced bats associated with haunting spirits that would choke them in the night.[72] One of the more troubling references of this type was to an "evil tenant" in the home who "is the devil he flaunt his self," which persisted over several years. The writer (56673) heard sounds in the house and felt a burning sensation when she walked in the yard.[73] "They is evil spirit," she wrote, and she felt only the Panacea Society's water kept her alive; "they can't overthrow me I am using the water after day [and] night."[74] Another woman (79154) reported that she was not superstitious but that she wanted help in dealing with a sister who "lives at the grave" of her son and was performing evil against her.[75]

Despite the great cultural differences separating the overseers of the Panacea Society in Bedford and the thousands of individuals who applied for the healing in Jamaica, the healing seems to have found a natural fit with the Jamaican religious and spiritual matrix. In some respects, the Jamaican example is most instructive about the reality of the negotiation and complex dynamism of people's religious lives and views, for it represents in effect a strikingly decentralized religious culture capable of being highly hospitable to new forms of religious expression and practice. Again, while there were many who applied to the healing from Jamaica who never made contact again, those who did evidenced a serious interest in the Panacea Society's healing offer. While the reference points are somewhat different, the dynamism in the Jamaican water-takers is not dissimilar to those apparent in their British counterparts.

FINLAND[76]

In Finland, a theosophical network had a significant part to play in the dissemination of the healing and its practical distribution. A branch of the Theosophical Society was opened in Finland in 1907, although Finnish people had been joining the Swedish branch of the Theosophical Society by 1892.[77] Tore Ahlbäck has observed that "the importance of the theosophical movement, as compared for example to the Lutheran state church, was purely marginal, quantitatively speaking"; nonetheless, as in England, Theosophy was significant in facilitating the introduction of novel religious ideas.[78] Maarit Leskelä-Kärki's refers to Theosophy as the "fundamental foundation" for occult alternatives to mainstream religion.[79] In Finland, the Panacea Society's healing was taken up by Pekka Ervast (1875–1934), a leading advocate for Theosophy and still recognized as a promoter of alternative religion in Finnish history.[80] Ervast established a spiritual society of his own, called Ruusu-Risti, when he left the Theosophical Society in 1920. His new group became enormously influential in Theosophy and broader alternative religious affiliation in Finland.[81] Ervast would manage the Panacea Society's activities in Finland from 1925 until his death in 1934. Thereafter, the Society used various translators as they managed the Finnish healing work directly from Bedford.[82]

There are frequent references to Ervast in letters from Finnish users of the healing in the Society's archive. It is evident from these that Ervast was important in sustaining and promoting the healing in Finland. He included an article he had written in February 1925 about the Panacea Society in *Ruusu-Risti*, the journal of the group he led, and shortly after that he submitted an application for the healing for himself.[83] Ervast continued to promote the healing in *Ruusu-Risti* and was himself a keen advocate.[84] Ervast wrote to the Society's leadership in October 1925 and offered to arrange translation and printing of the instruction leaflet for the healing. He said he would finance the cost of printing by raising funds "among the patients who have already been helped."[85] He printed one thousand copies of the leaflet by December and was appointed the Society's agent (Tower) in Finland.[86] After that, he was given a supply of blessed linen pieces to send out to the Finnish water-takers, and he reported regularly to the Society on applicants and their progression.[87] Ervast regarded the healing as successful in his homeland, reporting "wonderful cures here in Finland already" and that "we have reached the first thousand [Finnish members] now" in August 1926.[88]

The Society seems to have seen the Finns as having a special place in its understanding of Richard Brothers's doctrine that "the Lost Tribes of Israel settled in Britain" and that Anglo-Saxons were "the blood descendants of the Israelists."[89] An editorial note appended to an article by Ervast in *The Panacea* observed: "that the people of Finland are so wonderfully attracted to the Healing seems to point to some ethnological correspondence between our respective nations."[90] It was suggested in another article referring to Finland, published a few years later, that "we have a theory that a large number of the Lost Ten Tribes stayed in that far-off land and are now answering the Call."[91]

Ervast also made an association between an ancient magical and healing tradition in Finnish culture, the national foundation myth, the *Kalevala*,[92] and the apparent Finnish propensity to use the Society's healing. The text of the *Kalevala*, the "Finnish national epic," was compiled in the mid-nineteenth century.[93] Jeffrey Kaplan has discussed Ervast's use of the *Kalevala* and its interpretation as a parallel Christian text linked to "Finnish nationhood and the incarnation of the uniquely Finnish 'national genius.' "[94] Ervast wrote about the Finns and Lapps as having a special propensity to be "powerful magicians and sorcerers" and noted that "no other Christian nation has preserved as many magic formulas and incantations than our nation."[95] In 1925, Ervast linked the Society's healing to this element in Finnish culture in an article where he said:

> Our folk-healers and shamans have been curing people with their own remedies for centuries but their performance and procedures have always remained more or less esoteric, secret, so to speak. Their reputation has never spread great distances; if it has ever spread outside their home

boroughs, this has happened by itself with the aid of friends and thankful patients; never has it been intentionally spread. It seems to be a different case with the Southcottians [the Panacea Society] and their cure. Information on it is distributed as widely as possible and those suffering from illness are even invited to try it.[96]

Ervast referred to "conjurings ... to drive away bears, diseases and other evil from [adherents] and their friends" in an account he wrote of the types of ancient magic in Finland.[97] Ervast's observation that the Panacea Society's healing is equivalent to an intentionally spread version of local folk or shamanic practices in Finland suggests that he regarded the Society's healing as similar to those ancient practices from his own country.

THE PANACEA SOCIETY IN THE UNITED STATES, JAMAICA, AND FINLAND

In the American context, the Panacea Society's healing interacted with a range of diverse strands of religion and spirituality prevalent in that country. As might be expected, references to and echoes of well-known and well-studied forms of Christianity, and especially its various Protestant denominations, pepper letters of the water-takers from that country. In common with Jamaica and other countries, individual experiences of startling and somewhat confrontational encounters with spiritual forces are a presence for a number of writers. While the Panacea Society is little known in wider scholarship, the penetration of its offering into the House of David commune at Benton Harbor is not surprising. The House of David, like the Panacea Society and other groups, was one among a wide range of products of Joanna Southcott's work and the work of her successor prophets; that there was an easy interchange between these groups (despite the controls on communication at Benton Harbor) is a logical consequence of their shared ideological background.

Perhaps more surprising is the Panacea Society's reception in Jamaica. On a conventional understanding, a religious system formed by a middle-class community of committed (if restive) Anglicans in middle England would have little parley with a religious system built from African spirituality innervated by three hundred years of slavery and a dose of frequently antagonistic Anglicanism. What is evident, however, in the almost natural fit for the Panacea Society's healing in Jamaica, is that the social and cultural proving ground of a system of religion or spirituality is less important than its theology. It may be mere coincidence that the Panacea Society's theology and practice had multifarious contact points with Jamaican spirituality, and the discussion in this chapter has highlighted the shared doctrinal linking of (1) the connection between sickness or human tragedy and spiritual forces, (2) the importance of ritual for effective healing, and (3) the special significance of water as a source of spiritual power. Or these may reflect a long-standing and somehow fundamental aspect of human religious thinking. After all, the three elements are present to varying extents in a multitude of religious systems from the lost and ancient to the new and contemporary. Of course, after a time the Panacea Society withheld significant details about its theology from the literature it sent to Jamaican applicants, fearing the information's misuse. Nonetheless, and perhaps ironically, it did so in the context of a religious culture where literacy in written word was low while literacy in ritual act was high—and the physical ritual of the Panacea Society's healing was as much a statement of theological doctrine for many of its users as a written equivalent was for others.

While Finland had a superstructure of conventional Protestant Christianity and an effervescent interest in Theosophy, and thus had a *prima facie* congruence with the immediate and wider British context of the Panacea Society's healing formation, it is striking that there was next to no tradition of Southcottian spirituality in the country. While the Theosophists provided practical and administrative support for the dissemination of the healing in Finland, its popularity and the naturalness of its fit in the Finnish spiritual context were, in fact, understood in a way similar to the analysis of the naturalness of the fit for the healing in Jamaica presented here: the long history of spiritual practice linked especially to conceptions of magic and the cosmological power of water perceived to underlie Finnish spiritual thinking. Again, in Finland, as in each country studied here, what was happening for the individuals who tried out the healing was a practical and physical engagement with a theological statement expressed in actions (the water-taking ritual) and objects (the water and the linen) as much as in propositions of doctrine or theology. In the dynamic life of personal spirituality, each individual—in their communal and personal history, understanding, and experience—is the theological yardstick.

While much of the analysis presented in this chapter and the previous one has excluded those who applied but made no further contact, this group represents an important and somewhat silent constituency in the record. Indeed, it makes up a significant proportion of applicants; of the 3,894 individuals' records included in the index card sample used in these chapters, 40 percent (1,540) made no further contact. Though the assessment must be somewhat speculative, this group indicates a basic potential reason for people's interest in nonconventional and nonmainstream healing: people looking for healing of this type tend to do so due to a compelling health need that helps to overcome any skepticism they may have about a practice. Of course, some applications may have been frivolous or misplaced; nonetheless, we can surmise that many of the applicants would have commitments to other religious traditions or practices (or skeptical about religion more generally). Their communication with the Society suggests that their need for healing attracted them to approach this unfamiliar religious form. These contacts highlight the fact that an offer of healing can provide a basis for people to engage with an alternative spiritual practice that is not present in other spiritual systems. Discomfort or suffering caused by ill health might provide a strong motivation for trying a spiritual system more pressing than an instinct for spiritual quest on its own. As such, it also has the capability to reach potential subscribers outside sections of society who might be expected to engage in these kinds of spiritual practices.

Active participation in what are perceived as alternative or countercultural practices is likely to depend on the perceived opportunity the practices hold to meet a need that is not met elsewhere. For those who are actively skeptical about less authorized religious and spiritual practices, or simply those with little active interest in these kinds of alternatives, the simple fact of persistent or acute problems in their physical health or personal life may provide the basis to begin to engage with them. We can only speculate on the reasons those who applied and did not follow up failed to become more involved. Nonetheless, a host of practical and theological possibilities suggest themselves, in addition to a theorized creeping secularization of individuals' viewpoints—and there are some hints in the evidence; for example, Pekka Ervast comments in one letter on the "very few who on seeing the linen get shocked and don't use it at all."[98] We can surmise at least that (aside from cases of frivolous applications) an evaluation took place at the point of application, and that is evidence itself of a personal process of weighing and sifting practical and doctrinal ideas.

CHAPTER SIX

War and Anxiety

ADVERTISING AND WAR

During the period when the healing began to be made available to a wider public, the use of lucky charms and mascots, and some types of superstitious practice, was prevalent in Britain.[1] Geoffrey Gorer's somewhat anecdotal exploration of "English character" comments on the wide distribution of the "habit" of carrying lucky mascots and suggests that during the war "one serving man or woman in three had his or her private piece of solid magic."[2] Richard Sykes has observed the prevalence of popular superstition amid popular religion before and during the war.[3] With the public launch of the Panacea Society's healing in February 1924, the Society began a program of poster advertisements, leafleting, and newspaper advertisements. In the early days, the Society organized meetings open to the public and commissioned billboard advertisements.[4] An early advertisement in August 1924 proclaimed at an open meeting in the West End of London "Free healing of all diseases,"[5] and the publication of Octavia's *Healing for All* (1925) saw advertisements announcing " '*Healing for All*' sufferers from all diseases should read '*Healing for All*' Just published by the Panacea Society."[6]

The standard form of the early advertisement offered "slow but sure deliverance not miraculous, but by treatment, without money and without the price of accepting any particular belief" and listed a wide range of ailments (including cancer, consumption, and paralysis) but indicated that any could be treated. Applicants were asked to write to the Society with a list of their ailments and then to send updates on their health.[7] About the middle of the 1930s, there was a change of presentation in the advertisements: they took on a more religious tone compared to earlier emphasis on the medical and physical. Quoting from relevant biblical texts (for example, "Whosoever will, let him take the water of life freely"[8]), the new advertisement offered "Water and the spirit the new sacrament for the new dispensation" and advised people to write to the Society in

Bedford "for healing and deliverance in the tribulations preceding the coming of the Lord." The wording closed by noting that "there is nothing to pay." This last form of the advertisement was used in numerous newspapers and periodicals until the 1980s.[9]

To contemporary eyes, the large claims and the striking language in these advertisements are perhaps arresting. However, from the late Victorian period until the Second World War and beyond, advertisements for patent medicines making equally bold claims and using equally audacious language were not uncommon in Britain.[10] Thomas Richards's account of *The Commodity Culture of Victorian England* describes the openness of the British population to patent medicines that were widely believed to be of little curative value. He says that in the early years of the twentieth century "by any reckoning the English public bought more potions that it did legitimate drugs, and more pills per capita than any other nation in Europe. The makers of Beecham's Pills sold a million pills a day. Only alcohol was more popular and widely available."[11] T. R. Nevett's history of *Advertising in Britain* observes that many patent medicines "did not perform what was claimed for them" and notes that in the interwar period publications seeking the revenue that could be generated from advertising such medicines were often prepared to publish.[12] Of course, the nature of the cure offered by the Panacea Society was different in significant ways from its more medicinal rivals; not least, from a skeptical point of view, even if the blessed linen turned out to have no effect on health, it was also less likely to have any harmful effects compared to some of the patent remedies. And in many respects the claims of the Society were framed in more conventional and less hyperbolic language than those of the patent remedies. Indeed, the language of the patent remedy advertising could invoke supernatural or magical effects just as easily.

Thus, a Panacea Society advert like the one described earlier appeared in an issue of the *Daily Herald* in July 1939, which also carried advertising for a treatment for "summer catarrh" by quoting one purported user:

> Feeling stuffed up and getting prematurely old. I tried all kinds of so-called cures without any benefit. I decided to give Milton a trial. I have completely banished the catarrh. Now I can hear better, see better, and feel better in every way, and I feel life is worth while.[13]

The promotional text for another remedy for breathing difficulties said the product would "bring blessed relief and ease in a few seconds (this is so noticeable in some cases that it amounts almost to a miracle of healing) and ends the attack in a few minutes."[14] The previous day's *Daily Herald* had offered Beechams

Powders, which "sounds like 'Magic'—and it IS!," and Hall's Wine, which "acts directly on your blood-stream ... At once you feel a new life thrilling through you to every nerve, cell and tissue of your body. And this is no temporary fillip. Hall's Wine builds up all your vital forces."[15] A Panacea Society advert in the *Daily Mail* on the same day appeared in an issue with advertising that promoted a slimming aid with a testimonial:

> I am a continual source of amazement to my friends. As well as losing weight I seem to have lost years. I am told I look 10 years younger and my photographs seem to prove it. I feel wonderfully fit, I only take "SILF" 3 times a week now as I find it a splendid tonic.[16]

With the launch of the healing into public awareness in 1924, the Panacea Society entered a lively, thriving, and inventive marketplace for healing and spirituality that was of long standing and had a familiar vocabulary for the British public.

As we have seen, the Panacea Society had been advertising its healing widely in Britain from February 1924. The tone of the advertising remained fairly consistent over time, aside from an adjustment in the language in the mid-1930s. While the change at that point was immediately linked to changes at the head of the Society (Octavia died in 1934, and her deputy, Emily Goodwin, took over as senior Panacean in Bedford), it also coincided with a growing public awareness of an unstable geopolitical situation linked to the rise of fascism in Germany. The new advertisements included biblical quotes, and frequently these were on the theme of troubles and war: for example, "And the God of Peace shall bruise Satan under your feet shortly" (Rom. 16:20) and "Ye shall hear of wars and rumors of wars; see that ye be not troubled; for all these things must come to pass, but the end is not yet" (Matt. 24:6). As Panacean doctrine, in common with many millenarian religious movements, expected war and disorder as a sign of the dawn of the Millennium, it is likely that the change in the advertising was not an unconscious or an unsystematic attempt to market the Society in the light of prophecies about the end of the world that it believed were now coming to fruition. It made sense under those conditions that people's thoughts would turn more to matters religious and ultimate—and in that context the placement of advertising alongside news reports of war preparations at home and conflict overseas would have heightened its effect (and the Society's press cuttings books indicate a dramatic increase in the number of press advertisements for the healing published from June 1939).

Amid reports about the full mobilization of the Army and Air Force, the evacuation of children from cities, the introduction of conscription, and the

German attacks launched against Poland on multiple fronts, the *Daily Mail* for September 2, 1939, carried a large advertisement from the Panacea Society, a "NOTICE TO SEALED MEMBERS AND WATER TAKERS," advising that "Should a State of Emergency arise whereby communication with Head Quarters is interrupted or becomes difficult, continue to fill your bottle with Water as required and repeat the Blessing." It went on to enjoin them to "Sprinkle your Houses."[17] The same advertisement ran in the *Daily Telegraph* two days later, amid stories about fighting on various fronts, promises by allies to aid Britain, the first air raid warning in London, and "wild buying on Wall Street."[18] In fact, the Society ran a major newspaper advertising campaign during July, August, and September 1939, when more than two hundred of its advertisements for the healing appeared in national and local British newspapers and magazines.[19]

Again, it is instructive to note that the Panacea Society was not alone in detecting the need to adjust its message and exposure to respond to perceived existential threat. As early as July 1939, advertising for new homes on the south coast of England used anxiety about war to promote their products ("BUY A HOUSE ON THE COAST FOR HEALTH AND SAFETY"[20]). The *Daily Mail* advertisement advising water-takers of what to do "should a state of emergency arise" appeared in the same issue as an advertisement for Pontings department store that intoned: "If circumstances make it impossible to come to Pontings, remember that you can always keep in touch with Britain's best values through the post" (and promoted a special offer on waterproof blackout material).[21] Another page had an advert for British Cellophane Ltd recommending its products for protection of windows "against shattering by blast."[22]

Contemporary research in social psychology has given support to the idea that the existence of religion is linked to the anxiety and discomfort caused by the human awareness of death. Studies comparing groups of people who have spent time contemplating death and those contemplating neutral subjects under controlled conditions suggest that experimentally heightened awareness of death can make people more likely to agree with statements suggesting the existence of supernatural agents and other transcendent religious entities (God, heaven, hell, etc.).[23] The causal chain is summarized by Robb Willer:

> Fear of death creates significant anxiety in individuals. Individuals are motivated to come to conclusions that avoid negative arousal states. Therefore, greater fear of death should lead to greater belief in ideas that offer an escape from death anxiety, such as belief in an afterlife.[24]

With the Panacea Society's professed theology of relief from ailments and ultimately immortality, the offer of healing would have served as a natural inducement for those in fear of their own mortality—and, with the approach of war in the 1930s, the resonance of the association between existential anxiety and spiritual preservation was enhanced.

Rather contradicting the idea that war may be linked to enhanced religious belief, the classic historical understanding of the impact of the Second World War on religion and religiosity in general in Britain suggests that the disruption was a significant contributor to overall religious decline in the twentieth century. The first viewpoint is prevalent, for example, in the Mass Observation report *Puzzled People*, which is often cited for its account of "the explosion, or disintegration, of orthodox beliefs."[25] Edward Wickham's formative analysis of the decline of religion in Sheffield remarks on the disruptive effects of the Second World War; and Robert Currie, Alan Gilbert, and Lee Horsley's seminal statistical analysis of church affiliation after 1700 finds that "the two world wars had a most adverse effect on church growth."[26]

On the other hand, more recent work, often with a more inclusive definition of religion taking in wider folk (and less authorized) beliefs and practices, suggests that the Second World War was relatively insignificant in the trajectory of twentieth-century religion in Britain (i.e., reporting no special link between war and religious devotion). For example, Clive Field's overview of quantitative data about people's religious affiliation during 1939–1945 finds that "Christian membership fell during the war but not spectacularly."[27] Field finds support for his conclusions in more qualitatively framed studies such as Stephen Parker's *Faith on the Home Front*,[28] which observes that "in reality, the contours of wartime popular religion were similar to those of peacetime; 'diffusive Christianity' as such remained intact" and that "in the main the Christian religion . . . remained critical to the cultural life of the people in the mid-twentieth century and oral testimony underscores that it was a rich source of meaning and purpose in wartime."[29]

Furthermore, in studies suggesting a link between war and enhanced religious activity, the link is somewhat oblique and arguably value laden. Mass Observation's *Puzzled People* identifies an opportunistic and superstitious religion connected with the decline of traditional and institutional religion that found expression in astrology as much as in prayer.[30] And Field's assessment of the evidence related to Second World War religion, which makes significant reference to Mass Observation's research in this area (and *Puzzled People* in particular), comments that subjects treated Christian beliefs like "theological sweets to be tasted in almost any combination and rejected if found too bitter."[31]

Analysis of the sample of index cards discussed in the introduction and used earlier in much of the analysis of applications—but focused only on those who applied from addresses in Great Britain in the five years eight months of war as well as during the five years eight months before and after the war (i.e., a total period of seventeen years, from January 1934 to December 1950)—suggests that those who applied during the war years were more likely to make a committed attempt with the healing.[32] While the percentage of those who wrote just one letter after their initial application (indicating they made some kind of experiment with the healing) remained at 17 percent before and during the war, the proportion of applications who went on to write two or more letters increased by 7 percentage points (with a concomitant fall in those who applied and made no further contact). In the postwar years, the proportion of applicants who went on to write two or more letters returned to its prewar level. While the number in the postwar sample is perhaps too low for useful comparison (though the return to prewar figures is suggestive), the prewar and wartime samples are a good size and provide some support for the argument that war conditions elevated people's commitment to spiritual practice. While a theologian might consider the Panacea Society's belief system to have strayed some distance from conventional Christianity, *mutatis mutandis* this pattern of increased wartime commitment among users of the healing supports Parker's assessment of the continued value of religious commitment during war. On the other hand, there were significant drops in the average duration of contact, average number of

TABLE 6.1. Percentage of applicants writing no letters, one letter, or two or more letters for a sample of Panacea Society Healing users after applying from British addresses, analysed by period (pre-war, wartime, and post-war) of initial application.

	Number of Letters			
	0	1	2+	Number in sample
Jan 1934 to Aug 1939	33	17	49	207
Sep 1939 to Apr 1945	27	17	56	109
May 1945 to Dec 1950	32	18	50	34

letters written, and average intensity of contact (letters written per year) with the Society for those who applied during the war. While intensity was restored after the war (which is in line with the earlier finding that intensity remained fairly stable over the century), there was a small recovery in duration and none in the number of letters.

WAR AND THE HEALING

The Panacea Society's annual report for 1938–1939 noted that the Healing Department had "developed enormously" during the year—and it linked the growth to an increase in advertising, leafleting, and press articles, especially a large (and somewhat tongue-in-cheek) article in the *Daily Mail* in February.[33] In particular, the report records that the Society detected "many new applications, as well as letters from old patients asking for help and guidance" in response to the Sudeten Crisis and the Munich Agreement.[34] The annual report for the following year (covering July 1939 to June 1940) noted that the "outbreak of War has curtailed communications from European countries as they fell to the Nazis" but was linked to "a renewal of activity in the USA and UK."[35] The pattern is evident in the collated numbers of applications; worldwide, there was a very rapid increase from around one thousand applications in 1933 to more than eight thousand in 1939. During the buildup to war, there was a striking increase and then a peak in applications to the healing in the three countries that supplied the largest number of applicants overall during the twentieth century—the United States, Jamaica, and the British Isles.[36] However, the Jamaican peak was a little before the 1939

Table 6.2. Average duration of contact, number of letters written, and letters per year for a sample of Panacea Society Healing users applying from British addresses, analysed by period (pre-war, wartime, and post-war) of initial application. (Excludes applicants writing no letters after initial contact.)

	Duration (days)	Number of letters	Letters per year	Number in sample
Jan 1934 to Aug 1939	1,462	13.4	6.2	138
Sep 1939 to Apr 1945	969	9.3	5.2	80
May 1945 to Dec 1950	1,109	8.7	7.4	23

peak for the United States and the British Isles, and it was probably less linked to the growth of advertising than it was to local factors. (The causes of the boost in Jamaica over that period remain nonetheless unclear.)

The Society seems to have carried out very little international advertising[37]; thus, a direct link between war coverage, advertising, and the healing is only likely for water-takers in Britain. Nonetheless, take-up of the healing in other countries can only have come through personal recommendations between friends and family if advertising was not the main driver; as such, we would expect an indirect correlation at least between advertising in Britain and international take-up.

For some water-takers who otherwise expressed little everyday extension of the water and their use or understanding of the water into more metaphysical or transcendent territory, the outbreak of war, or fear of its outbreak, drew out their capacity to engage with the water in more complex ways and on more metaphysical terms. For example, an early applicant to the healing (30941), a woman

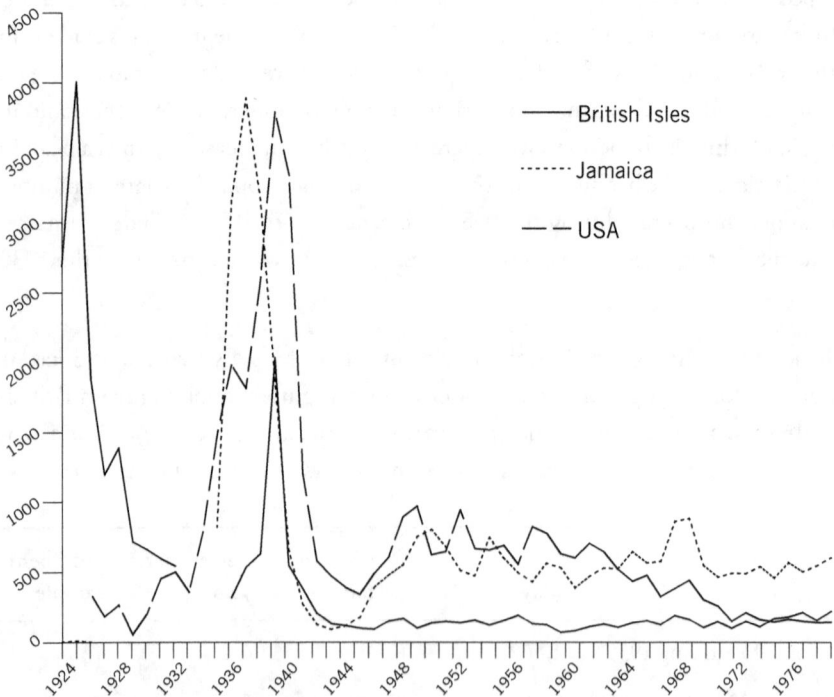

CHART 6.1. Annual number of British Isles, Jamaica, and USA Panacea Society Healing applications, 1924–78

who applied from Birmingham in the Midlands of England in 1924, later wrote letters that evidence the deep impact of the Second World War on her spiritual state. Her initial application had been based on deafness, and by 1940 difficulties with her legs also meant she relied on neighbors for help and errands. She retained faith in the Society and the healing, refusing to go to a bomb shelter because "the knowledge that your directions in my case-paper were carried out assures me of divine protection."[38] After ten days of continuous nighttime bombing, she wrote that though she could not hear the bombs, she felt the vibrations and her bed shaking, and "I feel no panic, just a tenseness and horror."[39] She prayed regularly for deliverance and understood the war in the context of the Society's apocalyptic vision: "How very thankful I am for the Knowledge the Panacea Teachings have brought me as to why it has come to pass, and what the future holds in store for Great Britain."[40] However, the start of the bombing activated spirits that troubled her.

> The room seemed full of presences, with umbrellas whirling them over one. Then night and early morning this phenomena would start with two presences. One would make passes over me and the other seemed to help in handing something that was whirled over my head. Then would follow much noise. Crowds of spirit people [were] passing through ... I have been powerless to stop it and at times feel that it is diabolical interference.[41]

After the death of Octavia in 1934, and while Emily Goodwin was the de facto leader of the Society, the Divine Mother (speaking through Goodwin) had advised the water-taker on these kinds of troubles. However, when Goodwin died in 1943 the Society no longer felt able to advise on such matters—though a note for a reply in the archives suggests that the Society assured the water-taker that the Divine Mother would still know the contents of her letters.[42] And the water-taker was reassured by the Society's report of the implications of Goodwin's passing in *The Panacea*:

> That the passing over of Mrs. Goodwin is part of the great work of the Divine Family for us in the setting up of the Kingdom and that all taking the water and following instructions already received will continue to gain the physical and spiritual benefits through the spirit in the water.[43]

Ultimately, the circumstances of the war and the death of Goodwin served to secure and fully validate this water-taker's faith in the water and the Society.

This early water-taker had applied to the Society after hearing of it in the theosophical journal *The Herald of the Star* in 1924, and in 1941 she reported that she had stopped reading other spiritual literature and would only accept the teachings of the Panacea Society.[44] Six months before she died in 1944, she wrote of the assurance she had found in the Society:

> I have tried theosophy two years, Christian Science many years ago (been under two different healers), Spiritualism longer. At a private seance I was told after some advice that I would find the pearl of great price! I have in the Blessed Water. Without it I could not have held on and endured the agony of suffering. As it is I have ... kept a grip on life, and hope for ultimate deliverance.[45]

A female nurse (19885) who applied from Cleveland, Ohio, sometime before 1932, and who had a daughter and a nephew who also took the water, relied on the water in great and small domestic matters for several years. Only with the beginning of the war in 1939 did she invoke the "Divine Mother and Father," asking them to "watch over our Dear body of Believers, through the awful Crisis in Europe. Also help and comfort all the rest."[46] And in 1942 she reflected on the distance between the American and European experiences of the war:

> Am feeling lots better and praying hard for God to come on this earth, to establish his Kingdom, and end this terrible War. Would not want to live, had I not hopes of something better.
> So far in America, we do not know the horrors our brothers across the water are going through, but some times I get thinking and the 91st psalm comes into my mind, and I know we who trust are safe.[47]

Though in time she would drift away from the Society, being baptized a Baptist in the early 1950s (against the specific instructions of the Society) after she married a member of that denomination, she kept in contact until 1971 and resorted to the water from time to time throughout her life.[48]

Another water-taker from Cleveland (33706), who appears to have initially applied in the 1930s, wrote mainly about physical and emotional preoccupations. It was with her unease about geopolitical instability in the 1960s that she began to discuss deeper cosmological concerns. She wrote in 1962 (perhaps overshadowed by the Cuban Missile Crisis) that "the world crisis gets worse all the time and we of the Panacea Society pray that it is at last signs of the end of evil rule and the return of our Lord God and King."[49] She returned to the theme in June 1967. As her physical complaints were improving, her geopolitical fears grew (perhaps the Six-Day War, which occurred during the weeks before she wrote, had affected her outlook), and she looked to an eschatological outcome.

> I am happy to report that my arthritis is considerably better am able to move around much easier and the pain has diminished thanks to the Divine Healing Water. Otherwise my general health is good and I thank God again that I am able to work.
>
> World conditions continue to worsen and now this middle East crisis could result in the finish of the end and then the return of the Divine Son to at last rule over this kingdom.
>
> I am very grateful for the Visitation, Healing Water and Divine protection.[50]

The letters in the archive from a Finnish woman (77067), who seems to have first come to the water in the 1930s, are marked as sent from British Columbia—though there may be unidentified or lost early letters from addresses in Finland. She wrote mainly about physical and emotional concerns during the 1930s, and she began to contemplate the healing in the context of larger cosmological concerns as the situation in Europe became unstable later that decade. In 1938, she linked the water to God's intercession in her prayers for peace: "I must express my pleasure about the European peace for which I thank and honour God. In drinking the Water I beg for His help and He has heard, thanks to you."[51] Later, in July 1939, she again linked her physical use of the water with her hopes for peace.

> I have used both waters, externally and internally, and I thank you for your help. God bless your work, in trying to alleviate the sufferings of the humanity. I am really in very good health, and I hope for the sake of every one, that their suffering will come to an end, so that they will be able to enjoy peace and happiness.[52]

Similarly, in 1952, perhaps amid reports of British and American developments in atomic weapons technology, she feared war and again linked the healing water to its avoidance: "I hope we shall be able to prevent war by using Panacea. These are very important days and let's hope He will be merciful to the human race."[53]

Others found a certain relief in the buildup to war, as they saw it as the culmination of their expectations and as the sign of God's impending return. A woman (87225) who applied from a town near Glasgow in Scotland, probably in 1934 or 1935, began to expect special messages from the Divine in 1937. "Please keep me informed. if you have got any special orders from The Lord my God and Saviour. He's a Friend indeed! Have you had any messages since Octavia died! Let me know when He sends out any special message to His Flock. (I'm one of His!!)."[54] Commenting a year later that "the World is Awful To-day. We have

'The Signs' so Redemption must be drawing nigh," she again expected messages, saying: "We are living in evil times and require a reliable guiding Hand."[55] By summer 1940, she felt the final fulfilment of her eschatological prophecies becoming a reality: "Spiritually I see things all in a different light. The Bible is certainly standing out. A living book. Christ is here with healing in his wings."[56]

Similarly, one of the more skeptical water-takers (72173) but no less committed (see chapter 7) who applied from Brighton on the south coast of England in March 1939, wrote in August of that year that he felt "perfectly confident to meet any crisis into which the world may be shortly plunged," and that "I am sure that the sands are fast running through now and that we are about to witness marvellous and terrible happenings."[57] And despite the absence of any physical benefits (he would later complain that he had taken the water for nearly a decade without benefit[58]), in 1940 he wrote that "spiritually I feel a great calm. / So confident am I of the nearness of the end of our troubles that the daily increasing gloom around has the reverse effect upon me. / I feel sure it is the power of the Almighty working through the water within me."[59]

Another woman (32463), who was married to a German and had been a pianist in Germany before the war, wrote from New York in November 1939 after a desperate departure from Nazi Germany—she was an American citizen but had been compelled to leave her Jewish husband and thirteen-year-old daughter behind.[60] The ailments she reported in January 1940 were "a broken heart, caused by my separation from my loved ones" and "having had to give up my Music."[61] Indications are that she had originally applied for the healing in the 1920s, and in one letter she linked her desperate plight to her neglect of the healing water: "Everything seemed to go right with me as long as I did so take the water. Whatever made me discontinue, I do not know. At any rate, ever since I stopped, I seem to have had bad luck."[62] She never saw her husband and child again, and her letters in the archive relate how she scraped a living in New York until the 1960s. Her preoccupations after the war were with her financial worries, difficulties in her rented accommodation, and small ailments; however, the Society provided a touchstone for a relieving metaphysical vision. When a dear friend died in the 1960s, she observed that "if it is true, that there is a Heaven, where perfect, + pure human beings from Earth go after death, that is where [he] is right now! This is my only consolation. – / I feel better now thanks to the prayer and to the water."[63]

In later years, it was a more personal and immediate expectation of death that induced an active use of the healing water and a developing spiritual state more generally in the Glasgow woman (87225). She seems to have been suffering with a heart complaint in 1949 and wrote to the Society that "I pray to be made a new creature. My out-look is the Coming of Christ to make all things new. I take the Water everyday and wash and bathe myself twice daily.... Pray the Lord to give me strength to endure. I'm so desirous of Life, hating the thought of death." She said in another letter: "I don't want to die, but I feel I need more Divine Help."[64] Though the archival indications are that she died a year later, she looked forward to the speedy coming of God before she passed away.

> I do get depressed at times with all these feelings and am inclined to cry. My outlook is Life I so much desire it. Not the grave. Hence my struggle.
>
> I get great comfort in reading The Scripts and its comforting to know that the Bible is being fulfilled.
>
> I pray for The Lord to come quickly and take This world under his immediate governance. I elect Him! man has failed.
>
> Please pray for me. That the Lord may add to my strength daily. / It's comforting to look to the Centre where The Power of The Lord is. / We are living in marvellous times—the passing of the old and The coming of The New.[65]

Similarly, the Finnish woman (77067) who wrote from British Columbia and who had linked the Panacea Society's healing to geopolitical anxieties began to reflect on her eschatological hopes as she aged and was diagnosed with heart trouble. Though she would live for many more years, she wrote in 1952, by then in her seventies:

> I think perhaps I am nearing my end . . . and as I am not perfect enough to live in this body on the arrival of our God. Perhaps I will be re-born. May His will be done. In any case I wish to thank Panacea for all the help I have received and may God bless your work in helping humanity.[66]

An archival draft response from the Panacea Society indicates the comforting vision it offered her—even though she might not live to see the perfect transformation and bodily preservation with the beginning of the Millennium.

> God knows all those who are hoping to live in His Kingdom on Earth—and <u>all</u> who have tried to serve Him will be perfectly satisfied whether they live in the Kingdom of Heaven, or the Kingdom on Earth—We hope indeed it will not be long before The Lord comes to reign on Earth for the devil's rule is very evil and causes much sin and suffering. [You] are in God's care.[67]

War, anxiety, and the anticipation of death were important impellers for some people to take up the Panacea Society's healing—and to that extent participation in nontraditional healing and spiritual practices, even without articulating a spiritual or metaphysical scheme, can be understood as a spiritual or metaphysical statement. Furthermore, as we have seen in the writings of a number of the healing users discussed in this chapter, fear of war and existential threat can provide a background against which to think about and articulate spiritual and metaphysical concerns. A study by Ryan Williams and Fraser Watts of the balance of people's religious and nonreligious explanations of meaningful events in their lives using the material in the Panacea Society's archive (from the 1920s, in particular) found that people were more likely to attribute positive events than negative events to religious causes (in line with earlier research in other contexts).[68] The authors of that article also report the unexpected finding that

> correspondents did not always make attributions to events when they occurred.... Despite people's natural inclination to explain events, sometimes the initial response is an emotive one, and we often found descriptions of feelings in the letters rather than causal inferences.[69]

In line with the qualitative impression suggested by the analysis of this chapter, Williams and Watts suggest that "when faced with a personal life crisis or serious physical or mental illness, often the initial response is an emotive one, and sometimes the suspension of judgment forms an ethical or religious response to suffering."[70] Theorists such as William Swatos and Kevin Christiano have argued that "existential questions" require "religious answers" because their "solutions lie beyond rational determination,"[71] and Peter Berger paints a picture of religion as "banners ... in the hands of men as they stand before death."[72] A number of social scientific studies also illuminate a link between contemplation of death and openness to the notion of transcendent realities. Thus, for example, Jonathan Jong, Jamin Halberstadt, and Matthias Bluemke discovered that while death priming (asking subjects to imagine and write about the experience of death) caused believers and nonbelievers to be more confident in their preexisting beliefs, implicit measures found it to cause increased belief in religious supernatural entities.[73]

Ara Norenzayan and Ian Hansen investigated the impact of awareness of mortality (by asking subjects to write about their own death) on belief in supernatural agents and found that it did indeed lead to "more religiosity, stronger belief in God, and in divine intervention."[74] Aaron Kay, Danielle Gaucher, Ian McGregor, and Kyle Nash's review of assessments of the relationship between religious belief and subjects' sense of control includes studies finding that asking subjects to remember a "positive event over which one had no control" is associated with "higher beliefs in the existence of a controlling God" compared to "remembering a positive event over which one does have control."[75] It must be observed that while arguably the difference is merely one of degree, there is a considerable difference between the insistent incomprehensibility of death (proposed by Swatos, Christiano, Berger, and others) and the gentle reflection on death engendered by studies such as that by Jong, Norenzayan, and their colleagues.

While the association between the increasing volume of applicants to the Panacea Society's healing and the escalating tension leading to global war in 1939 provides support for the findings of the empirical studies and the theorizing of the sociologists, the significant increase in the Society's advertising in the period clouds the value of that assessment. More telling is the complex picture painted in the case studies of Panacea Society healing users reflecting on war and geopolitical instability. What is evident in these letters is the way this kind of threat provides the context and premise for individuals to articulate ideas about transcendent or spiritual matters. And, though some of their experiences are no doubt of a highly emotional kind, these writers engage with ideas neither as individuals grasping at an alternative to rational answers nor as a baffled band of mortals holding secondhand banners in the face of death—but as calculating and rational individuals seeking personally satisfying religious solutions.

CHAPTER SEVEN

Religious Language and Metaphysics

RELIGIOUS LANGUAGE

The most important source of information about people's personal religious ideas about the Panacea Society's healing is the letters held in the Society's archives.[1] There are thousands of letters from thousands of correspondents, kept in sometimes irregular bundles wrapped together by Panacea Society healing workers from time to time over many years. While the index cards and register books can be used for systematized analysis, this is less possible for the letters, which offer a less ordered though far richer source of insight. Through a sustained process of sifting and interpretation, three broad categories of correspondence emerge from the letters. Perhaps the largest proportion are those making little or no reference to spiritual matters and remaining focused on the physical ailments the Society's healing was putatively there to minister to. This is unsurprising; applicants were asked to be brief and to restrict their comments to the matters at hand. Correspondents in this category did not use "religious" language; for example, they referred to the healing as medicine rather than as "spiritual healing" or a "divine cure," and others only used commonplace religious terms such as "thank God."

A middle group showed a more involved use of religious language than the first group. For example, a writer (90163) from Jamaica wrote in 1949: "I have heard of the wonderful work that is doing through the mighty hand of God in this work. Thank God for His Love towards mankind."[2] Another example is a writer (71480) from Sussex in England who in 1941 feared being evicted from her home: "So I ask you please when praying to ask 'The Divine Mother' to save us from such distress and allow us to stay here."[3] A third group displays more complex and extensive, detailed, or thoughtful use of religious language and phrases. An example is a woman from Finland (66461who applied in 1957; she wrote, "Have prayed that God would help me, but things only get worse. It may well be that God is training me in this way to obey and to be honest, although I believe I am honest."⁴ Another writer in this category was a man in India (93861) who initially applied in the 1930s. He wrote in 1938:

> I realise that I have done a very wrong thing in breaking away from the "Spirit + Water," and am very Sorry for doing so.
>
> I want to get rid of this great pest "Satan," I want our Lord to come down on earth, and turn this earth from unhappiness, to an Earth, so beautiful where there will be no sin, no unhappiness, no death, I want to live for ever under our Lords Rule.⁵

Most users of the healing water fall into the first category and either did not use religious forms of language, or they did so minimally or in passing and commonplace ways. An example is a farm worker (86153) who submitted an application from northwest England in 1932 and remained in contact until 1952. For this person, the healing was used as a direct alternative to conventional medicine, and he seems never to have talked about the healing in religious terms despite writing seventy-four letters during his period of contact. In 1934 he wrote to say: "I thank you very much for helping me which is very nice to think that there is someone very kind to help one through," and he observed that "before we knew any thing about it we used to spend many a shilling trying medicine we have given over since we found out about the water."⁶

Others in this group made use of some limited religious terms, perhaps using terminology from Panacea Society writings without indications of personal engagement, or using commonplace language that did not suggest association of the healing with a particular spiritual state. An example of this is a female water-taker (72913) from the southeast of England who submitted an application some time prior to October 1950, who said, "you also tell me fear is the devil's weapon which worry [*sic*] me very much." However, she did not concern herself with that point in any detail, remarking "I only hope that the Dear Lord will kindly make me well."⁷ A female water-taker (19298) from Bedfordshire found great benefit from using the water but was not drawn to make any overt religious observation when she remarked in 1929, "I must say I have not been too busy to take the Healing Water, as I feel now I could not live without it. It's wonderful what it has done for me. My trouble all comes back to me at times, but I take the water at once, it certainly gives me great relief."⁸

A married couple in Finland (89555 and 47077) introduced to the healing in the 1920s⁹ seem rarely to have used a religious term beyond the incidental despite using the healing for around forty years.¹⁰ Examples of these kinds of applicants in the Jamaican sample include a woman (54542) applying on behalf of her daughter and grandchildren. The daughter was focused on help for physical ailments—"I am still taking the medicine of the healing water I am suffering with my nerves, my head, my belly side hurts me at night my eyes are very bad and a lot of shade over them"—and was seeking a cure.[11]

Some who wrote to the Panacea Society employed religious language and referred to religious themes in more involved ways than the first category of correspondents. A user of the healing who applied from Yorkshire in 1928 communicated her poor health to the Society (92622; her husband wrote on her behalf): "I am requested to say with much regret that her health is generally worse than it was a month ago . . . However she intends to keep Hammering for Divine Help until her General Health is restored."[12] And a sufferer from osteoarthritis (94364) presented the Society's healing as part of her prayer life and associated it with a spiritual progression: "It is a painful complaint & has penetrated some of the joints as well as the muscles, but I pray earnestly for Divine Healing & strive to conquer when I fail in any way—Physically I may not be much better—but I know that, spiritually, I am prospering as some bad faults have utterly conquered."[13]

In the late 1950s, a female water-taker (28763) represented the healing as part of a divine power active in her life more generally. "I have received Divine healing and help through the Water. My feet are still painful . . . Feeling of sickness not so pronounced since I started drinking the Water." In the 1960s, she reported that "the spots on neck have lightened, the Divine Power is also helping finance."[14] A number of water-takers made use of conventional religious symbols and motifs in their communications. Discussing her headaches, one user (28763) wrote: "Am continuing with Panacea Treatment and am thankful for Christ's power which is helping me in my troubles."[15] Another user (65168) said, "I am very grateful for all this, and I feel as if protected by an angel."[16] An especially striking example (34035) was a user of the healing who discovered a religious renewal in her sense of the effectiveness of the healing.

> All the time I am conscious of the presence of the Almighty, His help and protection. All ills that I or any member of my family have had, have always been healed with the aid of the Divine water and prayer.
>
> It is most remarkable that I have got such a thirst for the Bible, and I read it many times a day.[17]

She wrote again to thank the Society, saying, "I have received so much through you both spiritually and mentally. I have found God."[18]

A Jamaican woman (73405) who applied in May 1954 wrote to the Society in 1956 saying: "At times the way seems dark but there is always something however small provided for me. So I am asking you all to continue to pray for me that the Lord will continue to bless me & that I will continue to derive benefits from the Blessed Water."[19] Another female water-taker (12608), who applied in February 1936, wrote in September of that year: "From I start my Divine Healing I can say thank God. I can say little by little I am [coming] on very well. because I believe that what my Healing has dones unto me no man on earth could ... do that unto me Praise God."[20]

The most developed forms of religious language are evident in those who go further than the middle category and show greater complexity of language, or a more involved application of their ideas to their experiences. In these correspondents it is common to see some level of conflict or grappling with their framing of the Panacea Society healing. A male furniture maker (35772) from Somerset, England, was among the few to explicitly assert his discontent before leaving the Society.

> I must say that as far as this family is concerned the Water and Packets have brought nothing but disaster. Ill luck of every description has beset the home since we sprinkled the water round the house, took the water internally and carried the packets. That financial matter mentioned in my first report has given an impossible amount of trouble. Before we got in touch with you things were going much more smoothly, the health of my wife and children has been worse.[21]

After the healing water apparently killed the family's Christmas tree, he withdrew from the Society entirely: "I will also admit that the fault of all this lies with us for substituting superstition in place of Faith, for even momentarily associating ourselves with a claim that has absolutely no Biblical support whatsoever."[22] Pekka Ervast's comment that "I have had many disappointments in my life, so I only can say as to the Panacea Movement, as long as it helps others I'll try and be among its helpers" is an example of this kind of standpoint (although he was less restrained in his comments in other places).[23]

For many, disagreement with the Society was a process of discussion and negotiation that could result in renewed affiliation or separation. All of these correspondents indicate by their skepticism the extent to which they have an active and dynamic personal sense of transcendent and metaphysical realities. As such, their language is often expressive of complex and dynamic attempts to formulate a theological language around their experience of the healing. A Finnish woman (44613) who applied in the 1930s wrote mainly about physical ailments, though she associated these with real spiritual powers.

> I would still like to add that lately I have had difficult[y] to breath[e] if I am doing something or even when waking. Being extremely tired, I had yesterday a rather bad spell of nervousness. It seemed as if something of the spirit world would have attacked me. Now I feel calm again.[24]

She had written to the Society to express some disagreement with its eschatology:

> The realisation of the Millennium and Christ's second coming on earth, I believe, is possible only after the elapse of immeasurable time, when the whole mankind is ready to receive Him. Until then, He comes, but only individually, to every one, who is seeking the Kingdom of God with all his might and will. Christ will be born in each of us if only our hearts are open to receive Him, with other words, we may experience God. But to achieve this we need self-discipline, and the teachings of Christ serve as our guide and form the criteria against which to check our mode of living. Thus our consciousness in God may grow until some day we may say: "I am living, however not I, but God in me." I do not know whether the above is in agreement with your views.[25]

When an x-ray discovered a "flaw" on her lung, she had a vision of a figure asking her, "Have you used Panacea as directed?," and subsequently she agreed to subscribe to the Society's beliefs on the grounds that the differences between her views and the Society's were slight.[26] And, towards the end of that year, having given the Panacea Society's water "to a little child who was dying, and had terrible pains" with the effect that "the end was much easier for him then," she approved her membership of the Society and said: "I join in everything that my innermost soul approves of."[27]

One of the earliest applicants to the Panacea Society's healing (64777) was a woman who applied from Hertfordshire in the south of England before September 1924. Though she came to the Society with concerns that were thoroughly corporeal ("I am getting rather fat! This is most uncomfortable and it upsets my husband"[28]), the death of her son and brother moved her concerns into highly spiritualized territory. She reported that since their deaths she had "realized a wider conception of the Truth" and that "God's Great Wisdom cannot be held by one portion of His Great Family. Each has some part of Truth, no one individual or Society can have the whole Truth revealed to them." Thus, while she expressed gratitude for "all you taught and showed me in the past, and for the help you gave us" and recognized some special color to the work of the Society, she dissolved her formal connection with it ("we no longer meet as often as we used to") but expressed "may we still be co-workers with Him in bringing His Kingdom."²⁹ Her language and conceptions in her final letter suggest that she had become much involved in Spiritualism: "All life here on Earth as on 'the other side' is all one and therefore death is only an event, a beginning not an end—and therefore nothing to dread and avoid. I have never felt my Son was dead but ... I feel he is more vitally living than ever before."³⁰

Another early applicant (57730) was a woman who applied in July 1924, also from an address in Hertfordshire. Four letters from her have been discovered in the archive. Though she became a sealed member at some point, she wrote in September 1929 to say: "I have been this summer listening to the beautiful and simple teaching of Krishnamurti." Moreover, she objected to what she saw as the Panacea Society's negative cosmology: "The longer I think about it, the more am I convinced that I could never accept unconditionally the teaching of the Panacea Society. To me the idea that the world is 'the Devil's world' is horrible"; rather, she wrote, "selfishness is the only Devil [and] when man learns to use his glorious gift of free will rightly and discipline himself then the world will be as God meant it." Though she was grateful for the kindness of the Society and said she would continue drinking the water (as it was also a part of "God's life"), she meant to follow Krishnamurti's teaching ("He who has himself attained to Liberation longs to set all men free from outside Authority") and gave up her membership in the Society.³¹

A man (72173) living in Brighton on the south coast of England applied during the buildup to war in 1939 saying, "I have never for a moment doubted the Power of God I only hope in these latter days of many false doctrines, I am applying to the right ones."³² He found some immediate emotional relief from using the water: "in these momentous days I am imbued with a feeling of great tranquillity knowing instinctively that I am protected."³³ However, in the summer of 1948, after using the healing water for nearly a decade, he queried its efficacy:

> In any case this is a tremendous lapse I admit, but as my health has not improved after taking the water for 9 years I fear I have become careless or apathetic in reporting.
>
> I have however been re-reading your literature & case paper + realise that the regular reporting is most essential.... In spite of not meticulously carrying out every detail of the treatment, it does seem not a little strange that after consuming such a quantity of water containing the Divine atom that no apparent benefit is manifest.

> I am not an unbeliever else I should never have applied to you, but being a reasoning human being it is difficult to understand why the spirit in the water should fail to operate unless I regularly contact other human beings.
>
> Were I to treat the matter irreverently or superficially I should not expect the spirit to operate but in view of my faith it does seem somewhat perplexing, after-all 9 years is a goodly time.[34]

In a later letter, he added that "the acceptance of all your teachings, this stands or falls naturally upon my complete cure since in a world full of doctrines and dogmas I accept little that cannot give tangible results" and noting that "of course it depends upon what you consider good health, personally if the healing is from God then I am satisfied with nothing less than perfection and not merely to be in a passable condition."[35] The Society's answer was apparently satisfactory, because he wrote back at the beginning of 1949 to say that "you were right in saying that my condition would probably have been worse during the last ten years had I not taken the water."[36]

A woman (14562) who was a member of an Elim Pentecostal church applied from southeast England in 1928 and had a brief correspondence of two or three letters before becoming disillusioned with the Society when it refused her request to visit in 1932 ("I should have thought that any Religious Society would have been pleased to welcome anyone interested in them, who felt anxious to meet them"[37]). Her final letter, written in October 1932, presented a systematic critique of the Society's claims in a leaflet she had been sent. She objected, for example, to a claim that the Society had power to "heal and to protect," as "only God can do this," and to the Society's practice of written confession "because that is contrary to the Bible, which tells us to confess to God, not to a human being."[38] Finally, she suggested the Society might be manifesting the false teaching predicted to occur at the culmination of history.

> I am sorry I cannot agree with the teaching of the Society as I have been very interested in it, in the past. But one would think to read this circular that the Panacea Society had been taught by God himself, that consequently all who believed differently although taking the Bible as their guide, were wrong.
>
> In these latter dates when Satan is so powerful, and when false teaching is continually springing up and many are being misled, we must stand firm on the Word of God, and accept nothing else.[39]

A male applicant from south London (84676), who appears to have applied for the healing in 1939, found a deterioration in his condition and came to reject the Society and its teachings. A longtime Methodist, he "worked in various causes in the Methodist Church" and had a palpable sense of evil powers assailing him. He wrote, "I am convinced that there is a real evil influence everywhere; and an evil spirit that is always waiting to suggest <u>powerfully</u> to me to act the wrong way, then to jeer at my folly. (please don't think this is fancy, it is a real fact.)."[40] Soon after applying to the Society, he expressed skepticism, found that the water "invariably gave me indigestion pains," and barely survived a ruptured ulcer. Though a neighbor believed "he had seen a miracle. He had seen the Dead brought to life," the man felt "justified in saying that the water did not heal me, but made me worse."[41] Despite making serious complaint about the Society's treatment, he still sought guidance from it:

> As to my present mental conflict: I cannot fathom it. I am urged to do a great & good work (from my point of view) yet everything hinders & frustrates me. Is it to try me? or, are the forces of evil to prevail? If God wants <u>me</u> to do it, why am I not helped? Can the <u>Oracle</u> tell you <u>what it is</u>? and if <u>I am to do it</u>? also, if the obstacles will [be] removed or, am I to abandon it? Nothing in the abstract, <u>please</u> this is the testing point, & I hope that <u>you piercing the veil</u>. Can give me a <u>definite</u> answer.[42]

Ultimately, though, he was unsatisfied with the Panacea Society's response—the Society suggested he keep taking the water and said "there is no compulsion for you to take up our teachings you can take the water for your health, if you persevere you will certainly receive benefit."[43] He broke off contact with the Society: "I must confess I have lost faith. One can't go on believing in promises in the face of repeated contradictions, & apparently hindered, not helped to do good."[44]

A farmer in the south of England (45913) who applied in January 1952 provided a detailed account of his ultimate skepticism about the Society's healing. There is evidence of military experience in his letters; as he was in his late teens in 1914 and about forty-two in 1939, he may have served in both of the twentieth century's world wars. When he applied, he described a developing spiritual discontent.

> In recent years I have rather lost faith in the purpose of life. I work hard and can, by the Grace of God, keep my wife and 3 children in reasonable comfort and happiness, but the recent war, and its treatment of human

life, has upset what I thought might be a gradual drift towards kindness amongst peoples generally, and I brood, (so my wife says,) too much upon these matters.[45]

He found real benefit from the water, emotionally and physically: "I felt a considerable calm settle over my nerves, and I have found this to be continuing. The change was really quite profound, and has I am sure assisted in the duodenal trouble."[46] Discussing the Panacea Society's alternative, he showed a creative and insightful theology based on his experience and reading:

> From what intuition I have, I deduce that the Linen (Christ's robe was linen) is blessed and portions provided and I see no reason to suppose that that, and faith, and a mystic emanation from the blessed linen will not have a very fortifying and beneficial effect upon anyone who has, and properly has, a mystic inclination most people who are not completely carnal do possess in varying degree an "inner light."
>
> Whilst I hope and trust that my life may be extended into infinity, yet with the microscopic effect I have had upon affairs in general, I should feel very presumptuous in declaring that I, for one, have earned everlasting life merely by taking the water regularly and writing once a month to you....
>
> I have spent many years of study in those things, which, one day when our bodies wear out, will become for us—facts. I think I have a fair expectation of what the future holds for me what I have passed on, and that it is governed by what I am, and not what I do.... Except perhaps involuntary things go very much deeper than the 10 commandments, or putting in appearances at church. I think that to say there is darkness and light (for example) beggars the question. They are indescribable in so much that Darkness is permanent unless light waves, atoms, rays, or what you like to call them, exist. Animal mechanical eyes are all that are necessary to see in the light, without them to the body—all is dark—but the true spirit knows NO darkness, only the lack of life in his or her own soul.[47]

For the water-takers showing these most developed forms of religious language, an important factor that distinguishes them from those who evidence less complex religious language is that they link the healing to grander spiritual ideas. These correspondents formed links between the spiritual powers they understood themselves to be harnessing and their everyday health and personal needs, and in doing so they expressed a process of formalizing religious accrual to a relatively idiosyncratic spiritual practice.

METAPHYSICS

In the analysis of religious language carried out in the previous section, three main types of correspondents can be identified in the letters: those making little or no reference to spiritual matters, those showing more involved use of religious language, and those evidencing complex and detailed religious language. In a similar way, a review of the ways water-takers linked their use of the healing to spiritual or religious elements beyond their immediate physical or psychological context and needs—and, in that sense, the gradations of metaphysical extension of the healing—suggests that three broad categories of writers can be identified. The first category made no explicit link between the healing and anything greater. This is not to suggest that these people did not have such ideas or instincts; rather, it is an indication of the extent to which there is evidence for this in the letters.

People in the second category expressed an understanding of the healing as a spiritual rather than just a physical practice—they made these kinds of links but still showed signs of preoccupation with their individual circumstances. A Finnish writer (13228) who applied in the 1930s wrote, for example, "I am glad to be a member of your Society and pray that I could be a faithful member and that I could bear all the difficulties of life.... I often think why does God punish me so terribly."[48] And a Jamaican woman (66162) wrote to the Society in 1951: "I could not work I could not do any thing, and now I can do anything now praise and thanks my Heavenly Master."[49] The third category showed evidence of the basic maneuver carried out by the second category in extending the significance of the healing to a somewhat transcendent spiritual context, but went further in terms of the range of that extension into the world and the cosmos. Examples of this latter group include a Finnish woman (18076) who joined in 1958.

> I am very grateful to you and to God and may God bless your work to help suffering humanity ... Thank you for your help. I also thank God—He is good. I await the time when evil will be overcome on this earth. God is almighty and He can also help me.... God has been kind to give me this remedy and take me from the edge of the precipice ... I am happy about the second coming of our Lord and hope I shall be ready. Then this strife would end for ever.[50]

And a woman (87225) writing from Scotland in 1950 said:

> My out look is Life I so much desire it. not the grave. hence my struggle. I get great comfort in reading The Scripts and its comforting to know that the Bible is being fulfilled.
>
> I pray for The Lord to come quickly and take This world under his immediate governance. I elect Him! man has failed.[51]

As might be expected, there is a significant overlap between the two systems of classification: those with a low rating for their use of religious language would be unlikely to indicate metaphysical understandings in the middle or higher category, and vice versa. Similarly, those using the most developed religious language were more likely to refer to a metaphysical horizon of the middle or higher category. Indeed, of the 450 correspondents examined who withheld the use of religious language, all but five fell within the minimal category for their metaphysical extension of the healing. A striking example of one of these exceptions is a correspondent from New York (81539), for whom there are just four letters in the archive between 1936 and 1951, who shows little extensive use of religious language. He wrote in 1935, "I am feeling at this time like a new man thanks to the water and the Spirit[;] my eye is getting on nicely that is the only thing that is not altogether well but now it is."[52] He clearly became deeply involved in the Society's teaching, as the same letter also referred to a "second order of books"; however, evidence of his allocation to the middle category for his metaphysical ideas stems from his adaptive use of the water. He reported in 1949: "On February 7th 1935 was the last connection, I had with the Society, the war started [and] everything went out of order with me continuing to correspond with the Society.... I've been going without the section from 1937 until now, but still using the water without the section."[53] His use of the water without the linen was in line with recommended practice by the Society; nonetheless, doing so (or even just claiming to do so) over a period of more than a decade suggests a highly metaphysical implicit understanding of the plane of operation of the healing.

Another example of a relatively low categorization for religious language alongside a high category for extension of the healing's significance is a male correspondent from London (96608). His religious language use was almost casual; however, in two letters in 1952, he wrote: "I desire to be of benefit to humanity in the ways of which I am capable," and "Is it possible to add to church blessings by using the water—I wish to be of help to humanity as far as I can?"[54] So he clearly extended the implications of the healing to a horizon beyond his own.

The other counterintuitive combination is those who used the most developed religious language combined with the most limited evidence of metaphysical range. Of the 129 correspondents showing signs of this level of religious language, forty-nine showed the most highly developed metaphysics and sixty-seven were categorized in the middle group—just thirteen were identified in the minimal metaphysical category. One example of this group of correspondents is a woman (79369) from Bronx in New York (originally from the West Indies) who applied in 1959 and continued to write a total of seventy-seven letters until 1985. She had a highly dynamic religious life, tithed at her church, and would freely quote scripture in her letters.[55] She went so far as to apply special divine intervention in her circumstances as the outcome of religious practices.[56] However, the evidence from her letters is that her metaphysical horizon did not extend beyond her immediate circumstances and needs—hence, the developed religious language is connected to the minimal metaphysical horizon. Another of those combining the most complex religious language and the least complex metaphysical range was simply too preoccupied by personal difficulties to develop any extended metaphysics. This was a woman in Jamaica (55730), who applied in 1936 and wrote about her husband's infidelity and her reaction to it.

> I do not pay them any mind. I never mention her to my husband I treat the situation with contempt. I have nobody in this world but god. If He is my Creator and will allow human power to harm me, well Amen, so let it be. I try my best not to worry over my condition, because I believe that God will deliver me some day.[57]

Thus, the overwhelming nature of her personal predicament limited the range of her extension of the healing beyond her own circumstances. (This is not to suggest that any of these writers could not or did not make this kind of suggestion in other contexts.)

For many who used the Society's healing, it represented a simple and effective physical remedy with an agreeable and malleable spiritual perspective. At the age of seventy-two, a woman (54811) from Swansea in Wales, who had been a member of the Salvation Army since her forties, was convinced by some of the Panacea Society's writings and left the former in 1940.

> After reading your books over twice I am convinced that there is a great opportunity before mankind, to reach a perfection which is essential to live a life which I would cherish as a true Christian and ready for his

second coming.... I have been for 26 years a member of the Salvation Army which I do not regret because it have been an instrument to keep me from sin, but your books shows me that there is a higher standard to reach and a different outlook for a Christian to look for, than merely have his sin forgiven. I hope you will lead me into greater knowledge of the love of God, where he leads I will follow.[58]

There is limited evidence of her developing any complexly articulated metaphysical perspective, but she did find "a new outlook on the spiritual entirely to what I seen on life before," and "I am letting go the material easier than I used to and clinging more to the spiritual."[59] Against the background of her own expectation of death, and perhaps similar mechanisms to those visible in the context of existential threat discussed in an earlier chapter, she was able to give up a long-held and relatively conventional religion to seek something less authorized but more meaningful to her. In the context of discussions about the dynamic form of religion encountered in contemporary societies, this is no mere bricolage or exercise of choice for its own sake—it is an attempt to reach a personally satisfying metaphysical and spiritual settlement.

Amid the difficulties of poverty and deprivation, a woman (57683) in Kingston, Jamaica, looked to God for help: "I can't find the doctor bill because we are having it very rough in Jamaica[,] especially we the poorer class[;] no work and business places closing down account of that crime rate is very high we are afraid to walk on the street[;] its only God can undo all these wrongs."[60] Though preoccupied with her own troubles, she invoked a grander vision of creation in her request for intercession.

> Please continue to pray with me for all loving people of Panacea Society my husband ... [five] children ... my [five] sisters ... also their children and grand children and the only little grand daughter of mine ... and her mother ... the world and its people, animals, birds and all the beautiful things in the world the government of every country. God bless you all in the name and through the power of Jesus Christ.[61]

In this writer, there is an easy transition to transcendent thinking from her own family to the physical things of the world and then to its public social institutions ("the government of every country") and ultimately to God and Jesus Christ. This is not a parley or negotiation between the things of this world and things beyond it, or a tension between the secular and the spiritual, but a religion and a metaphysics of the everyday.

In Khargapur, India, in the 1920s, a number of British expatriates adopted the Panacea Society and its healing, and they formed a nucleus of highly committed affiliates.[62] While precise numbers are hard to estimate, it is clear that there was a sizeable and recognizable community of Panaceans there; one member (96017) reported their preservation during an earthquake in 1934: "Many towns to the North of Bihar have suffered greatly. Muzzafapore [sic] seems (from the papers) to have been demolished and in Jamalpur [sic] only 50 houses were left standing. We felt the shock here and it was fairly severe for about 3 1/2 minutes."[63] However, Panacea Society members were preserved:

> It was very remarkable that Panacea Members were not alarmed or panicky, but others were terrified and rushed out of their houses. We thanked the whole Divine Family for the protection we had received, and we realised that if we were not in this wonderful mission how alarmed and anxious we would have been. I pray that right-minded people will be brought to realise that these are warning and that they will cry out to Almighty God for help and seize hold of the priceless gift, which is being offered without money and without price.[64]

This member worked as a teacher and applied from Khargapur in the late 1920s; she expressed her relief at having found the Society in 1929:

> I cannot express the joy I feel in having found "that" which I have sought for, and I cannot thank you sufficiently for having been the means of removing the scales from my eyes.
>
> I was much against the Panacea Society, and took the Water very indifferently, but after reading the 1st volume of the Panacea I felt a different being. Both my husband and I devoured the five volumes and still we thirst for more. . . .
>
> I am taking the Water regularly and according to the Instructions, + find that constipation is a thing of the past, and my sight is improving.
>
> Ah! how much I regret that I have allowed so many months to have slipped past in indifference and apathy.[65]

In time, she became something of a leader among the Panaceans in the town, and her husband seems to have led meetings of an active group of water-takers there.[66] They integrated the Society and its theology with their understanding of the British Empire, commenting about preparations for the Silver Jubilee of King George V, that "we do humbly pray that King George V may receive power from the Divine Family whereby he may become ruler under God of all his dominions."⁶⁷ Another member of the group (81845) suggests that the Khargapur members were interpreting and reinterpreting the Panacea Society's cosmology in light of their own notions of the Empire:

> I cannot tell you what a shock King George's death was to all of us, especially as I had been told by a member that it was predicted by the Society that the King would never die, but would hand over the reins of government to our Lord, at first I was doubtful, but as I thought of all that had been accomplished in my own family and all that I had read, I thought that there must be some reason for what had happened and my faith in the society was not shaken.⁶⁸

This is a luminous example of an individual process of continual and dynamic interpretation and reinterpretation. The Panacea Society provided a catalyst for this group's members to examine the power structures they were part of and to frame them in the context of a complex cosmology involving a personal and intervening God. Understanding the geopolitical and cosmological perspective of the British Empire as a theocracy, these women also wrote of the power of the water in their everyday lives. So the writer shocked at the death of her king (81845) used the water to successfully modify the behavior of her unfaithful and unpleasant husband; similarly, the teacher (96017) gave the water to her son and found "a great difference in his general behavior,"⁶⁹ and she looked forward to an individual transformation as a result of the water.

> I am longing to have an entirely new character. What a joy it will be to have the mind that was in our Lord and saviour Jesus Christ, and to be good. As we go further in this wonderful work we are realising what a terrible enemy we have to fight in the Self. How terrible our condition would have been if we had not the mighty Weapons given us to fight with, the power of the spirit in the Blessed Water and the formula.⁷⁰

In a parallel move to the Jamaican woman (57683) discussed earlier, these correspondents make a transition from worldly events to a transcendent perspective—in this case, from the death of the king to the government of the world by God. Thomas Luckmann referred to the changing nature of articulations of "wild experiences of transcendence,"⁷¹ yet these kinds of accounts display the difficulty of separating an experience of transcendence from its interpretation. Although correspondent 96017 recognized a consistent struggle in working towards the transformation, the Panacea Society's healing provided a powerful support. Commenting on how working in a school provided "opportunities for overcoming faults and failings. Impatience, irritability, temper etc.," she noted that the "falls are many, but it is very encouraging to know from the Scripts that one falls forward and not backwards and that we can pick ourselves up and struggle on."[72] When she learned of Octavia's death in 1934, she looked "forward to Her return in Power and Glory."[73] In 1938, the writer and her husband visited the Society in Bedford, and with the war looming they moved to the Society's headquarters permanently in the summer of 1939; records indicate that she died shortly after the war.

Another woman (20109), who got in touch with the Society after returning from India, showed a very complex attitude towards spiritual matters. She wrote in the first place because her husband was largely absent, working in India, and when he was physically present he was emotionally distant and rather imperious.[74] She admitted "I do not understand in the least how you can help me," but noted that "I see from your pamphlet that that does not matter, and nothing is required of me but a certain obedience, and that I am willing to give."[75] Although she self-identified as a member of the Church of England, she had investigated many other religions and conceded that "my beliefs are not orthodox."[76] And amid the physical trials of rheumatism and malaria contracted while in India and the household work of raising five children, an overriding concern was a complex set of thoughts about sin and guilt.

> I do not believe it possible for any human being to be "damned," in whatever sense each religion takes the word, eventually, God gave us our life, character, and conditions. He sends us our temptations, we have little choice in these matters, so I cannot believe He would allow any one of us, however bad, to "die" spiritually. I have read many books written by Roman Catholics, Protestants, Theosophists & Christian Scientists, but no one seems to reach the root of the matter i.e. how it was that we were ever permitted to become "sinners," and even leaving that question, is not "sin," as we call it, part of God's plan anyhow? For why make us only to "die"? A great many of us certainly would "die" with the weaknesses we have allotted to us at a birth, for which we are not responsible.[77]

She articulates a profound sense of the complexity of her own outlook and experience of life and its relation to a transcendent power. It was with some relief, one senses, that she discovered the Panacea Society made no doctrinal demand and only asked for "a certain obedience." The detachment of the Society from doctrinal prescription provided her with something she sought in her spiritual life, and it was part of the offering of contemporary spiritualities—the freedom from constraints on belief, faith healing for the faithless. Her words suggest that we need to reverse the conventional formula for understanding what religion or chosen spirituality does; this is less like a person with personal (perhaps "spiritual") needs seeking a religion with a cosmological system that helps them to live with those needs, and more like a person confronted by complex and half-articulated metaphysics seeking a working religion to bed down in.

The depth of the spiritual penetration of the Panacea Society's healing is especially evident in correspondents who expressed their most profound sense of sin. A woman (22807) who would become one of the long-standing users of the healing, writing more than one hundred letters between the 1930s and the 1970s, found remarkable help from the water:

> I am very thankful to you and to God that I have received such great help and alleviation in my illness, because I was at absolutely the lowest ebb both mentally and physically, and the doctors did not even know what was wrong with me. The water gave me immediate relief.[78]

After many years of contact she felt induced to confess what is condemned as a terrible crime in many conventional contexts—and no less in Finland in the interwar period:

> You asked me earlier to tell you what was on my mind, though I have not got down to it until now. The worst of my sins has worried me [many] years. Now I feel I must be honest and confess. For a number of reasons I had an abortion. It was only after committing this act that I realized the horror of it.... I do not feel I am fit to live again, because I know the wages of sin—death. I am deeply grateful to you and to God for the help received in spite of being a sinner. I respect you for the time and trouble expended in helping us sinners. I shall continue to use the Water until you tell me not to.[79]

And the Panacea Society provided her with a doctrinal space—the woman's letter bundle in the archive includes a note for a draft response from the Society. They thanked her for expressing her fears and urged her to write down her sin and to ask for forgiveness. The Society's response expressed certainty that she would be forgiven and counseled her to continue with the Water.[80]

One of the virtuoso water-takers was a woman with an address in western Jamaica who applied in 1936 when she was in her mid-thirties (32171). She was poor and made a little money from sewing, and she wrote to the Society asking "for a special prayer" to help her in a time of difficulty. She understood her life and world in a highly religious and spiritual way, consoling herself "with daily prayer to God, for he alone sees and knows that was never my wish."[81] Indeed, the Society's intervention provided positive support ("I certainly feel much happier, since I come connected to this society"[82]; "I try to use water in every way possible, I always use it to wipe my sewing table and a little in the floor water, it has made a wonderful change over the home"[83]) and met a spiritual need she had felt for a long time.

> From my childhood days I wish to have the real true love of Christ Jesus, and often wonder why is it I go to church always take active parts, join the different organisations and yet I always feel that is not enough for till I feel wanting of something, but truly I now feel a different feeling all together, when I read my Bible, I feel that I understand it more, and feel much lighter and happier in mind and body daily, daily when I go in silence to God explaining my life to him, and only he who can assist us in all things. . . . I certainly feel a new person since I am connected to your society, and no power will get me sever from this, May Gods true blessings rest in this society "the Panacea" always and for ever.[84]

This culminated in the early 1940s when she felt called to missionary work and set out as a pilgrim to minister in poor and rural parts of Jamaica.[85]

> I must now report that I am now a changed person, I am in the world but not of the world any more, I have been called in the Holy Spirit and is now doing the work of the Lord Jesus sincerely since January, my life is just devoted in the work of the Lord Jesus and every day I find it much happier, in the work, I am doing missionary work in a very poor district a few miles from my home.[86]

And she felt guided in her work by a transcendent source:

> Happy to say the great trouble I had in understanding the Bible is all or nearly passed away from me. I can hear and understand plainly, voices speaking within me all the while since I have had the out pouring of the holy spirit "chapters" are always given to me. Which I find very helpful and just in the times when needed.[87]

This was a renewal of a lifetime of visions, encounters, and experiences with spirits and devils. She reported, for example, that she had a premonition of an impending death in her family—and had had these since childhood—and a feeling that devils were fighting over her since a neighbor had put evil magic on her.[88]

In the early 1940s, she wrote to say she was answering a need of her followers and was to begin building a temple, and the following year she collaborated with a male prophet she had met on her travels to hold general prayer meetings.[89] From the reports in her letters, and ultimately from the Society's alarmed reaction (though slow to respond, no doubt in part due to the war), it is clear that her mission met with considerable success. In effect, the woman formed herself into a de facto Tower in Jamaica, and she preached and distributed the Society's healing water to all comers.[90]

A severe letter finally arrived from the Society in March 1945 rebuking the woman for her arrogation of spiritual power. Though the Society was limited in its response by the fact that Octavia and the Divine Mother were no longer available to making a ruling (they had died in 1934 and 1943, respectively), it relied on the teachings the two women had left behind to object that the Jamaican woman had usurped the Society's (and individuals') role in providing divine succor to people.

> When you wrote to us in an earlier letter that you were having prayer meetings we thought you were just having meetings with your friends for Bible reading and prayer, as many people like to do if they are of the same mind. We did not think you were having meetings in connection with our work. Do you not see that in doing so and in giving out the Blessed Water from your own supply, you are making yourself a providence to them in the place of God, who has begun this great work in the world from a Centre—one place only—to which those who seek His help and Word should turn. Those people in Kingston that you speak of are not turning to God, they are turning to you. Can you see that?[91]

The Society urged her instead to attend to a quiet home life ("A perfect home life is God's idea for His Kingdom. To live as those who are waiting for the Lord and preparing themselves and their homes according to His Will, takes all one's time"[92]). Following her husband's sudden death, she said that much of the blame for her overreaching rested on him, as he had begun charging people for the healing they provided, and he had even gone so far as to distribute linen squares he took from her sewing box and consecrated himself.[93]

While the Society's rebuke had some effect in quieting the woman's active missionary life, she seems to have continued to attract people seeking healing and to have ministered to them—eventually gathering a more or less settled congregation around her.

> It is most wonderful to see the people of the better classes coming in to me daily, and making themselves so very homely here, many say they have spent hundreds of pounds and no deliverance on their bodies and they find great changes in coming, many say they would be glad to live here, through the calm cool feelings of Unity here, I do thank the Supreme Spirit Divine, for The power and gift of explanation, many come burdened in tears, we only go in quiet talks on the obedients of God's Divine Words.[94]

Her practice became a mixture of traditional Jamaican healing and the Panacean techniques. One account explains how she treated a sufferer from ringworm under divine guidance:

> He was a real stranger to me then, But as I saw him my spirit was led to go in the garden I picked a large green leaf from a creeper vine, I ask him to let me put it on his chest when he opened his shirt I saw on his chest a shape and a size ring worm blotch the very same size and shape of the leaf. he looked at me and tears roaled from his eyes for he knew he told me nothing, my sister and myself went in prayers with him to God, he says he feals he is to be [cured] here by Gods own help I was led to give him some water I bathed the suffering body and tapped it with olive oil well he came several times.[95]

However, when he asked to have some of the healing water to take home, she told him to write to the Panacea Society in Bedford.[96] And, though the process of her association with it is difficult to discern, she came to have charge of a balmyard of her own with a regular group of members to whom she provided healing and forgiveness of sins.[97] (She was rebuked again for this, and she apologized.) Her correspondence with the Society carried on for years, and in 1968, after around 175 letters and a relationship with the Society lasting over thirty years, she wrote a final letter reporting a serious and painful illness, closing with the words, "I feel this case belongs to Dr. Divine. I thank you ever so much."[98] She represents, perhaps, the apotheosis of the malleability of the healing offered by the Society as a catalyst of personal religious expression that was articulated in terms of an old and sophisticated culture of spirituality such as that found in Jamaica. We see in this user of the healing the full range of personal and public religious processes taking place, in the conventional grammar of Jamaican spirituality but with the transmitted spiritual power of Panacean healing. This woman carried on a long and complex process of religious and metaphysical interpretation, reinterpretation, and ritual activity that incorporated the fundamental task of a healing ministry and an energetic missionary spirit.

Among those who showed the deepest affiliation with the healing, and who made the most involved adoption of it as a religious practice, were those who did not use complex language and perhaps had little exposure to conventional and mainstream religions. An American woman (72150) was one of the Society's virtuoso water-takers; she applied from Chicago, Illinois, in November 1958, and remained in contact until May 1985, writing about 140 letters in total. In an early letter, she wrote to ask for help winning a lottery game[99] (a practice the Society frowned upon), but though her financial situation hardly improved, she developed a deep and tranquil relationship with the transcendent constellated around the water.

> I'm very poor don't have much of anything but I feel very rich because I have peace with God, in my heart and with my ups and downs I am able to bare my [burden] with ease cause I know God is with me and you have helped me to be a little closer to Christ. I thank God for everything.[100]

Ultimately, the Panacea Society enabled the correspondent to develop a theodicy of the small and large sufferings of the world. She said in 1961, "I'm more thankful to God, each day for the Blessings he has given me ... I thank him for making me able to stand the storms of life because the sunshine is always shining from above."[101] She observed five years later that

> I'm glad I am able to have a peaceful heart and a contented mind, as most people of today have forgotten god, fighting with each other, against races and churches and everything, and the reason some may give is no reason at all just full of hate. I pray for all, and in time god, will take care of everything. I'm happy to be alive.[102]

The full extent of the Panacea Society's healing in her personal practice and self-understanding is evident in a remark during March 1965: "The water has become a part of me now."[103]

As a record of the spiritual and religious lives of people from all walks of life and in a multitude of personal and cultural contexts, the letters of the Panacea Society's Healing Department provide a deep and possibly unique source. The study of religion outside conventional structures has gradually dropped its reliance on numerical and institutional reference points and is recognizing the need to understand religion not merely as a social object but as something embedded in people's lives. The focus in this chapter has been on those who offer us considered articulations of this kind of religiosity in their own lives, showing how this doctrinally undemanding religious system could articulate with the most complex and challenging attempts to understand and coexist with the transcendent.

This chapter's concern has been not so much with the history of the Panacea Society's healing in people's lives, but with the light that their articulations of moments in those histories can shed on the dynamic processes they worked with. A number of the theorists examined in chapter 3 engaged with the problem of the nature of a theorized movement or oscillation between secular and sacred, between sacred and profane, in societies. The examples discussed in this chapter indicate that the distinction has had little real significance in the personal context. Secular or profane life is in each case part of an attempt to understand the world, and if that understanding stretches to transcendent horizons, then the secular or profane is part of that arc. In these writers, the religious project that is underway is not the mere search for a pleasing and undemanding form of religious activity but an unavoidable metaphysical task. The formal metaphysics or doctrines of transcendence encountered in churches is not relevant or irrelevant; it is a background reality in some lives and takes a different form in each, but it remains a background for the personal task of working out a theory of the transcendent and its relationship to an individual's life.

CHAPTER EIGHT

Theories of Transcendence

═══ CONTEMPORARY SPIRITUALITY AND THE HEALING ═══

The example of the Panacea Society's healing water shows how a healing practice has the capacity to become a personal nucleus around which people can attach religious and spiritual ideas. Indeed, some of the individual stories discussed in this book show that the healing could function not just as an attachment point for religious thinking but as a full form of religious affiliation in itself. For some users of the healing, it was the center of a dynamic and complex religious practice and belief embedded in their lives. Chapter 3 examined the ways that the religious change characteristic of recent times, which was for a long time presented as a form of religious decline by theorists, can instead be understood as a process of developing dynamic forms of individual religiosity. Chapter 3 proposed that this is in fact the essential insight of the secularization thesis. The examples of personal religion show how religion more or less detached from traditional and institutional structures is truly religion in the lives of those who practice it—and not simply a decayed or eviscerated institutional form of it.

The broad terms of the potential for a healing practice to be extended in this way have been discussed by a number of theorists. Marion Bowman discusses how elements of contemporary alternative healing can be seen as a reemergence of nineteenth- and twentieth-century conceptions of healing. She notes that "healing has often been related to religion and complementary resources used at times of need."[1] Meredith McGuire's article on "Health and Spirituality as Contemporary Concerns" observes that "to many contemporary Americans, health and healing appear to be salient metaphors for salvation and holiness."[2] Christopher Partridge's account of the re-enchantment of the West comments on the democratization of "strategies for healing, health, and wellbeing," and he observes that in the contemporary context, "because the embodied self is understood to be the site of spiritual transformation, central to notions of wellbeing is a growing emphasis on spiritual health."³ The suggestion of the spiritual salience of healing is strongly proposed in a study by Brian Hughes, who argues that complementary and alternative medicine might be considered to be "filling a 'mysticism void' left by the decline of orthodox religion."⁴ And Wouter Hanegraaff has proposed that " 'personal growth' can be understood as the shape 'religious salvation' takes in the New Age movement . . . therapy and religious 'salvation' tend to merge to an extent perhaps unprecedented in other traditions."⁵

Hughes raises the conundrum of accounting for the growing popularity of complementary and alternative medicine despite its poor performance in clinical trials, and he suggests that, rather than interpreting the rise "in terms of consumers' changing levels of regard for science," there may be a complex dynamic of mysticism and caregiving social roles at play.⁶ Hughes proposes approaching these kinds of healing as outlets for an inherent human need, previously associated with traditional religion but now expressed in alternative ways, "to explain part of [users'] lives in terms of assumptions for which there is no clear evidence."⁷ As he says, "if events in a given society negatively reinforce participation in formal religions (such as might be said to be the case in societies that are becoming more secular), then individuals in that society may turn to other belief systems with which to give expression to their mystical propensities."⁸ The letters of the users of the Panacea Society's healing illustrate this kind of process and demonstrate the personal thinking and experience that can lie behind the accrual of religious meaning to a healing system beyond the administration of physical healing alone. For a number of those users, the healing does not come across as a mere compensation for some inadequacy elsewhere, but it is engaged with as an important and dynamic element of their wider spiritual view.

The Panacea Society's healing has much in common with theoretical analyses of the defining characteristics of contemporary and New Age spiritual movements; it can be understood as a precocious or nascent version of New Age spirituality. In her discussion of healing as a metaphor for salvation and holiness, McGuire suggests that the emergence of this kind of thinking is a direct response to the larger forces of institutional differentiation identified by sociologists. While "health, healing, and well-being were traditionally interwoven with other institutional domains, especially religion and the family," modernization has, she suggests, entailed the separation and specialization of the domains: "biomedicine claimed control over the health and curing of physical bodies; a separate science claimed the health and well-being of minds; and religion was relegated to the sphere of the purely spiritual."⁹ The process has located disease in the body and "the body can be understood and treated separately from the person inhabiting it"—"these assumptions exclude social, psychological, spiritual, and behavioral dimensions of illness."[10] McGuire argues that the growth of individualized and eclectic forms in recent times is "an expression of dissent from the medicalized conception of health and healing" distinct from what came before.[11]

Hanegraaff makes a similar point when he discusses the importance of the distinction between the modern biomedical model of healing disease, which refers to "abnormalities in the structure and/or function of organs and organ systems," and the alternative model, which refers to "a person's perceptions and experiences of certain socially disvalued states."[12] Hanegraaff suggests that the increasing polarization between the former and the latter has led to a reaction in alternative movements that seeks to reemphasize the traditional function of healing illness. In this respect, he says, "in their implicit criticism of official western medicine, New Age healing practices not surprisingly evince a rather close affinity to those of traditional cultures which western medicine has sought to replace."[13] To the extent that the Panacea Society's healing performed the function of a dynamic, participatory, and inclusive form of healing beyond mere physicality in the lives of its users—and arguably even among those who inquired but failed to take up the healing in earnest—it is a form of the contemporary search outside conventional biomedicine.

Ellie Hedges and James Beckford suggest (quoting Michael York) that the unifying factor in New Age spirituality is "the vision of 'a radical mystical transformation on both the personal *and collective levels*'" and "the claim that 'the New Age is always ultimately directed toward the communal, that is, toward something greater or more inclusive than merely the self.'"[14] Similarly, McGuire concludes by suggesting that "perhaps the contemporary linkage of religion and health may also be understood as one form of identity work by which the individual pursues the ongoing project of constructing his or her self."[15] So far as the Society understood the meaning of the healing, personal and collective transformation at the physical and spiritual levels was literally what they believed individuals taking the water were engaged in. In the individual lives of the committed users of the healing, there is a consistent sense of a pressing need to change and transform.

The Panacea Society's healing was a mass-market phenomenon. However, the Panacea Society retained its exclusivity at the center; full membership was restricted to a limited number of proficient correspondents, and core membership at headquarters was limited to a very restricted coterie. Perhaps counterintuitively, this exclusivity was combined with the extraordinarily accessible healing practice. While in many ways the Panacea Society retained or imitated the sectarian and authoritarian tendencies of the hegemonic religious forms it was seeking to supplant—most notably in the highly authoritarian central administration—in the nonprescriptive attitude to doctrine embodied in the healing there are commonalities with the proliferation of eclectic and relatively novel religious forms. In this respect, the Panacea Society's healing is an aspect of the kind of spirituality characteristic of New Age movements.

Commenting on new positive-thinking movements emerging in the 1980s, Hanegraaff notes that often these presented "the 'growth' of spiritual insight as a dialectical rather than a one-way process" to help overcome "deep-seated emotional patterns [that] may simply make it impossible for us to be open to healthy positive beliefs."[16] In its presentation of the water as the medium that took the healing to those who tried it, who were in effect passive recipients, the Panacea Society's framing of the healing was one-sided. However, the water-takers in fact employed the water as part of their own dynamic process as they worked their way through a spiritual landscape of their own. This latter process exemplifies what Partridge calls "malleable spirituality," associated with more recent forms of spiritual activity that are "always chosen spirituality, continually constructed and reconstructed."[17] As the example of the Panacea Society's healing shows, centralized organization and leadership are not incompatible with the absence of binding doctrines; however, the nonbinding nature of those doctrines becomes a doctrine itself. While the *Panacea Society* may not have epitomized characteristics associated with recent and New Age spiritual movements, the *users* of its healing did.

James Lewis has commented that the New Age movement

> emerged out of a preexisting occult-metaphysical subculture that—especially in such institutional embodiments as the Theosophical Society, New Thought churches, traditional Spiritualist denominations, and so forth—was affected by, but was never completely absorbed into, the New Age.[18]

He concludes, therefore, that it "makes sense to distinguish the New Age from its predecessor movements."[19] Though there may be theoretical advantages in making the distinction, new religious and spiritual forms arguably never completely absorb their predecessors in any case. And while they may have had important origins in some particular culture (in this case a "preexisting occult-metaphysical subculture"), that is not the entirety of their origin. In individual lives, a great range of mainstream and subcultural elements and themes are collapsed into religious and spiritual feeling and understanding. In the case of a historical study like this one, reifying the theoretical distinction would obscure the practical confusion.

We can recognize dual doctrines in the example of the Panacea Society's relationship to its healing: centralized authority balanced by decentralized individualism amongst its affiliates, and a pedigree in ancient esoteric belief alongside amenability to individual contexts. The healing can therefore be thought of as a hybrid between more conventional pre–"New Age" forms of spiritual framing and more liberal "New Age" movements. While the Panacea Society retained an authoritarianism and a sectarianism at its headquarters, the permission it gave for users of the healing to have heterodox beliefs (from the Society's point of view) or even no beliefs, and its radical association of healing with spiritual reform, indicates how the Panacea Society's healing should be understood as part of the ecosystem of eclectic and "new" religious forms, even though its flowering occurred sometime before that ecosystem is usually understood to have established itself.

TRANSCENDENCE

Thomas Luckmann describes the shift in contemporary religiosity not simply as the rise of alternative spiritualities that develop to displace mainstream and traditional forms, but rather as a general disarticulation or loosening of systems of the sacred in which traditional religions have taken part (see the previous discussion of chapter 3). While traditional societies contain "well-articulated themes that form a universe of 'ultimate' significance that is reasonably consistent in terms of its own logic" in the modern "sacred cosmos," while it "also contains themes that may be legitimately defined as religious," these themes "do not form a coherent universe" that is "internalized by potential consumers as a whole." Instead, "the 'autonomous' consumer selects ... certain religious themes from the available assortment and builds them into a somewhat precarious private system of 'ultimate' significance."[20] Traditional religions, in Luckmann's account, are not replaced as such; rather, they partake in the process as their own status is changed:

> They no longer transmit, as a matter of course, an obligatory model of religion. They are forced to compete, instead, with many other sources of transcendence reconstructions for the attention of "autonomous" individuals who are potential consumers of their "product."[21]

In effect, the dominance of the traditional religions is displaced; according to Luckmann, they "no longer represent the socially dominant form of religion" and "become institutions among other institutions."[22] Luckmann's account of the nature of modern religious change describes a structure of individual relationships to transcendent experiences. This structure is a scale from the smallest transcendences of everyday life ("There is a 'before' and 'after' and 'behind' one's ongoing actual experience"[23]) to the largest ("transcendences of life and death"[24]). As discussed earlier, according to Luckmann, while the traditional religions articulated the great transcendences, the modern shift in religion has been down the scale to the smaller ones. "Modern religious consciousness is characterized by a radically shrunken span of transcendence ... away from the 'great' other-worldly transcendences to the 'intermediate' and, more and more, also to the minimal transcendences of modern solipsism."[25]

No doubt the evidence of the majority of the Panacea Society's healing users, those who only flirted with the healing or showed little proof of employing it in the context of great transcendences, could be understood as evidence supporting that proposition. However, it is clear that a number of users went much further and associated the healing with the widest and deepest perspectives. To the extent that both viewpoints are in play (those who engaged with minimal transcendences, and those who parlayed with the greatest), the evidence of the Panacea Society's healing users can only indicate the presence of both kinds and makes no assertion about any measurable trajectory of change—though the fact that some healing users associated the healing with great transcendences suggests there is no inherent disconnection between nontraditional, nonmainstream religion and the great transcendences.

While this book questions, then, Luckmann's claims about diminishing metaphysical range, it endorses his implicit assertion that, whatever is going on, it is about transcendence. Luckmann's analysis represents a useful reminder that engaging with transcendent experience is not the preserve of the grand institutions of religious history but is in fact the property of ordinary people in their everyday lives. This is perhaps the pressing finding of the contemporary study of spirituality—we no longer suspect the conversation with transcendence to be the property of a particular class of (educated and ordained) individuals. Hanegraaff observes his own use of "the spectacular products of unquestionably gifted individuals" with accessible published writings, but he argues that "when talking of spiritualities" we are "in principle ... dealing with a common everyday phenomenon: every person who gives an individual twist to existing religious symbols (be it only in a minimal sense) is already engaged in the practice of creating his or her own spirituality."[26] This insight was encountered in the discussion in chapter 3 of Hugh McLeod's reference to personal testimony not relying on "celebrities or activists"[27] and Jeremy Morris's observation that "there is no intrinsic reason to believe that the spiritual world of the poor was any less complex ... than was that of the rich and educated."[28] While these authors are referring more explicitly to postmodern forms of religious expression, the same idea lies behind Kelly Besecke's identification of "the noninstitutional-but-public kind of religion" and David Lyon's everyday "meaning routes."[29] It is plainly and richly demonstrated in the letters of the Panacea Society's healing users.

In the introduction to *Vernacular Religion in Everyday Life*, Marion Bowman and Ülo Valk trace the trajectory of the academic study of forms of religion that are not identified with mainstream and authorized forms.[30] They emphasize the problem of defining these "non-official" religious forms as if they are in open opposition to "official" religions. Starting with Don Yoder's contestation of "the tendency to pathologize folk beliefs as primitive superstitions," Bowman and Valk note his agenda to present such beliefs as "in a dynamic relationship with institutionalized Christianity" in an attempt to overcome the artificial dichotomization of the realms.[31] Nonetheless, Yoder's definition of folk religion, as "the totality of all those views and practices of religion that exist among the people apart from and alongside with strictly theological and liturgical forms of the official religion,"[32] may provide definition to the subject but does not embed the dynamic interaction of domains. A recent attempt to analyze the complex nature of the religious forms encountered and expressed in individuals' daily lives, and to overcome the reification of categories, is that offered by Bowman, in a chapter on "Phenomenology, Fieldwork and Folk Religion."[33] Bowman proposes that the field be "viewed in terms of three interacting components":

> official religion (meaning what is accepted orthodoxy at any given time, although this is subject to change), folk religion (meaning that which is generally accepted and transmitted belief and practice, regardless of the official view) and individual religion (the product of the received tradition, plus personal beliefs and interpretations).[34]

As discussed in chapter 3, the debate is developed further by Leonard Primiano, who proposes a category of "vernacular religion": "religion as it is lived: as human beings encounter, understand, interpret, and practice it."[35] In a sense, in an attempt to analyze something that is authentically close to religion as people encounter and experience it in an everyday way, Primiano indicates the need for a dissipation of categories of interpretation.

Behind each of these attempts to penetrate the definition or essential category of vernacular religion is the consistent (even if implicit) reference to something that may be, in any case, a phantasm—that is, any kind of official, orthodox, generally recognized, mainstream religion. The subject of study, then, might be thought of as that which is going on *outside* a church on a Sunday morning (at least in a traditionally Christian context), while those on the inside express something else—official and authorized. However, for all their efforts, no doubt each individual inside the building (consciously or otherwise) interprets, accepts, or rejects what he or she hears moment to moment, and on his or her own intuitive terms. And, though even the authorized officiant may read from sanctioned texts, who is to say that that individual is any less subject to his or her personal processing of each and every sanctioned phrase? The object of the studies discussed here is summarized by Bowman and Valk:

> The myths, personal experience narratives and more casual verbal expressions of belief, or material culture and actions related to, arising from or inter-related with beliefs, shed valuable light on religion in everyday life, practical religion, religion as it is lived. In this context, the stress is not on artificial expectations of theological homogeneity or "orthodoxy," nor is it perpetuating judgements as to what counts as "real" religion at the expense of what people actually do in relation to extra-liturgical praxis. In the tradition of folklore and ethnology, the stress, the overriding interest, is on what people in a variety of cultural, religious and geographical landscapes do, think and say in relation to what they believe about the way the world is constituted.[36]

This book subscribes to this representation, but not the need to deemphasize "artificial expectations of theological homogeneity or 'orthodoxy'" nor the perpetuation of "judgements as to what counts as 'real' religion," because these kinds of religious inclination (i.e., "religion in everyday life, practical religion, religion as it is lived") occur in churches, too. The expectations of theological homogeneity (however artificial researchers or practitioners may feel them to be) are simply another valid influence on all forms of religious practice alongside all the others. Indeed, we can even recognize that *rejection* of "artificial expectations of theological homogeneity" and "judgements as to what counts as 'real' religion" are themselves expressions of religious beliefs (or at least of metaphysical commitments), and that the *perpetuation* of such expectations must be as much a part of "vernacular" religion as its opposite. The subject under inquiry need not be defined by a reference of those who do it ("popular," "vernacular," "folk," etc.), because in truth there is no one outside these categories. Rather, perhaps aside from some special moments when we might for the sake of argument allow that an individual embodies the abstract theology of a defined religious discourse, the kind of religion examined in this book is that which happens every day, whether to a pope, a reiki healer, a worried parent, an unworried secularist, or to someone drinking water into which they have dipped sacred linen sent from Bedford—and all of these *are* religion.

As a case study of the nature of quotidian religion, the Panacea Society and its healing ministry reflect something that is perhaps not recognized enough in the study of popular religion, that the two-tier model of religion (an authorizing priestly elite and an interpreting participant class) is present in many forms of popular and folk religion. The question is mainly of the degree to which the participants believe they subscribe to what is handed down from the priestly class. The Panacea Society shows that it need not hand down a great deal beyond a model of ritual—so participants do not need to believe to be members.

This book provides striking evidence of how religion is a negotiation. Chapter 4 (in the context of a discussion of people's spiritual and intellectual trajectories through Christian Science, Spiritualism, and Theosophy) and chapter 6 (in a discussion of the heightened awareness of death) bring to the fore the processes by which individuals continuously negotiate with a sensed transcendence, with the reality of death, with moments of personal and social transformation, and with the small failures and triumphs of domestic life. Perceived static points at each end of a spectrum, from pure atheism to monolithic theism, or from religious societies to secular societies, are heuristics generated by theorizing about religion and religious change. In fact, in people's lives there is a perpetual meditation on the places where the everyday aspects of existence run up against the imponderable and the unfathomable—sometimes large and sometimes small, but always encountered as transcendent to the normal run of events. As chapter 7 shows, that negotiation requires a working theory, more or less articulated—a quotidian metaphysics or a domestic theory of transcendence. This goes beyond Jane Shaw's observation of the ways the Society's membership in Bedford "refracted" their religious thinking and experience "through a domestic lens."[37] It is in the immediacy of encounter with transcendence, whether articulated or not.

If we grant the strong model, that religiousness persists because everyone fears death (discussed in chapter 6), one way of "buffering death anxiety"[38] is to keep yourself alive. To that extent, especially among the destitute and those living in precarious societies, the mere act of seeking food and shelter to continue life is a response to death anxiety, and it can be thought of as a practical metaphysical statement. Similarly, the basic maintenance of life having been attended to, responding to illness, especially to potentially life-threatening illness, can be considered a response to death anxiety and thus a metaphysical statement—in this case one that can be met in medical or religious ways. When these two threats are adequately managed, if the individual has the resources to do so, the practical metaphysics can be followed by an intellectual metaphysics—that is, a search for existential and metaphysical accounts that adequately assuage anxiety about the great diversity of discomfiting experiences on the edges of control or understanding. Individuals may find these in religious or secular ways, in conventional or unconventional practices, and, while the secular routes are obscured in the evidence of the Panacea Society's healing letters, the letters open a window onto the ways individuals seek to address the presence of the unknown in their lives.

Steve Bruce has argued that "a chosen religion is weaker than a religion of fate because we are aware that we chose the gods rather than the gods choosing us." This is countered by Partridge's claim that chosen spirituality is stronger because people who choose their spirituality "understand the spiritual life to be *their choice, their responsibility, their journey* towards wholeness and wellbeing."[39] Similarly, Lyon has objected to the early Berger's assumption that "the spiritual supermarket prefigured a situation of increasing pluralism, which would irreversibly undermine conventional forms of religiosity . . . and accelerate secularization," suggesting instead that "today's religious choices may reflect a seriousness of faith that did not figure in the lives of those involved in organized religion from the cradle."[40] In the case of water-takers like those discussed in chapter 7—such as the Jamaican woman (57683) in straitened circumstances and with worries about a beloved family, or the long and complex spiritual life of another water-taker from Jamaica (32171) who gathered followers, mixed traditional and Panacean healing methods, and founded a balmyard—there is no question of a chosen religiosity or bricolage project. The spirituality and long-range metaphysical thinking come naturally and potently, built out of old and new, personal and consensual.

The purpose of this research has been to access practical lived religion, not as a proposition presumptive of some conceptual homogeneity, but as a vernacular and quotidian expression of people's basic and individual experience and understanding of the world. As such, the project addresses the growing contemporary shift in the scholarly study of religion "from religion as systematic and coherent doctrine, to its individual meanings, experiential core and expressive forms" to take account of "the perceptions, beliefs and behaviour of those practising it."[41] The book touches on the themes of the increasingly significant study of late modern spirituality and tests the notion that expressions of this kind of spirituality are "manifestation[s]" of an alternative tradition that "flows like an underground river through the Christian centuries."[42] While, to a significant extent, it is in line with accounts like these, we also observe that a shift in the way religion is *studied* (from a focus on organized systems to a focus on individual experiences) does not imply that a similar shift has taken place in religiosity or spirituality in any structural sense; the varying interests of scholars of religion (be they sociologists, anthropologists, or theologians) may or may not reflect an oscillation in people's religious lives.

Similarly, the theorized occasional manifestation of a persisting alternative stream, while perhaps not historically inaccurate, may simply reify the occult tradition as much as conventional approaches reify mainstream religious traditions. Both of these (occult and conventional traditions) are really the epiphenomena of personal religious thinking and experience; they are more or less organized expressions of domestic theories of transcendence, or of everyday metaphysics. With an adequately rich and deep source of insight into individual stories and personal metaphysical ideas—such as that provided by the letters of the Panacea Society—we can see that personal religion or spirituality is not the residue of a withering institutional religion; rather, those institutional forms are straitened versions of perennial, dynamic, and personal transcendent thinking.

POSTSCRIPT

The End of the Healing

As the twentieth century went on and as the original members of the Society grew elderly and died, a succession of water-takers moved to Bedford to take over managing the healing and the Society more broadly. The last head of the healing, and the last Panacean to live at the Society's campus in Bedford, was Mrs. Ruth Klein, a retired nurse, who had become a water-taker in the early 1970s and moved to Bedford in 1996 to take over the oversight of the Society's teachings and rituals from the previous two or three elderly members. In 2001, the Society appointed an administrator who was not a believer in the Society's doctrines to oversee the financial and legal side of the Society's charitable work, and with Ruth Klein's death in 2012, the healing and the religious function of the Society effectively ceased. The Society continues as a charitable institution at its original headquarters in Bedford.[1]

Ruth Klein had continued the long-standing system of recording and managing water-takers' information on index cards stored in tidy drawers in a room adjacent to the kitchen in the Society's main administrative office at 16 Albany Road. The index cards she used indicate that, in the ten years before she died, 283 individuals made contact with the Society, either to apply or to report on their progress. Of those, 130 had identification codes used by the Society for those applying from the West Indies and most wrote from addresses in Jamaica—though some wrote from London or other places in England, and a few from the United States. Fifty-three of the correspondents had codes indicating they had originally applied for the healing from Africa, and they principally wrote from addresses in Ghana and Nigeria. American water-takers remained an important constituency, and 48 people made contact with the Society's healing with U.S. codes, most writing from the U.S. mainland, though some had Jamaican addresses. Aside from four Canadians; one person each from Finland, France, the Netherlands, and New Zealand; and one with no address; the remaining 43 correspondents in that final decade had British numbers. It is remarkable to note that nine of those had in fact first applied in the interwar period—including some who had originally applied when they lived in Khargapur in India, Kingston in Jamaica, County Cork in Ireland, Canada, Britain, and elsewhere. The longest-serving water-taker in evidence among these was a woman (86904) in England. In 1924, when she was four years old, her mother had applied for healing on her behalf, and she wrote 376 letters before she stopped writing in the final years of the healing.

In 2003, a documentary broadcast on British television, called *Maidens of the Lost Ark*, caused a considerable increase in the volume of applications—and the Society's lay administrator was even called on to assist with their processing. While many of these applicants quickly stopped writing, a small number became relatively committed and continued to maintain contact with Bedford. The Society's administrator, who worked closely with Ruth Klein, recalled the decision to take part in the documentary as part of Klein's final attempt to renew and invigorate the membership—though he also noted her sense that the healing was in long-term decline and that this was perhaps a final opportunity to tell the story of the Society. The last water-takers who wrote to the Healing Department were ultimately sent a letter informing them of its closure and given a few pieces of linen—though many thousands of these remain in storage in Bedford.[2]

APPENDICES

These lists are compiled from the multitude of index cards, register books, consolidated counts, and other records stored in the Panacea Society's General Archive and Healing Collection (in Bedford). While there are some clear and continuous sources for some countries for some time periods, the records are frequently discontinuous or duplicated. Every effort has been made to avoid duplication and to identify individual applicants by their actual country of residence at the time of application.

TABLE A.1. Alphabetical list of countries/territories showing year of first registered application received in Bedford and total number of known applications.

Country/Territory	Number of applications	Year of first application
Algeria	160	1925
Antigua	1	1935
Argentina	2	1925
Aruba	1	1936
Australia	1,597	1924
Austria	21	1924
Bahamas	11	1957
Bangladesh	3	1925
Barbados	9	1935
Belgium	21	1926

continued on next page

Table A.1 (continued)

Country/Territory	Number of applications	Year of first application
Belize	3	1939
Benin/ Dahomey	423	1947
Bermuda	1	1953
Borneo	7	1937
Brazil	53	1925
British Guiana	18	1939
British Honduras	13	1938
British Isles	23,385	1924
Bulgaria	1	1925
Burma	26	1925
Cameroon	1	1965
Canada	1,353	1924
Canary Islands	1	1925
Cayman Islands	1	1977
Chile	2	1931
Cocoa Islands	1	1925
Costa Rica	9	1924
Cuba	45	1937
Curaçao	2	1939
Cyprus	2	1929
Czechoslovakia	11	1925
Democratic Republic of Congo	5	1926
Denmark	169	1924
Dominica	2	1958

Country/Territory	Number of applications	Year of first application
Ecuador	1	1925
Estonia	120	1924-28
Finland	3,186	1924
France	3,030	1924
Gabon	2	1949
Germany	1,766	1924-25
Ghana/Gold Coast/ British Togo	2,863	1930
Greece	5	1928
Grenada	3	1937
Guinea	1	1966
Haiti	12	1938
Honduras	2	1960
Hong Kong	2	1939
Hungary	16	1924
Iceland	1	1926
India	1,445	1924
Indonesia	89	1924
Italy	63	1924
Ivory Coast	19	1939
Jamaica	33,074	1924
Japan	1	1939
Kenya	3	1945
Latvia	3	1926
Liberia	4	1948

continued on next page

Table A.1 (continued)

Country/Territory	Number of applications	Year of first application
Lithuania	5	1926
Malaysia	3	1930
Mali	6	1971
Malta	1	1958
Mauritania	1	1972
Mauritius	1	1938
Mexico	1	1952
Morocco	17	1925
Nepal	1	1932
Netherlands	865	1924
New Guinea	1	1933
New Zealand	662	1924
Nigeria	1,456	1933
Norway	2,494	1924
Pakistan	29	1924
Palestine/Israel	1	1941
Panama/Canal Zone	197	1931
Paraguay	2	1926
Peru	1	1935
Poland	2,302	1924
Portugal	2	1939
Puerto Rico	1	1941
Republic of the Congo	4	1972
Romania (+ Bessarabia)	263	1925
Russia	4	1925

Country/Territory	Number of applications	Year of first application
Rwanda	1	1982
Senegal	83	1962
Sierra Leone	12	1945
South Africa	289	1924
Spain	3	1925
Sri Lanka/ Ceylon	30	1924
St Kitts	1	1932
St Vincent	40	1935
Sweden	652	1924
Switzerland	110	1924
Togolese Republic	651	1938
Trinidad	8	1955
Tunisia	34	1924
Turkey	5	1925
Ukraine	1	1925
Upper Volta	1	1966
USA	39,055	1924
Virgin Islands	1	1974
Yugoslavia/Serbia	24	1925

TABLE A.2. Total number of applications by year, 1924–1998

Year	Applications	Year	Applications	Year	Applications
1924	4,712	1949	2,047	1974	1,022
1925	5,424	1950	1,835	1975	1,169
1926	4,305	1951	1,780	1976	1,150
1927	3,197	1952	2,208	1977	1,178
1928	2,886	1953	1,832	1978	1,260
1929	2,348	1954	1,790	1979	367
1930	2,460	1955	1,650	1980	306
1931	2,159	1956	1,579	1981	329
1932	2,022	1957	1,677	1982	360
1933	1,049	1958	1,697	1983	205
1934	1,206	1959	1,525	1984	199
1935	2,760	1960	1,320	1985	125
1936	5,782	1961	1,467	1986	118
1937	6,563	1962	1,491	1987	64
1938	6,923	1963	1,311	1988	51
1939	8,465	1964	1,394	1989	63
1940	4,692	1965	1,394	1990	25
1941	1,943	1966	1,174	1991	20
1942	990	1967	1,593	1992	4
1943	741	1968	1,644	1993	6
1944	672	1969	1,164	1994	1
1945	692	1970	1,136	1995	9
1946	1,179	1971	1,005	1996	0
1947	1,459	1972	1,138	1997	0
1948	1,857	1973	1,019	1998	5

NOTES

INTRODUCTION

1. See Lockley's discussion of the Panacea Society's archives (and other Southcottian archives) in Lockley, "Southcottian Archives."
2. The theology professed by the Society, which offered an explanation of how the healing was thought to work, is discussed in detail in chapter 2.
3. C.S.S. Juniors, "More Peeps behind the Scenes III," 59.
4. C.S.S., "Peeps behind the Scenes in the Healing Department II," 106.
5. "Panacea Society Annual Report 1940," TS, F.3.2.6, Panacea Society General Archive (henceforth PSGA).
6. England was by far the predominant source of applicants from the British Isles; the sample includes records for just fifty-four applicants from Ireland (Irish Free State and Northern Ireland—the sample captured no applicants from the southern twenty-three counties after 1924), Scotland, and Wales combined.
7. The term was taken from Psalm 48:12 (Fox, *How We Built Part I*, 22).
8. A.E.J., "Peeps behind the Scenes," 128.
9. C.S.S., "Peeps behind the Scenes in the Healing Department III," 128. See also C.S.S., "Peeps behind the Scenes in the Healing Department II," 106.

CHAPTER ONE

1. Elements of the research discussed in this chapter first appeared in Lockhart, "Southcottian Healing Panacea," published by I.B. Tauris.
2. 98356 to Panacea Society (henceforth PS), August 12, 1939, September 14, 1939, MS letters, Panacea Society Healing Archive (henceforth PSHA). Panacea Society archive identifiers correlating with the random reference codes used in the text for purposes of anonymization, and document locations for each correspondent, are held by the Panacea Charitable Trust archivist.
3. "Divine Deliverance," printed leaflet, PSGA, 1. Archive location details are provided in the bibliography for all items.
4. "Divine Deliverance," printed leaflet, PSGA, 2.

5. 16746 to PS, September 14, 1939, MS letter, PSHA.
6. "Divine Deliverance," printed leaflet, PSGA, 2.
7. 44871 to PS, various TS letters, PSHA.
8. "Divine Deliverance," printed leaflet, PSGA, 1, 2.
9. 42811 to PS, September 1943, December 1943, MS letters, PSHA.
10. "Divine Deliverance," printed leaflet, PSGA, 2. Hot dry sponging involved soaking a sponge or flannel in a solution of "two tablespoons of Water B added to boiling water, wringing it out, and placing it on the affected part (night and morning), counting 4 slowly, 4 times."
11. 40371 to PS, January 20, 1936, MS letter, PSHA.
12. "Divine Deliverance," printed leaflet, PSGA, 1, 2.
13. 17930 to PS, August 20, 1955, TS letter, PSHA.
14. "Divine Deliverance," printed leaflet, PSGA, 2.
15. C.S.S., "Children"; C.S.S., "Our Children."
16. C.S.S., "C.S.S. Postbag IV Africa," 84.
17. "Sidelights upon the Healing," 229.
18. 44613 to PS, May 16, 1938, TS letter, PSHA.
19. 44613 to PS, July 1, 1938, TS letter, PSHA.
20. 19880 to PS, January 10, 1956, February 23, 1956, MS and TS translations of MS letters, PSHA.
21. 19880 to PS, January 10, 1956, MS translation of MS letter, PSHA.
22. 19880 to PS, July 17, 1956, TS translation of MS letter, PSHA.
23. See Fox, *Finding of Shiloh*, 34–40, 71–74.
24. Shaw, *Octavia: Daughter of God*, 3.
25. Ibid., 5.
26. Ibid., 4–6.
27. Ibid., 8–9, 27–31, 276.
28. Shaw, *Octavia: Daughter of God*, 8–9, 11; Shaw, "Seymour, Alice (1857–1947)"; Shaw, "Southcottians in the Early Twentieth Century," 165–66.
29. Shaw, *Octavia: Daughter of God*, 5, 13; Shaw, "Southcottians in the Early Twentieth Century," 166.
30. Shaw, *Octavia: Daughter of God*, 26–27; Shaw, "Southcottians in the Early Twentieth Century," 167; Fox, *Finding of Shiloh*, 120.
31. See Fox, *Finding of Shiloh*; Fox, *Sufferings and Acts*; Fox, *How We Built Part I*; Fox, *How We Built Part II*.
32. Fox, *Finding of Shiloh*, v–xii; Shaw, *Octavia: Daughter of God*, 28–29, 34–35.
33. C.S.S. Seniors and Juniors, "Our Work at Home," 276, 277. See also Shaw, "Southcottians in the Early Twentieth Century," 175.

34. "Divine Deliverance," printed leaflet, PSGA, 4. The Society's attention to detail was such that the instructions also advised that "lodgers and those living in flats can sprinkle the water outside their rooms." See also Shaw, *Octavia: Daughter of God*, 170.

35. "Divine Deliverance," printed leaflet, PSGA, 4. See also "Divine Protection Divine Healing," 227; "Editorial," *Panacea* 2, issue 22, p. 220; Fox, *Sufferings and Acts*, 527; Fox, *How We Built Part I*, 27–28; Shaw, *Octavia: Daughter of God*, 256.

36. "Divine Deliverance," printed leaflet, PSGA, 4. See also Shaw, *Octavia: Daughter of God*, 171.

37. C.S.S., B.E.G., and I.N.M., "Peeps behind the Scenes VI," 276.

38. "Divine Deliverance," printed leaflet, PSGA, 4. See also Shaw, *Octavia: Daughter of God*, 172.

39. "Divine Deliverance," printed leaflet, PSGA, 4. Shaw provides additional detail about the "protection work" of the Society in *Octavia: Daughter of God*, 173–74, 255–56.

40. "Editorial," *Panacea* 5, issue 52, p. 75.

41. "Editorial," *Panacea* 2, issue 17, p. 100.

42. "Editorial," *Panacea* 6, issue 63, p. 51.

43. Octavia, *Healing for All*, 7, 10, 70–72.

44. M.L.H., "Peeps behind the Scenes," 11; H.G., "More Peeps behind the Scenes," 57. Very few Confidential Department records are available in the Society's archives.

45. M.L.H., "Peeps behind the Scenes," 11.

46. 98356 to PS, September 14, 1939, MS letter, PSHA.

47. 16746 to PS, October 12, 1939, MS letter, PSHA.

48. MS note (filed with 16746 to PS, October 12, 1939, MS letter, PSHA).

49. 44871 to PS, September 1, 1924, TS letter, PSHA (original emphasis).

50. See various 44871 letters in PSHA.

51. 42811 to PS, December 1943, MS letter, PSHA.

52. Ibid. (spelling and grammar adjusted).

53. Draft reply, MS (attached to 42811 to PS, December 1943, MS letter, PSHA).

54. 42811 to PS, March 1943, MS letter, PSHA. Gender differences are discussed in more detail in chapter 3.

55. 40371 to PS, June 7, 1936, MS letter, PSHA.

56. 40371 to PS, March 30, 1937, MS letter, PSHA.

57. 17930 to PS, August 20, 1955, TS letter, PSHA.

58. 17930 to PS, March 5, 1961, MS letter, PSHA.

59. 17930 to PS, December 30, 1955, TS letter, PSHA.
60. Draft reply, MS (attached to 17930 to PS, December 30, 1955, TS letter, PSHA).
61. 17930 to PS, April 6, 1956, MS letter, PSHA.
62. Ibid.
63. 17930 to PS, March 5, 1961, MS letter, PSHA.
64. 44613 to PS, October 26, 1938, MS translation of letter, PSHA.
65. 44613 to PS, December 29, 1938, TS letter, PSHA.
66. 44613 to PS, August 20, 1946, MS translation of letter, PSHA.
67. 19880 to PS, March 22, 1956, TS translation of letter, PSHA.
68. 19880 to PS, July 17, 1956, TS translation of letter, PSHA.
69. 19880 to PS, November 19, 1957, TS translation of letter, PSHA.
70. 19880 to PS, September 22, 1958, November 20, 1958, MS and TS translation of letters, PSHA.
71. The use of linen (and, originally, cardboard) to transmit the divine healing power was explained by citing the various media of healing mentioned in the Bible: clay (John 9:6–7), pitchers of water that became wine (John 2:7–9), handkerchiefs or aprons taken from Paul's body to heal the sick (Acts 19:12), and the use of wood (Exodus 15:23–25) or salt (2 Kings 2:20–22) in the Old Testament. See Fox, *How We Built Part I*, 203.
72. Fox, *Sufferings and Acts*, 208–9; "Important Dates," n.d., TS, F.1.3.21, PSGA; "History of the Reports Department," n.d., TS, F.1.4.4, PSGA; Notes in "Clerical Desk Diary 1940," F.2.3.14, PSGA.
73. Shaw, *Octavia: Daughter of God*, 151–80.
74. Ibid., 151; see also 163–66, 170.
75. Ibid., 153
76. Ibid., 156.
77. Ibid., 160–61, 176–80.
78. Arguably, the insistence in the advertisement that the healing was "not miraculous, but by treatment, without money and without the price of accepting any particular belief" may have invoked a question about the opposite notion in the minds of the readers.
79. See the "first advertisement" in Octavia, *Healing for All*, 119.
80. "At the Church Congress," 679. See the Society's account of the same event in Fox, *How We Built Part I*, 90, and Jane Shaw's account of the Society at this and other Church Congresses in Shaw, *Octavia: Daughter of God*, 295.
81. The appendices include tables showing the number of applicants from each country/territory up to 1998, with year of first application for each (Table A1) and the overall number of applicants each year up to 1998 (Table A2).

82. In 1953, the Society was worried that patients in the West Indies might have made multiple applications, which could have inflated the numbers to some extent (although the Society took measures to combat the problem). See "Panacea Society Annual Report 1953," TS, F.3.2.10, PSGA. See also comments on West Indian patients moving to Britain in "Panacea Society Annual Report 1955," TS, F.3.2.11, PSGA.

83. The index card sample suggests that England contributed more than 95 percent of applications from the British Isles.

84. See appendix A for other countries and numbers of applications. For the USA, see "USA Register of Applicants for Healing" (7 volumes), A.4.4.18; "USA Panacea Healing Department," A.4.5.1; "Panacea Society Healing Department from 15,191 to 30,456," A.4.5.1. For Finland, Great Britain, and Jamaica, see "The Divine Mother's Record of Applications" (also labelled with "Healing Index") (3 volumes), A.4.2.2–4; *Weekly Post* record books [without accession number]; various volumes in A.4.5.2 (Jamaica only); "Finland Alphabetical Register of Applicants for Healing," C.4.4.10 (Finland only). All in PSGA.

85. These figures have been compiled from a sifting of the various MS registers in PSGA. See Weekly Post record books [without accession number] and "The Divine Mother's Record of Applications" (also labelled with "Healing Index"), 3 volumes, A.4.2.2–4. For Chile, Malaysia, Nigeria, and Rwanda in particular, see A.4.4.17: "Applications Con 1–2599"; "Con. Application Book" (with red cover); "Con. Application Book" (with blue cover); "Miscellaneous Countries ("Con") Alphabetical Register of Applicants for Healing 1939–1940 Vol 1"; "Miscellaneous Countries ("Con") Alphabetical Register of Applicants for Healing 1950 Volume 2"; "Miscellaneous Countries ("Con") Alphabetical Register of Applicants for Healing 24th April 1970 (Onwards) Volume 3."

86. The records for active water-takers at the time of the healing's closure consist of uncatalogued index cards in PSHA.

CHAPTER TWO

1. Fox, *Finding of Shiloh*, 107. For more on Octavia's period in the asylum, see Shaw, *Octavia: Daughter of God*, 16–24.

2. Extract from notebook of Mabel Barltrop reported in Fox, *Sufferings and Acts*, 162–63. See also Shaw, *Octavia: Daughter of God*, 151.

3. "302. – March 23rd, 1921," 341. Also reported (with slight variation) in Fox, *Sufferings and Acts*, 164.

4. Fox, *Sufferings and Acts*, 361.

5. Hirst, *Jane Leade*, 1.
6. Lockley, "Jane Lead's Prophetic Afterlife," 241, 246–48, 252–55.
7. Fox, *Sufferings and Acts*, 159.
8. Temme, "From Jakob Böhme," 104.
9. Hirst, *Jane Leade*, 7, 56.
10. Hopkins, *Woman to Deliver*, 3, 17.
11. Hopkins, *Woman to Deliver*, 18, quoting Southcott to a friend, October 8, 1803, University of Texas Southcott Collection, 339, ff. 118–19; Brown, *Joanna Southcott*, 9; Harrison, *Second Coming*, 88; Lockley, *Visionary Religion*, 4.
12. Hopkins, *Woman to Deliver*, 20–33; Bowerbank, "Southcott, Joanna (1750–1814)"; Lockley, "Southcottians in Britain," 35; Niblett, *Prophecy and the Politics of Salvation*, 32–33.
13. Harrison, *Second Coming*, 88; Matthews, *English Messiahs*, 47.
14. Hopkins, *Woman to Deliver*, 73; Bowerbank, "Southcott, Joanna (1750–1814)."
15. Hopkins, *Woman to Deliver*, 75; Lockley, *Visionary Religion*, 4.
16. Hopkins, *Woman to Deliver*, 76.
17. Hopkins, *Woman to Deliver*, 76–77. See also Lockley, "Southcottians in Britain" on membership patterns.
18. Juster, *Doomsayers*, 171.
19. Thompson, *Making of the English*, 420, 421. In light of Thompson's comments about Southcott, his observation that she was "the greatest Prophetess of all" must be somewhat tongue-in-cheek (*Making of the English*, 420; cf. Bowerbank, "Southcott, Joanna [1750–1814].")
20. Hopkins, *Woman to Deliver*, 112.
21. Allan, "Southcottian Sects from 1790," 218.
22. Niblett, "Joanna Southcott's Apocalyptic Theology," 13. See also Niblett, *Prophecy and the Politics of Salvation*, 13.
23. Harrison, *Second Coming*, 96, quoting Southcott, *Strange Effects of Faith*, 16. See also Hopkins, *Woman to Deliver*, 112–13; Niblett, *Prophecy and the Politics of Salvation*, 134–39.
24. Harrison, *Second Coming*, 96, quoting Southcott, *Full Assurance*, 45.
25. Harrison, *Second Coming*, 96, quoting Bennett, *Cross and the Crown*.
26. Hopkins, *Woman to Deliver*, 199. See also Lockley, *Visionary Religion*, 4–5; Niblett, "Joanna Southcott's Apocalyptic Theology," 28–29; Niblett, *Prophecy and the Politics of Salvation*, 130.
27. Hopkins, *Woman to Deliver*, 202; Niblett, "Joanna Southcott's Apocalyptic Theology," 31; Niblett, *Prophecy and the Politics of Salvation*, 155–56.

28. Brown, *Joanna Southcott*, 264–68. Hopkins says that 17 out of 21 physicians who examined her confirmed the pregnancy (*Woman to Deliver*, 200). See also Allan, "Southcottian Sects from 1790," 219; Matthews, *English Messiahs*, 73–74; Niblett, *Prophecy and the Politics of Salvation*, 159.

29. See Hopkins, *Woman to Deliver*, 269n71.

30. Hopkins, *Woman to Deliver*, 210; Niblett, "Joanna Southcott's Apocalyptic Theology," 29.

31. Harrison, *Second Coming*, 135–36; Hopkins, *Woman to Deliver*, 210–11; Brown, *Joanna Southcott*, 300; Matthews, *English Messiahs*, 80; Lockley, *Visionary Religion*, 5; Lockley, "Southcottians in Britain," 40–41; Allan, "Southcottian Sects from 1790"; Niblett, *Prophecy and the Politics of Salvation*, 162–64. Lockley's *Visionary Religion* provides a good detailed account of numerical and membership patterns in the movement.

32. Octavia, *Healing for All*, 40.

33. Harrison, *Second Coming*, 58; Stunt, "Brothers, Richard (1757–1824)"; Allan, "Southcottian Sects from 1790," 216–17; Lockley, "Southcottians in Britain," 57.

34. Harrison, *Second Coming*, 58, 59.

35. Ibid., 59.

36. Octavia, *Healing for All*, 41.

37. Allan, "Southcottian Sects from 1790," 217; Madden, "Emergence of Southcottian Israelite Theology." Niblett discusses Southcott's objection to Brothers' Israelism in *Prophecy and the Politics of Salvation*, 147, 151–52.

38. Lockley, *Visionary Religion*, 36–37; Madden, "Southcottian Methodist"; Harrison, *Second Coming*, 119; Allan, "Southcottian Sects from 1790," 220–21; Lockley, "Millenarian Religion," 46; Lockley, "Southcottians in Britain," 41; Niblett, *Prophecy and the Politics of Salvation*, 164–65.

39. Harrison, *Second Coming*, 121; Lockley, *Visionary Religion*, 64; Lockley, "Southcottians in Britain," 42; Madden, "Emergence of Southcottian Israelite Theology," 79.

40. Octavia, *Healing for All*, 48. See also Lockley, *Visionary Religion*, 36–37, 88; Madden, "Southcottian Methodist," 69–70.

41. See Allan, "Southcottian Sects from 1790"; Madden, "Southcottian Methodist," 73; Lockley, *Visionary Religion*, 108–9n36.

42. Allan, "Southcottian Sects from 1790," 222; Harrison, *Second Coming*, 136.

43. Octavia, *Healing for All*, 48–49.

44. Harrison, *Second Coming*, 138–40; Lockley, *Visionary Religion*, 104–8.

45. Allan, "Southcottian Sects from 1790," 222; Harrison, *Second Coming*, 141; Lockley, "Southcottians in Britain," 42–49; Madden, "Emergence of Southcottian Israelite Theology."

46. Harrison, *Second Coming*, 141; Lockley, *Visionary Religion*, 104, 110–21.
47. Lockley, *Visionary Religion*, 162–65.
48. Octavia, *Healing for All*, 49–50.
49. Octavia, *Healing for All*, 51. Original emphasis. See also Madden, "Emergence of Southcottian Israelite Theology."
50. Octavia, *Healing for All*, 51–52, 53. Original emphasis.
51. "Dear Friend," draft letter "from C.S.S. c/o J. Carpenter-Smith Esq.," n.d., F.1.3.21, PSGA.
52. Stunt, "Jezreel, James Jershom (1848x51–1885)"; Allan, "Southcottian Sects from 1790," 222; Windscheffel, "Jezreelites and Their World," 116.
53. Octavia, *Healing for All*, 55.
54. Stunt, "Jezreel, James Jershom (1848x51–1885)"; Allan, "Southcottian Sects from 1790," 222–23; Windscheffel, "Jezreelites and Their World," 120.
55. Allan, "Southcottian Sects from 1790," 225.
56. Octavia, *Healing for All*, 57.
57. Ibid., 58.
58. Shaw, *Octavia: Daughter of God*, 31. See also Octavia, *Healing for All*, 60–65.
59. Shaw, *Octavia: Daughter of God*, 28–31, 32–35; Allan, "Southcottian Sects from 1790," 224.
60. "Dear Friend," draft letter "from C.S.S. c/o J. Carpenter-Smith Esq.," n.d., F.1.3.21, PSGA.
61. "Dear Friend," draft letter "from C.S.S. c/o J. Carpenter-Smith Esq.," n.d., F.1.3.21, PSGA (emphasis in original).
62. Fox, *Finding of Shiloh*, 273 (original emphasis). See also Shaw, *Octavia: Daughter of God*, 39.
63. Fox, *Finding of Shiloh*, vii, 263–67; Fox, *Sufferings and Acts*, 145; Shaw, *Octavia: Daughter of God*, 37–41; Shaw, "Southcottians in the Early Twentieth Century," 168.
64. Fox, *Sufferings and Acts*, 69–70, 72; Shaw, *Octavia: Daughter of God*, 29, 34.
65. Shaw, *Octavia: Daughter of God*, 6, 8, ch. 14, 329; Shaw, "Southcottians in the Early Twentieth Century," 176–78.
66. Shaw, *Octavia: Daughter of God*, 8.
67. Ibid., 16, 24–26, 29–32.
68. Ibid., 33–34.
69. Fox, *Sufferings and Acts*, 69, 72, 102–3, 198–200; Shaw, *Octavia: Daughter of God*, 71–74, 80, 112. The campus remains intact; it is preserved by the present-day trustees of the Society's successor charitable trust.
70. Fox, *Sufferings and Acts*, 88–91; Shaw, *Octavia: Daughter of God*, 327.

71. The Society had instituted a system of "sealing" based on Southcott's equivalent practice. See Shaw, *Octavia: Daughter of God*, 110–11.
72. See Shaw, *Octavia: Daughter of God*, 327.
73. Owen, *Place of Enchantment*, 86.
74. Ibid.
75. Roden, "Kiss of the Soul," 39.
76. Owen, *Place of Enchantment*, 87.
77. See Roden, "Kiss of the Soul," 39.
78. Owen, *Place of Enchantment*, 90.
79. Ibid.
80. Shaw, *Octavia: Daughter of God*, 84, 83.
81. Ibid., 247.
82. Ibid., 85.
83. Sutcliffe and Bowman, "Introduction," 4 (emphasis added).
84. Ellwood, "How New Is the New Age?" 59.
85. Ellwood, "How New Is the New Age?" 59.
86. Owen, *Place of Enchantment*, 15.
87. Hanegraaff, "New Age Religion and Secularization," 293.
88. Hanegraaff, "New Age Religion and Secularization," 294. See also Hanegraaff, *New Age Religion and Western Culture*, 517–21.
89. Octavia, *Early Dawn*, ii.
90. Ibid.
91. Ibid., iii. See also viii.
92. Octavia, *Early Dawn*, v. See also iv: "The PRIEST has had a long innings and now the PROPHET takes the field and none too soon, for the mechanism of the Church is faulty, the Priests are on the wrong road and the government we are under is Satanic."
93. Octavia, *Early Dawn*, iv. See also viii.
94. Ibid., vii (original emphasis).
95. Ibid.
96. Ibid., iv (original capitalization). See also iv: "Let not any suppose that those who follow these teachings, desire to live for ever in a diseased body amid distressing circumstances!"
97. Ibid., vi (original capitalization).
98. Ibid., vi.
99. Ibid.
100. Ibid., v. See also vii: "If you belong to the Incorruptible fold, that is, if you are going to die, all this will not interest you—you were not taught it in spirit

before you came down and it will sound ridiculous to you, but if you are destined, *pre*-destined to live and not to die, you will feel stirred and will never rest till you know more, for these things being "brought to your remembrance," you will recognize them as *being for you* and you will know that the call has come to gather "the Elect" from all places where they are scattered" (original emphasis).

101. Ibid., vi.
102. Ibid., viii. See also viii, n.
103. Ibid., vii, viii.
104. Ibid., ix.
105. Ibid.
106. Higher Thought makes the same error as the Behmenists in this respect. See Octavia, *Early Dawn*, ix.
107. Octavia, *Early Dawn*, ix.
108. Ibid., v.
109. Octavia, *Healing for All*, 74, 121, 125.
110. "Divine Deliverance," printed leaflet, PSGA, 1.
111. Ibid., 4.
112. Fox, *Sufferings and Acts*, 362. See also Shaw, *Octavia: Daughter of God*, 151–52.
113. On the quaternity, see Fox, *How We Built Part I*, 12.
114. Fox, *Sufferings and Acts*, 139. See also 286–87.
115. Southcott, *Answer to Mr. Brothers's Book*, 22 (the original refers to 1 Corinthians 14:20). See also Southcott, *Long-Wished-For Revolution*, 19, 83; Southcott, *Answer of the Lord*, 105–6. See Niblett, "Joanna Southcott's Apocalyptic Theology," 17–22, and Niblett, *Prophecy and the Politics of Salvation*, 39–67, for a discussion of Southcott's gendered interpretation of the Fall. See Shaw, "Southcottians in the Early Twentieth Century," 169–71, on Barltrop's theology.
116. Octavia, *Healing for All*, 31. See also 32–35.
117. Fox, *Sufferings and Acts*, 362 (emphasis added).
118. Fox, *Sufferings and Acts*, 356, 364, 373–74; "The Script."
119. C.S.S., "Notes from My Case-Book Defects," 262. Indeed, obedience was *all* that was required of water-takers (Fox, *How We Built Part I*, 21–22; Octavia, *Healing for All*, 122).
120. "Our cry is, 'Back to Eden before the fall, back to health of soul and body, back to the world as God made it, back to the only religion that was, and is, and ever will be true religion'" ("The Title of the Magazine," 11). See also Shaw, *Octavia: Daughter of God*, 4.

121. "Divine Deliverance," printed leaflet, PSGA, 3. On Leviticus 15, see Fox, *Finding of Shiloh*, 362–64.
122. "Divine Protection Divine Healing," 225.

CHAPTER THREE

1. McLeod, *Secularization in Western Europe*, 3. McLeod names Peter Berger, Harvey Cox, Thomas Luckmann, and Bryan Wilson among recent theorists (in addition to Dietrich Bonhoeffer, Auguste Comte, Émile Durkheim, W. E. H. Lecky, Karl Marx, and Max Weber).
2. Carroll, *Protestant Modernity*, xiii, 17.
3. Berger, *Social Reality of Religion*, 113.
4. Bruce, *Secularization*, 11.
5. Gorski and Altinordu, "After Secularization?," 57.
6. Warner, "Work in Progress," 1045, 1048, citing Berger, *Sacred Canopy* (1969 ed.); Berger, *Rumor of Angels*.
7. Lyon, *Jesus in Disneyland*, 19.
8. Lyon, *Jesus in Disneyland*, 104.
9. Kaplan, "Radical Religion in Finland?," 121.
10. Kääriäinen, Niemelä, and Ketola, *Religion in Finland*, 112–13.
11. Ibid., 112.
12. Duke, Johnson, and Duke, "World Context of Religious Change," 147, 153, 163–64.
13. Taylor, "British Churches and Jamaican Migration," 194.
14. Ibid., 199.
15. Shaw, *Octavia: Daughter of God*, 328.
16. Ibid., 327.
17. In individuals, membership of groups is not necessarily exclusive.
18. Cox, *Secular City*, 69.
19. Heelas and Woodhead, *Spiritual Revolution*, 45.
20. Houtman and Mascini, "Why Do Churches Become Empty," 455.
21. Ibid., 459.
22. Ibid., 468.
23. Partridge, *The Re-enchantment of the West*, vol. 1, p. 3, 4.
24. Ibid., vol. 1, p. 4. See also Partridge, *The Re-enchantment of the West*, vol. 2, p. 2.
25. Asprem, *Arguing with Angels*, 78.
26. Hanegraaff, "New Age Religion and Secularization," 301.

27. Voas and Chaves, "Is the United States a Counterexample," 1520, 1523, 1551.
28. Bruce, *Secularization*, 48–49. Note Partridge's response to Bruce on this point in Partridge, *The Re-enchantment of the West*, vol. 2, 9.
29. Morris, "Secularization and Religious Experience," 204.
30. Ibid., 209.
31. Goldstein, "Secularization Patterns," 158, 175–76.
32. Ibid., 160–63. In addition to Peter Berger and Thomas Luckmann (who are discussed later), Goldstein refers to Robert Bellah, Richard Fenn, Niklas Luhmann, David Martin, Talcott Parsons, and Bryan Wilson.
33. Goldstein, "Secularization Patterns," 166, referring to Berger, *Sacred Canopy* (1967 ed.).
34. Goldstein, "Secularization Patterns," 169.
35. Ibid., 167, with quotation and citation of Berger, *Rumor of Angels*.
36. Goldstein, "Secularization Patterns," 167.
37. Ibid., 168.
38. Goldstein, "Secularization Patterns," 168, citing Tschannen, "Secularization Paradigm," 412–13; Luckmann, "Shrinking Transcendence, Expanding Religion?," 135, 138.
39. Goldstein, "Secularization Patterns," 175.
40. Tschannen, "Secularization Paradigm," 413.
41. Ibid., 413.
42. Wilson, "Secularization and the Survival," 8, quoted by Tschannen, "Secularization Paradigm," 412.
43. Luckmann, *Invisible Religion*, 26–27.
44. Ibid., 39, 45, 51, 52.
45. Ibid., 51, 52.
46. Ibid., 55, 56.
47. Ibid., 87.
48. Ibid., 39, 95. See also Luckmann, "Shrinking Transcendence, Expanding Religion?," 133.
49. Luckmann, *Invisible Religion*, 99. See also Luckmann, "Shrinking Transcendence, Expanding Religion?," 134–36.
50. Luckmann, *Invisible Religion*, 99.
51. Ibid., 104–5.
52. Ibid., 104. See also Luckmann, "Shrinking Transcendence, Expanding Religion?," 133.
53. Luckmann, "Shrinking Transcendence, Expanding Religion?," 129.
54. Ibid., 130.

55. Ibid., 132.

56. Ibid., 132. Citing Luckmann, "Secolarizzazione: un mito contemporaneo," Luckmann calls this "an etiological myth of modernity."

57. Luckmann, "Shrinking Transcendence, Expanding Religion?," 132 (original emphasis).

58. Ibid., 130.

59. For example, "Subjective experiences of transcendence are universal. It can hardly be doubted that human beings have had and still have such experiences everywhere" (p. 130), and "the offer of the traditional social constructions of the great transcendences ... still remains open" (p. 138).

60. Luckmann, "Shrinking Transcendence, Expanding Religion?," 135.

61. Berger, *Social Reality of Religion*, 115, 133.

62. Ibid., 113.

63. Berger, *Desecularization of the World*, 2. He offers a *mea culpa* on the same page: "in my earlier work I contributed to this literature."

64. Ibid., 2–3.

65. Berger, *Social Reality of Religion*, 37.

66. Ibid., 60.

67. Ibid., 131, 145, 156.

68. Berger, *Desecularization of the World*, 3.

69. Ibid., 9, 10.

70. Durkheim, *Elementary Forms*, 22, quoted in Thompson, *Emile Durkheim*, 125.

71. Durkheim, *Elementary Forms*, 474–75, quoted in Thompson, *Emile Durkheim*, 135.

72. Lukes, "Durkheim's 'Individualism and the Intellectuals,'" 25.

73. Ibid., 25.

74. Ibid., 25.

75. McGuire, "Health and Spirituality as Contemporary Concerns," 151–52. McGuire compares contemporary spiritual well-being movements to Durkheim's "L'individualisme et les intellectuels" on p. 153.

76. Hanegraaff, "New Age Religion and Secularization," 305, referring to Durkheim, *Les formes élémentaires de la vie religieuse*, 63–65.

77. McLeod, *Religious Crisis*, 4.

78. Francis Kilvert's *Diary*, the diary of Francis Chavasse, an oral history interview, Lockhart's biography of Cosmo Gordon Lang, and a letter of John Betjeman.

79. Morris, "Secularization and Religious Experience," 215–17, citing Kilvert, *Kilvert's Diary, 1870–1879*; Smith and Taylor, *Evangelicalism in the Church of*

England; Williams, *Religious Belief and Popular Culture*; Lockhart, *Cosmo Gordon Lang*; Wilson, *Betjeman*.

80. Morris, "Secularization and Religious Experience," 217.
81. Lyon, *Jesus in Disneyland*, 18, 91.
82. Besecke, "Seeing Invisible Religion," 182.
83. Ibid., 188. See also 190.
84. Ibid., 182.
85. Shaw, *Octavia: Daughter of God*, 83, 84.
86. Yoder, "Toward a Definition of Folk Religion," cited by Bowman and Valk, *Vernacular Religion*, 4–5.
87. Primiano, "Vernacular Religion," 42. See also Bowman and Valk, *Vernacular Religion*, 4–5.
88. Bowman and Valk, *Vernacular Religion*, 5.
89. Primiano, "Vernacular Religion," 39.
90. Ibid., 42. Primiano discusses other uses of the term vernacular religion in 42n5.
91. Crystal, *Dictionary of Linguistics*, 326, quoted by Primiano, "Vernacular Religion," 42.
92. Primiano, "Vernacular Religion," 42.
93. Ibid., 43.
94. Ibid., 47.
95. Ibid., 52.
96. Primiano, "Afterword: Manifestations of the Religious Vernacular," 384.
97. See Candelaria, *Popular Religion and Liberation*, 2, quoted by Primiano, "Afterword: Manifestations of the Religious Vernacular," 387.
98. The index card sample suggests that England contributed more than 95 percent of applications from the British Isles.
99. See appendix A for other countries and numbers of applications. For the United States, see "USA Register of Applicants for Healing" (7 volumes), A.4.4.18; "USA Panacea Healing Department," A.4.5.1; "Panacea Society Healing Department from 15,191 to 30,456," A.4.5.1. For Finland, Great Britain, and Jamaica, see "The Divine Mother's Record of Applications" (also labelled with "Healing Index"), 3 volumes, A.4.2.2–4; *Weekly Post* record books [without accession number]; various volumes in A.4.5.2 (Jamaica only); "Finland Alphabetical Register of Applicants for Healing," C.4.4.10 (Finland only). All in PSGA.
100. This sample is discussed in the introduction.
101. Other prolific bodies of correspondence discovered in the index cards (but not included in the index card sample referred to here) include 228 letters from a

woman (97298) who applied from Jackson, Mississippi, in 1956, and remained in contact with the Society until 1988, and another female applicant (36607) who wrote 225 letters after applying in 1940 and maintained contact until 1998.
102. The number of letters per year is calculated as the average of the average number of letters written each year by each applicant included in the sample.
103. Trzebiatowska and Bruce, *Why Are Women More Religious than Men?*
104. Frisk, "New Age Participants in Sweden," 243; McGuire, *Ritual Healing in Suburban America*, 12; Heelas and Woodhead, *Spiritual Revolution*, 94, see also 169n13.

CHAPTER FOUR

1. Elements of the research discussed in this chapter first appeared in Lockhart, "Religious and Spiritual Mobility" published by Taylor and Francis.
2. The discussion in this paragraph refers to water-takers in the British Isles (England, Northern Ireland, Irish Free State/Republic of Ireland, Scotland, and Wales). Sampling from a different source in the archive (the index card sample discussed in the introduction) suggests that England contributed more than 95 percent of applications from the British Isles, and that applications from Republic of Ireland/Irish Free State and Northern Ireland made up less than half of one percent of British Isles applicants. The main part of the discussion in this chapter refers to Great Britain (England, Scotland, and Wales) only.
3. There is no complete data available for 1933–1935.
4. Numbers collated from "Divine Mother's Record of Applications" (also labelled with "Healing Index"), 3 volumes, A.4.2.2–4, PSGA (for 1924–1932), and from *Weekly Post* records [without accession number], PSGA (for 1935–1978). Partial data for 1978.
5. The index card sample is described in the Introduction. The analysis in this paragraph includes cards from water-takers identified as applying from Great Britain (England, Scotland, and Wales). The sample includes 1,255 water-takers and is heavily weighted to England (1,206) with Scotland contributing 22, and Wales 27.
6. As the Society's requirement was that a water-taker would have consumed the water several times a day and used it on their body twice a day for a month by the time they made their first report to the Healing Department, this was not an insignificant level of commitment.
7. Again, the sample is overwhelmingly made up of applicants from England.

8. That is, the first letter extant in the archive for an individual, which is not in every case the first letter to the Society.

9. This assessment excludes wartime work, which obscures the socioeconomic indication associated with employment as people took jobs outside their likely peacetime profile; for example, 28332 was a singer before the war and worked in a canteen during the war.

10. Partridge, *The Re-enchantment of the West*, vol. 1, 4.
11. Shaw, *Octavia: Daughter of God*, 11.
12. Dixon, *Divine Feminine*, 4.
13. Hanegraaff, *New Age Religion and Western Culture*, 97.
14. Lewis, "Approaches to the Study of the New Age Movement," 3.
15. Santucci, "Theosophy," 236.
16. Ryan, *H. P. Blavatsky and the Theosophical Movement*, 1.
17. Ransom, *Short History of the Theosophical Society*, 1, 5.
18. Taylor, "Besant, Annie (1847–1933)"; Ryan, *H. P. Blavatsky and the Theosophical Movement*, 282–83.
19. Currie, Gilbert, and Horsley, *Churches and Churchgoers*, 193.
20. Octavia, *Early Dawn*, v–ix.
21. Ibid., ix.
22. Ibid., ix.
23. Ibid., ix.
24. Fox, *How We Built Part I*, 45.
25. Ibid., 44. See also Shaw, *Octavia: Daughter of God*, 176–80.
26. Nelson, *Spiritualism and Society*, 3–5, 7, 89–91.
27. Lodge, "Christianity and Spiritualism," 168.
28. Ibid., 169, 171.
29. Octavia, *Early Dawn*, ix.
30. Fox, *Sufferings and Acts*, 8–9.
31. The report is identified by Smith, *Historical Sketches*, 231.
32. Mews, "Revival of Spiritual Healing," 310; Wilson, *Sects and Society*, 140; Smith, *Historical Sketches*, 232–33.
33. "Directory of Professional Services." See also Wilson, *Sects and Society*, 152.
34. Orme, "Christian Science," 8.
35. Ibid., 8–9; Fox, *How We Built Part I*, 190.
36. Shaw, *Octavia: Daughter of God*, 161, 176–80.
37. Ibid., 176.
38. 30941 to PS, February 20, 1924, MS letter, PSHA.
39. 30941 to PS, June 10, 1943, MS letter, PSHA.

40. 30941 to PS, January 8, 1941, MS letter, PSHA.
41. 27312 to PS, March 23, 1924, MS letter, PSHA.
42. 16377 to PS, March 16, [1925?] and April 17, [1925?], PSHA.
43. 57730 to PS, September 12, 1929, PSHA.
44. 38978 to PS, August 29, 1934, MS letter, PSHA.
45. 19077 to PS, July 10, 1930, MS letter, PSHA.
46. 60756 to PS, August 16, 1939, MS letter, PSHA.
47. 41680 to PS, July 5, 1941, TS letter, PSHA.
48. 41680 to PS, August 9, 1941, TS letter, PSHA.
49. 20109 to PS, October 7, 1929, PSHA.
50. 54577 to PS, October 11, 1930, PSHA.
51. 54577 to PS, June 15, 1932, PSHA.
52. 51835 to PS, February 24, 1931, PSHA.
53. 51835 to PS, March 8, 1931, PSHA.
54. 51835 to PS, February 24, 1931, PSHA.
55. "Editorial," *Panacea* 1, issue 8, p. 172 (emphasis added). See also Octavia, *Healing for All*, 15–16.
56. "Editorial," *Panacea* 1, issue 8, p. 172. See also Fox, *How We Built Part I*, 3–4.
57. See, for example, "Editorial," *Panacea* 1, issue 10, p. 219; "Editorial," *Panacea* 5, issue 49, p. 3.
58. "Mortal (or Dying) Life," 159. See also "Editorial," *Panacea* 2, issue 22, p. 219.
59. Octavia, *Healing for All*, 7, 10, 70–72.
60. Shaw, *Octavia: Daughter of God*, 80.
61. Ibid., 81.
62. Ibid., 294.
63. Byrne, *Modern Spiritualism*, 3.
64. Kollar, *Searching for Raymond*, 3, 6.
65. Mews, "Revival of Spiritual Healing," 312.
66. Mews, "Religion, 1900–1939," 481; Mews, "Revival of Spiritual Healing," 310–11.
67. See Mews, "Revival of Spiritual Healing," 304; Hickson, *Heal the Sick*.
68. *Conference of Bishops of the Anglican Communion*, 41 [resolution 55].
69. Ibid., 42 [resolution 57].
70. Ibid., 43 [resolution 65].
71. Ibid., 43 [resolution 61].
72. Ibid., 43 [resolution 63]. The growth of new forms of religion and healing had attracted the attention of the Anglican bishops as early as 1908.

The American bishops attending the Lambeth Conference in 1908 requested special discussion of spiritual healing to guide them in their response to the emergence of Christian Science (see Mews, "Revival of Spiritual Healing," 312). The 1930 Conference showed a similar, though less explicit, concern. See *Lambeth Conference 1930*, 61 [resolution 73], 182–83.

73. *Ministry of Healing*, 16.
74. 99009 to PS, October 3, 1932, PSHA.
75. 58019 to PS, April 30, 1940, PSHA.

CHAPTER FIVE

1. A single shoebox of U.S. index cards was discovered in PSHA in the course of this research.
2. The index card sample is described in the Introduction. The sample contained index cars for 1,893 Jamaican water-takers.
3. "Healing Department 1937–1938," MS, F.3.2.4, PSGA.
4. "Panacea Society Annual Report 1948," TS, F.3.2.8, PSGA.
5. Finnish application figures from "The Divine Mother's Record of Applications" (also labelled with "Healing Index"), 3 volumes, A.4.2.2–4, and *Weekly Post* record books [without accession number]. All in PSGA.
6. The index card sample is described in the Introduction. The number of Finns included is substantially fewer than the 1,893 Jamaicans and 1,255 from Great Britain. A larger sample is discussed in Lockhart, "Heterodox Healing"; this shows equivalent values of 40 percent, 14 percent, and 46 percent.
7. See Ahlbäck, "Origins of the Theosophical Society," 144; Helve, "Formation of Religious Attitudes," 386; Holm, "Religion in Finland," 10–13; Kääriäinen, Niemelä, and Ketola, *Religion in Finland*, 112, 113; Kaplan, "Radical Religion in Finland?," 121. These are also discussed in Lockhart, "Heterodox Healing."
8. The discussion in this chapter of Southcottians in the United States draws on Lockhart, "Southcottian Healing Panacea."
9. 64297 to PS, March 3, 1924, MS letter, PSHA.
10. 61458 to PS, June 8, 1958, MS letter, PSHA.
11. 86317 to PS, n.d., MS letter, PSHA.
12. Jesse Green was well known to the Society. He had pestered Octavia with letters written from Chicago in 1920 and had been involved in a male homosexual subculture within the community in Bedford which threatened Octavia's leadership a few years later. Following discovery of the situation, Green was among

those expelled from the community. He returned to the United States in 1923. See Shaw, *Octavia: Daughter of God*, 125, 135–40, 142.

13. Shaw, *Octavia: Daughter of God*, 143.
14. "Panacea Society Annual Report 1943," TS, F.3.2.6, PSGA.
15. 98027 to PS, February 27, 1940, MS letter, PSHA.
16. 53443 to PS, December 24, 1964, MS letter, PSHA; 25630 to PS, January 1, 1962, MS letter, PSHA.
17. 25630 to PS, January 1, 1962, MS letter, PSHA.
18. PS to 25630, MS draft reply, appended to 25630 to PS, August 16, 1962, PSHA.
19. See Windscheffel, "Jezreelites and Their World"; Sutton, *Heartland Utopias*, 152; Madden, "Israelites in America," 140–47; Adkin, *Brother Benjamin*, 5–8, 13–17; Fogarty, *Righteous Remnant*, 43–48, 58.
20. Adkin, *Brother Benjamin*, 30; Fogarty, *Righteous Remnant*, 52–53. Philip Lockley has discussed the carrying of Jane Lead's writings and ideas to the United States, including their association with the Wroe, Jezreel, and the Benton Harbor communities. See Lockley, "Jane Lead's Prophetic Afterlife," 242, 244, 252–59.
21. Adkin, *Brother Benjamin*, 127.
22. Sutton, *Heartland Utopias*, 152; Adkin, *Brother Benjamin*, 33; Fogarty, *Righteous Remnant*, 54.
23. Sutton, *Heartland Utopias*, 152; Fogarty, *Righteous Remnant*, 53.
24. Adkin, *Brother Benjamin*, 20–30.
25. Sutton, *Heartland Utopias*, 154; Madden, "Israelites in America," 154–56; Adkin, *Brother Benjamin*, 79–93, 127–47; Fogarty, *Righteous Remnant*, 80–87, 89–103.
26. Adkin, *Brother Benjamin*, 106, 114, 145, 191–92; Fogarty, *Righteous Remnant*, 111–20; Sutton, *Heartland Utopias*, 156.
27. Adkin, *Brother Benjamin*, 195.
28. Sutton, *Heartland Utopias*, 156–57; Madden, "Israelites in America," 156–58; Adkin, *Brother Benjamin*, 210–14; Fogarty, *Righteous Remnant*, 121. Adkin reports that in 1990 the two communities had a total of 39 members (plus a number of family members and associates who were not formal members), including 18 who joined during Benjamin Purnell's lifetime (Adkin, *Brother Benjamin*, 324). Sutton reports a total of about 50 people in the two groups (Sutton, *Heartland Utopias*, 157).
29. 76110 to PS, December 17, 1934, MS letter, PSHA.
30. 62253 (originally 43594) to PS, September 7, 1925, MS letter, PSHA.
31. 62253 (originally 43594) to PS, n.d., letter, PSHA.

32. 62253 (originally 43594) to PS, n.d., letter, PSHA.
33. 62253 (originally 43594) to PS, n.d., letter, PSHA.
34. 81193 to PS, n.d., from TS summary of MS letter, PSHA.
35. 45518 to PS, September 10, 1924, MS letter, PSHA.
36. 45518 to PS, February 17, 1925, MS letter, PSHA.
37. "Jamaican Report," TS, F.3.2.4, PSGA. (Emphasis in original.) See also comments on the expense of communicating with Bedford for Jamaicans in "Panacea Society Annual Report 1943," TS, F.3.2.7, PSGA.
38. "Panacea Society Annual Report 1937–1938," TS, F.3.2.5, PSGA.
39. "Panacea Society Annual Report 1945," TS, PSGA. See also loose TS notes filed with "Panacea Society Council Meeting Minutes, 26th Council Meeting," F.3.1.22, PSGA. The *Writings of the Holy Ghost* were divine communications taken down by Octavia under divine inspiration.
40. "Panacea Society Annual Report 1947," TS, F.3.2.7, PSGA.
41. "Panacea Society Annual Report 1952," TS, F.3.2.10, PSGA.
42. Smith, "Preface," xiii.
43. Stewart, *Religion and Society*, xv.
44. Ibid., xv.
45. Ibid., xvi. In the nineteenth century, systematic Christian evangelism was not coherently implemented by the white ruling groups, who were even deliberately holding this kind of evangelism back. Wesleyan and Baptist missionary work was more systematically implemented. See Stewart, *Religion and Society*, 2–8.
46. Taylor, "British Churches and Jamaican Migration," 13. See also Stewart, *Religion and Society*, 1–13; Morrish, *Obeah, Christ and Rastaman*, 23–35.
47. Austin-Broos, *Jamaica Genesis*, 7; Smith, "Preface," xiii, xiv.
48. Smith, "Preface," xiv.
49. Austin-Broos, *Jamaica Genesis*, 1, 4, 53.
50. Stewart, *Religion and Society*, 110.
51. Ibid., xviii, 136 (emphasis added). See also Austin-Broos, *Jamaica Genesis*, 54.
52. Austin-Broos, *Jamaica Genesis*, 4.
53. Ibid., 52.
54. Phillippo, *Jamaica*, 263, quoted by Austin-Broos, *Jamaica Genesis*, 52.
55. Austin-Broos, *Jamaica Genesis*, 63, citing Long, "Balm Jamaica Folk Medicine."
56. Austin-Broos, *Jamaica Genesis*, 64.
57. Barrett, "Portrait of a Jamaican Healer," 9.
58. Ibid.

59. Morrish, *Obeah, Christ and Rastaman*, 108.
60. Barrett, "Portrait of a Jamaican Healer," 17–18.
61. Stewart, *Religion and Society*, 135–36. Cf. Konadu, *Akan Diaspora*, 146, for a discussion of the Komfo river ritual.
62. Austin-Broos, *Jamaica Genesis*, 204, citing Mbiti, *African Religions and Philosophy*.
63. "Panacea Society Annual Report 1947," TS, F.3.2.7, PSGA.
64. 73405 to PS, June 30, 1956, MS letter, PSHA.
65. 12608 to PS, September 16, 1936, MS letter, PSHA.
66. 47040 to PS, October 24, 1934, TS letter, PSHA.
67. 16880 to PS, March 16, 1958, MS letter; 98286 to PS, January 1, 1959, MS letter; 56842 to PS, April 6, 1965, MS letter; 91921 to PS, August 9, 1965, MS letter. All PSHA.
68. 84805 to PS, February 11, 1950, MS letter, PSHA.
69. 53777 to PS, May 15, 1954, MS letter, PSHA.
70. 52353 to PS, November 24, 1964, MS letter, PSHA.
71. 97655 to PS, April 10, 1962, MS letter, PSHA.
72. 39408 to PS, July 23, 1968, MS letter, PSHA.
73. 56673 to PS, June 15 and August 28, 1976, July 4, 1978, MS letters, PSHA.
74. 56673 to PS, July 4, 1978, September 17, 1978, MS letters, PSHA.
75. 79154 to PS, August 17, 1946, MS letter, PSHA.
76. The discussion of Finland in this chapter and elsewhere draws on Lockhart, "Heterodox Healing" published by Suomen Kirkkohistoriallinen Seura/Societas Historiae Ecclesiasticae Fennica (Finnish Society of Church History).
77. Ahlbäck, "Origins of the Theosophical Society," 127.
78. Ibid. 144.
79. Leskelä-Kärki, *Kirjoittaen maailmassa*, 254. See also Kaplan, "Radical Religion in Finland?," 125; Ahlbäck, "Origins of the Theosophical Society," 144; Sohlberg, "Esoteric Milieu in Finland Today," 205.
80. Ahlbäck, "Origins of the Theosophical Society," 128, 134–37, 143; Kaplan, "Radical Religion in Finland?," 125; Sohlberg, "Esoteric Milieu in Finland Today," 205; Reijonen, "Pekka Ervast."
81. Ervast, "Finland," 228. See also Reijonen, "Pekka Ervast," 6–7. For a discussion of the upheavals in the Theosophical Society, see Santucci, "Theosophy," 238–39; Santucci, "Theosophical Society," 1121. For a discussion of Ruusu-Risti, see Sohlberg, "Esoteric Milieu in Finland Today," 209–10; Junnonaho and Gullman, "Ervast, Pekka (1875–1934)," 654–55. For more on Ervast's biography and significance, see Kaplan, "Radical Religion in Finland?," 125–28.

82. See Ervast to PS, September 21, 1933; Reijonen to PS, June 2, 1934; Translator to PS, March 23, 1996, February 28, 1994, May 9, 1996. All PSHA. See also Lockhart, "Heterodox Healing."
83. Ervast, "Finland," 229; "Finland: Alphabetical Register of Applicants for Healing," A.4.4.10, PSGA.
84. Ervast to PS, August 12, October 1, and December 19, 1925, April 6, 1926, PSHA. Ervast wrote to the Society in English.
85. Ervast to PS, October 1, 1925, PSHA.
86. Ervast to PS, December 7, 19, 1925, PSHA.
87. Ervast to PS, December 7, 1925, April 6, 1926, PSHA.
88. Ervast to PS, April 6, 1926, August 7, 1926, PSHA
89. Shaw, *Octavia: Daughter of God*, 250.
90. Ervast, "Finland," 231n.
91. C.S.S., "The Healing," 58.
92. *Kalevala: The Epic Poem of Finland.*
93. Branch, "Kalevala," 1.
94. Kaplan, "Radical Religion in Finland?," 126. A similar point is made by Sohlberg, "Esoteric Milieu in Finland Today," 210. This linking of religion and nationalism was not unique to Ervast. Aila Lauha writes of the Lutheran Church's notion that the "building up of Finland, the fatherland, was ... a worthy, almost a holy mission" and its teaching "that the country, her language and culture were God's good gifts for which one had to be grateful and for which one should work" (Lauha, "Lutheran Church of Finland," 82, 83).
95. Ervast, *Key to the Kalevala*, 204.
96. Ervast, *Tietäjän Aarteisto*, vol. 2, 436.
97. Ervast, *Key to the Kalevala*, 205.
98. Ervast to PS, February 1, 1927, letter, PSHA.

CHAPTER SIX

1. Gorer, *Exploring English Character*, 265 (Gorer uses research carried out in 1950); Bourke, *Fear*, 252, citing Balleine, *What is Superstition?*, 7.
2. Gorer, *Exploring English Character*, 265.
3. Sykes, "Popular Religion in Decline," 305–6.
4. Fox, *How We Built Jerusalem ... Part I*, 19–22; "Panacea Society the Twelfth General Meeting 22 July 1937," F.3.2.4, PSGA; "Panacea Society Annual Report 1938–1939," TS, F.3.2.5, PSGA; "Panacea Society Annual Report 1946," TS, F.3.2.8, PSGA; Shaw, *Octavia: Daughter of God*, 152, 157–58.

5. The Society's healing advertisements are collected in its Press Cuttings Books, numbered 1–5 [without accession number], PSGA. This example is identified as *Morning Post*, August 7, 1924. Advertisements were normally published with varying capitalization and emphasis; this has been standardized for all advertising quoted in the text.

6. See *Eastbourne Chronicle*, February 7 to May 2, 1925; *Eastbourne Gazette*, February 11 to May 6, 1925; *Finchley Press*, February 20 to May 15, 1925; *Christian World*, July 2, 9, 15, 23, 1925 (Press Cuttings Books, PSGA).

7. The "first advertisement" is reproduced in Octavia, *Healing for All*, 119.

8. Revelations 22:17.

9. There are numerous examples in the *Daily Express, Daily Mail, Daily Telegraph*, and a number of local and regional papers from summer 1939 to 1945. The last advertisement for the healing known to this research appears in the *Harrow Weekly Post*, November 12, 1980.

10. See Nevett, *Advertising in Britain*, 145–68; Richards, *Commodity Culture of Victorian England*, 168–204.

11. Richards, *Commodity Culture of Victorian England*, 172.

12. Nevett, *Advertising in Britain*, 163.

13. *Daily Herald*, July 15, 1939, 1. (The Panacea Society advertisement appears on p. 9.)

14. Ibid., 5.

15. *Daily Herald*, July 14, 1939, 13, 15.

16. *Daily Mail*, July 15, 1939, 6. (The Panacea Society advertisement appears on p. 7.)

17. *Daily Mail*, September 2, 1939, 5, 9.

18. *Daily Telegraph*, September 4, 1939, 9.

19. See Panacea Society press cuttings book "Newspaper Advertisements 2" [without accession number], PSGA.

20. *Daily Mail*, July 15, 1939, 15.

21. *Daily Mail*, September 2, 1939, 1 (original emphasis).

22. Ibid., 3.

23. Norenzayan and Hansen, "Belief in Supernatural Agents"; Willer, "No Atheists in Foxholes"; Vail, et al., "Terror Management Analysis"; Jong, Bluemke, and Halberstadt, "Fear of Death and Supernatural Beliefs."

24. Willer, "No Atheists in Foxholes," 244.

25. Blackman, "Preface."

26. Wickham, *Church and People*, 211; Currie, Gilbert, and Horsley, *Churches and Churchgoers*, 30.

27. Field, "Puzzled People Revisited," 460–61. Field comments on the opposition between his conclusions and those in Currie, Gilbert, and Horsley, *Churches and Churchgoers*, 113–15.
28. Field, "Puzzled People Revisited," 473, citing Parker, *Faith on the Home Front*, 59, 213–15, 217, and Snape and Parker, "Keeping Faith and Coping," 401.
29. Parker, *Faith on the Home Front*, 18, 60.
30. *Puzzled People*, 60.
31. Field, "Puzzled People Revisited," 457.
32. The sample included 350 individuals (applying from England, Scotland and Wales), 93 percent of whom applied from England.
33. *Daily Mail*, February 23, 1939, 9.
34. "Panacea Society Annual Report 1938–1939," TS, F.3.2.5, PSGA.
35. "Panacea Society Annual Report 1939–1940," TS, F.3.2.5, PSGA.
36. The British Isles and the USA peaked in 1939, Jamaica in 1937.
37. Advertisements in the international edition of the *Daily Sketch* for September 14, 1955, and the continental edition of the *Daily Mail* for December 7, 12, 20, 1946, and December 18, 1952, are included in the Society's cuttings books, and a number of periodicals with healing advertisements no doubt had an international circulation. (Press Cuttings Books, numbered 1–5 [without accession number], PSGA.)
38. 30941 to PS, August 24, 1940, MS letter, PSHA.
39. Ibid.
40. Ibid.
41. 30941 to PS, March 24, 1943, MS letter, PSHA.
42. MS notes appended to Ibid.
43. 30941 to PS, February 9, 1943, MS letter, PSHA.
44. 30941 to PS, February 20, 1924, January 8, 1941, MS letters, PSHA.
45. 30941 to PS, June 10, 1943, MS letter, PSHA.
46. 19885 to PS, September 2, 1939, MS letter, PSHA.
47. 19885 to PS, June 17, 1942, MS letter, PSHA.
48. 19885 to PS, August 22, 1954, MS letter, PSHA.
49. 33706 to PS, October 29, 1962, MS letter, PSHA.
50. 33706 to PS, June 19, 1967, MS letter, PSHA.
51. 77067 to PS, October 4, 1938, TS translation of MS letter, PSHA.
52. 77067 to PS, July 31, 1939, TS translation of MS letter, PSHA.
53. 77067 to PS, May 6, 1952, TS translation of MS letter, PSHA (emphasis in original).
54. 87225 to PS, August 5, 1937, MS letter, PSHA.

55. 87225 to PS, August 8, 1938, MS letter, PSHA.
56. 87225 to PS, May 31, 1940, MS letter, PSHA.
57. 72173 to PS, August 24, 1939, MS letter, PSHA.
58. 72173 to PS, July 24, 1948, MS letter, PSHA.
59. 72173 to PS, July 26, 1940, MS letter, PSHA.
60. 32463 to PS, November 12, 1939, MS letter, PSHA.
61. 32463 to PS, January 7, 1940, MS letter, PSHA.
62. 32463 to PS, November 12, 1939, MS letter, PSHA.
63. 32463 to PS, March 13, 1966, MS letter, PSHA.
64. 87225 to PS, March 3, 1949, May 27, 1950, MS letters, PSHA.
65. 87225 to PS, February 27, 1950, MS letter, PSHA.
66. 77067 to PS, October 29, 1952, TS translation of MS letter, PSHA.
67. PS to 77067, n.d. (filed with 77067 to PS, October 29, 1952), MS draft letter, PSHA (emphasis in original).
68. Williams and Watts, "Attributions in a Spiritual Healing Context."
69. Ibid., 105.
70. Ibid.
71. Swatos and Christiano, "Secularization Theory," 217.
72. Berger, *Social Reality of Religion*, 60.
73. Jong, Halberstadt, and Bluemke, "Foxhole Atheism, Revisited."
74. Norenzayan and Hansen, "Belief in Supernatural Agents," 174 (from the abstract).
75. Kay, Gaucher, McGregor, and Nash, "Religious Belief as Compensatory Control," 39, citing Kay, Gaucher, Napier, Callan, and Lautin, "God and the Government."

CHAPTER SEVEN

1. Elements of the research discussed in this chapter first appeared in Lockhart, "Religious and Spiritual Mobility," and Lockhart, "Southcottian Healing Panacea."
2. 90163 to PS, October 26, 1949, MS letter, in PSHA.
3. 71480 to PS, May 3, 1941, MS letter, PSHA.
4. 66461 to PS, November 17, 1960, TS translation, PSHA.
5. 93861 to PS, August 15, 1938, MS letter, PSHA.
6. 86153 to PS, January 12, 1934, March 12, 1934, MS letters, PSHA.
7. 72913 to PS, July 17, 1953, MS letter, PSHA.
8. 19298 to PS, August 8, 1929, MS letter, PSHA.

9. See entries for 89555 and 47077 in "Finland: Alphabetical Register of Applicants for Healing," A.4.4.10, PSGA.
10. 89555 and 47077 in PSHA.
11. 54542to PS, October 27 1965, MS letter, PSHA.
12. 92622 to PS, March 18, 1928, MS letter, PSHA.
13. 94364 to PS, July 11, 1944, MS letter, PSHA.
14. 28763 to PS, September 12, 1959, September 21, 1966, PSHA.
15. 28763 to PS, August 11, 1959, PSHA.
16. 65168 to PS, December 1, 1976, TS translation of MS letter, PSHA.
17. 34035 to PS, September 17, 1956, PSHA.
18. 34035 to PS, October 1, 1956, PSHA.
19. 73405 to PS, June 30, 1956, PSHA.
20. 12608 to PS, September 16, 1936, PSHA.
21. 35772 to PS, March 14, 1930, MS letter, PSHA.
22. Ibid.
23. Ervast to PS, February 20, 1926, PSHA (emphasis in original).
24. 44613 to PS, July 1, 1938, TS letter, PSHA.
25. 44613 to PS, September 6, 1938, TS letter, PSHA.
26. 44613 to PS, October 26, 1938, MS translation of MS letter, PSHA.
27. 44613 to PS, December 29, 1938, TS translation of MS letter, PSHA. This applicant is also discussed earlier.
28. 64777 to PS, November 22, 1924, MS letter, PSHA.
29. 64777 to PS, June 22, 1932, MS letter, PSHA.
30. Ibid.
31. 57730 to PS, September 12, 1929, PSHA.
32. 72173 to PS, March 13, 1939, MS letter, PSHA.
33. 72173 to PS, April 13, 1939, MS letter, PSHA.
34. 72173 to PS, July 24, 1948, MS letter, PSHA.
35. 72173 to PS, September 23, 1948, MS letter, PSHA.
36. 72173 to PS, January 23, 1949, MS letter, PSHA.
37. 14562 to PS, October 19, 1932, MS letter, PSHA.
38. Ibid.
39. Ibid. Cf. Matthew 24.
40. 84676 to PS, August 18, 1939, MS letter, PSHA (emphasis in original).
41. 84676 to PS, July 26, 1940, MS letter, PSHA.
42. Ibid. (emphasis in original).
43. PS to 84676, MS draft letter annotation added to 84676 to PS, July 26, 1940, MS letter, PSHA.

44. 84676 to PS, March 2, 1941, MS letter, PSHA.
45. 45913 to PS, January 7, 1952, MS letter, PSHA.
46. 45913 to PS, February 10, 1952, MS letter, PSHA.
47. 45913 to PS, November 12, 1952, MS letter, PSHA.
48. 13228 to PS, no date, TS translation of letter, PSHA.
49. 66162 to PS, August 2, 1951, MS letter, PSHA.
50. 18076 to PS, no date, TS translation of letter, PSHA.
51. 87225 to PS, February 27, 1950, MS letter, PSHA. The passage is also discussed in an earlier chapter.
52. 81539 to PS, October 31, 1935, MS letter, PSHA.
53. 81539 to PS, May 1, 1949, MS letter, PSHA.
54. 96608 to PS, January 12, 1952, February 11, 1952, MS letters, PSHA.
55. 79369 to PS, April 19, 1962, February 14, 1964, MS letters, PSHA.
56. "I got mixed up with a man and I had to leave him in June 1960 he did me every thing that was wicked under the sun I mysteriously got out of his clutches by prayer and fasting" (79369 to PS, May 11, 1962, MS letter, PSHA).
57. 55730 to PS, August 11, 1936, MS letter, PSHA.
58. 54811 to PS, May 6, 1940, MS letter, PSHA.
59. 54811 to PS, December 21, 1940, MS letter, PSHA.
60. 57683 to PS, November 14, 1977, MS letter, PSHA.
61. Ibid.
62. Jane Shaw discusses some of the Panacea Society's links with India in *Octavia: Daughter of God*, 154–55, 160–62.
63. 96017 to PS, January 18, 1934, MS letter, PSHA.
64. Ibid.
65. 96017 to PS, June 19, 1929, MS letter, PSHA.
66. 81845 to PS, May 31, 1930, MS letter, PSHA.
67. 96017 to PS, April 18, 1935, MS letter, PSHA.
68. 81845 to PS, January 28, 1936, MS letter, PSHA.
69. 96017 to PS, June 19, 1929, MS letter, PSHA.
70. 96017 to PS, April 19, 1933, MS letter, PSHA.
71. Luckmann, "Shrinking Transcendence, Expanding Religion?," 130.
72. 96017 to PS, July 19, 1933, MS letter, PSHA.
73. 96017 to PS, December 27, 1934, MS letter, PSHA.
74. 20109 to PS, October 7, 1929, MS letter, PSHA.
75. Ibid.
76. Ibid.
77. Ibid.

78. 22807 to PS, March 3, 1950, TS translation of MS letter, PSHA.
79. 22807 to PS, c. March 18, 1966, TS translation of MS letter, PSHA.
80. PS to 22807, c. March 18, 1966, draft letter filed with 22807, PSHA.
81. 32171, August 16, 1936, MS letter, PSHA.
82. 32171, September 27, 1936, MS letter, PSHA.
83. 32171, August 23, 1937, MS letter, PSHA.
84. 32171, September 27, 1936, MS letter, PSHA.
85. 32171, August 9, 1942, MS letter, PSHA.
86. 32171, August 21, 1940, MS letter, PSHA.
87. 32171, March 15, 1941, MS letter, PSHA.
88. 32171, August 21, 1938, MS letter, PSHA.
89. 32171, August 9, 1942, December 28, 1943, MS letters, PSHA.
90. 32171, February 13, 1945, December 28, 1943, MS letters, PSHA.
91. PS to 32171, March 23, 1945, duplicate TS letter, attached to letters of 32171, PSHA.
92. PS to 32171, March 23, 1945, duplicate TS letter, attached to letters of 32171, PSHA.
93. 32171, November 13, 1945, April 10, 1946, MS letters, PSHA.
94. 32171 to PS, December 19, 1951, MS letter, PSHA.
95. Ibid.
96. Ibid.
97. 32171 to PS, December 9, 1952, March 21, 1955, MS letters, PSHA.
98. 32171 to PS, August 22, 1968, MS letter, PSHA.
99. 72150 to PS, May 10, 1959, MS letter, PSHA.
100. 72150 to PS, January 30, 1961, MS letter, PSHA.
101. 72150 to PS, June 4, 1961, MS letter, PSHA.
102. 72150 to PS, July 31, 1966, MS letter, PSHA.
103. 72150 to PS, March 15, 1965, MS letter, PSHA.

CHAPTER EIGHT

1. Bowman, "Healing in the Spiritual Marketplace," 342.
2. McGuire, "Health and Spirituality as Contemporary Concerns," 144 (from the abstract).
3. Partridge, *The Re-enchantment of the West*, vol. 2, 4.
4. Hughes, "Regional Patterns of Religious Affiliation," 553.
5. Hanegraaff, *New Age Religion and Western Culture*, 46.
6. Hughes, "Regional Patterns of Religious Affiliation," 550, 551.

7. Ibid. 551.
8. Ibid.
9. McGuire, "Health and Spirituality as Contemporary Concerns," 146, 146–47.
10. Ibid., 147.
11. Ibid., 150.
12. Hanegraaff, *New Age Religion and Western Culture*, 42, citing Young, "Anthropologies of Illness," 264–65.
13. Hanegraaff, *New Age Religion and Western Culture*, 43.
14. Hedges and Beckford, "Holism, Healing and the New Age," 173, quoting York, *Emerging Network*, 39, and York, "New Age and the Late Twentieth Century," 414–15.
15. McGuire, "Health and Spirituality as Contemporary Concerns," 154.
16. Hanegraaff, *New Age Religion and Western Culture*, 239.
17. Partridge, *The Re-enchantment of the West*, vol. 2, 10.
18. Lewis, "Approaches to the Study of the New Age Movement," 3.
19. Ibid.
20. Luckmann, "Shrinking Transcendence, Expanding Religion?," 134.
21. Ibid.
22. Ibid., 135.
23. Ibid., 128–30.
24. Ibid., 130.
25. Ibid., 135.
26. Hanegraaff, "New Age Religion and Secularization," 300.
27. McLeod, *Religious Crisis*, 4.
28. Morris, "Secularization and Religious Experience," 217.
29. Besecke, "Seeing Invisible Religion," 182; Lyon, *Jesus in Disneyland*, 91–95.
30. Bowman and Valk, *Vernacular Religion*, 1–19.
31. Ibid., 4. They refer to Yoder, "Toward a Definition of Folk Religion," 2–15.
32. Yoder, "Toward a Definition of Folk Religion," 14, quoted by Bowman and Valk, *Vernacular Religion*, 4.
33. Bowman, "Phenomenology, Fieldwork and Folk Religion."
34. Ibid. quoted by Bowman and Valk, *Vernacular Religion*, 4.
35. Primiano, "Vernacular Religion," 37–56, 44, quoted by Bowman and Valk, *Vernacular Religion*, 5.
36. Bowman and Valk, *Vernacular Religion*, 5.
37. Shaw, *Octavia: Daughter of God*, 84.
38. See Vail, et al., "Terror Management Analysis," 88, 91.

39. Partridge, *The Re-enchantment of the West*, vol. 2, 9, quoting Bruce, "Pluralism and Religious Vitality," 170 (Partridge's emphasis).

40. Lyon, *Jesus in Disneyland*, 77.

41. Bowman and Valk, *Vernacular Religion*, 6, 7. See also Bowman, "Taking Stories Seriously," 125–42.

42. Ellwood, "How New Is the New Age?," 59.

POSTSCRIPT

1. Author's personal interview with David McLynn, Panacea Charitable Trust Business Manager, May 3, 2013.

2. Ibid.

BIBLIOGRAPHY

PANACEA SOCIETY ARCHIVES

Held by the Panacea Charitable Trust at 14 Albany Road, Bedford, MK40 3PH, United Kingdom.

Ervast   packet "Letters from the Tower for Finland" in box "Finland F2800–3099 Non-reporting; PA/TO; Tower Notes."

Reijonen   packet "Letters from the Tower for Finland" in box "Finland F2800–3099 Non-reporting; PA/TO; Tower Notes."

Translator packet "Finland" in box "Finland F3100–3499 Non-reporting; PA/TO; Passed Over."

To preserve anonymity randomly allocated identification numbers have been used for all other correspondents. Archive locations and references for each identification number used in the text are held by the Panacea Charitable Trust archivist.

PANACEA SOCIETY PUBLICATIONS

Published by the Panacea Society, though often with a limited circulation. All held at 14 Albany Road, Bedford, MK40 3PH, United Kingdom.

"302. – March 23, 1921." *Writings of the Holy Ghost* 2, no. 11: 340–41.

A.E.J. "Peeps behind the Scenes in the Healing Department IV. – Foreign Correspondence." *The Panacea* 9, issue 6 (n.d.): 128–29.

C.S.S. "Children." *The Panacea* 6, issue 70 (n.d.): 240.

C.S.S. "C.S.S. Postbag IV Africa." *The Panacea* 5, issue 52 (n.d.): 83–84.

C.S.S. "Notes from My Case-Book Defects." *The Panacea* 6, issue 71 (n.d.): 262–63.

C.S.S. "Our Children." *The Panacea* 7, issue 75 (n.d.): 63–64.

C.S.S. "Peeps behind the Scenes in the Healing Department II. – Organization of Correspondence." *The Panacea* 9, issue 5 (n.d.): 106–7.

C.S.S. "Peeps behind the Scenes in the Healing Department III. – Our Correspondence Overseas." *The Panacea* 9, issue 6 (n.d.): 128–29.

C.S.S. "The Healing." *The Panacea* 8, issue 87 (1931?): 57–58.

C.S.S., B.E.G., and I.N.M. "Peeps behind the Scenes VI Report from the Healing Department on the Work for the Year." *The Panacea* 5, issue 60 (n.d.): 276–77.

C.S.S. Juniors. "More Peeps behind the Scenes III: The Report Department." *The Panacea* 6, issue 63 (n.d.): 59–61.

C.S.S. Seniors and Juniors. "Our Work at Home and Abroad in 1929." *The Panacea* 6, issue 72 (n.d.): 276–77.

"Divine Protection Divine Healing Divine Sealing." *The Panacea* 2, issue 22: 224–27.

"Editorial." *The Panacea* 1, issue 8 (n.d.): 170–72.

"Editorial." *The Panacea* 1, issue 10 (n.d.): 218–29.

"Editorial." *The Panacea* 2, issue 17 (n.d.): 98–100.

"Editorial." *The Panacea* 2, issue 22 (n.d.): 218–21.

"Editorial." *The Panacea* 5, issue 49 (n.d.): 2–4.

"Editorial." *The Panacea* 5, issue 52 (n.d.): 74–76.

"Editorial." *The Panacea* 6, issue 63 (n.d.): 50–51.

Ervast, Pekka. "Finland." *The Panacea* 5 issue 58 (1929?): 228–31.

Fox, Rachel J. *The Finding of Shiloh, or the Mystery of God "Finished."* London: Cecil Palmer, ca. 1921.

———. *How We Built Jerusalem in England's Green and Pleasant Land Part I.* London: Cecil Palmer, 1931.

———. *How We Built Jerusalem in England's Green and Pleasant Land: Part II.* Bedford: Garden Press, 1934?.

———. *The Sufferings and Acts of Shiloh-Jerusalem (a Sequel to "The Finding of Shiloh")*. London: Cecil Palmer, 1927.

H. G. "More Peeps behind the Scenes: Review of the Society's Work." *The Panacea* 8, issue 87 (n.d.): 57.

M. L. H. "Peeps behind the Scenes in the Healing Department Inquiries." *The Panacea* 9, issue 1 (n.d.): 9–11.

"Mortal (or Dying) Life and Immortal (or Undying) Life." *The Panacea* 11, issue 7, no. 127 (n.d.): 158–59.

Octavia [Mabel Barltrop]. *Early Dawn of the Great Prophetical Visitation to England.* n.p., 1922.

———. *Healing for All: The Story of the Greatest Discovery of Any Age.* 2d ed. London: Panacea Society, 1925.

———. *Writings of the Holy Ghost*, 16 vols. [Bedford: Panacea Society], 1919–1934.

Orme, C. "Christian Science—A Successful Error." *The Panacea* 2, issue 13 (n.d.): 7–10.

"Sidelights upon the Healing 'Water-Babies.' " *The Panacea* 1, no. 10 (n.d.): 229.

"The Script." *The Panacea* 11, issue 7, no. 127 (n.d.): 159.

"The Title of the Magazine." *The Panacea* 1, no. 1 (1924?): 11–12.

PUBLISHED SOURCES

Adkin, Clare E. *Brother Benjamin: A History of the Israelite House of David*. Berrien Springs, MI: Andrews University Press, 1990.

Ahlbäck, Tore. "The Origins of the Theosophical Society in Finland." In *Beyond the Mainstream: The Emergence of Religious Pluralism in Finland, Estonia, and Russia*, edited by Jeffrey Kaplan, 127–44. Studia Historica 63. Helsinki: Suomalaisen Kirjallisuuden Seura, 2000.

Allan, Gordon. "Southcottian Sects from 1790 to the Present Day." In *Expecting the End: Millennialism in Social and Historical Context*, edited by Kenneth G. C. Newport and Crawford Gribben, 213–33. Waco, TX: Baylor University Press, 2006.

Asprem, Egil. *Arguing with Angels: Enochian Magic and Modern Occulture*. Albany: State University of New York Press, 2012.

"At the Church Congress." *British Medical Journal* 2, no. 3328 (11 Oct 1924): 679–80.

Austin-Broos, Diane J. *Jamaica Genesis: Religion and the Politics of Moral Orders*. Chicago: University of Chicago Press, 1997.

Balleine, G. R. *What Is Superstition? A Trail of Unhappiness*. London: Board of the Church Assembly, 1939.

Barrett, Leonard. "The Portrait of a Jamaican Healer: African Medical Lore in the Caribbean." *Caribbean Quarterly* 19, no. 3 (1973): 6–19.

Bennett, G. *The Cross and the Crown*. n.p., 1848. Broadsheet in Greater London Record Office 1040/301.

Berger, Peter L. *The Desecularization of the World: Resurgent Religion and World Politics*. Grand Rapids: William B. Eerdmans, 1999.

———. *A Rumor of Angels: Modern Society and the Rediscovery of the Supernatural*. Garden City, NY: Anchor/Doubleday, 1970.

———. *The Sacred Canopy: Elements of a Sociological Theory of Religion*. Garden City, NY: Anchor, 1969.

———. *The Sacred Canopy: Elements of the Sociological Theory of Religion*. New York: Anchor Books, 1967.

———. *The Social Reality of Religion*. Harmondsworth: Penguin, 1973.

Besecke, Kelly. "Seeing Invisible Religion: Religion as a Societal Conversation about Transcendent Meaning." *Sociological Theory* 23, no. 2 (2005): 179–96.

Blackman, H. J. Preface to *Puzzled People: A Study in Popular Attitudes to Religion, Ethics, Progress and Politics in a London Borough (Prepared for the Ethical Union)*, by Mass Observation, 7–9. London: Victor Gollancz, 1947.

Bourke, Joanna. *Fear: A Cultural History*. London: Virago, 2005.

Bowerbank, Sylvia. "Southcott, Joanna (1750–1814)." In *Oxford Dictionary of National Biography*, edited by David Cannadine. Oxford: Oxford University Press, 2004. Accessed May 15, 2017. http://www.oxforddnb.com/view/article/26050.

Bowman, Marion. " 'Healing in the Spiritual Marketplace': Consumers, Courses and Credentialism." *Social Compass* 46, no. 2 (1999): 181–89.

———. "Phenomenology, Fieldwork and Folk Religion." In *Religion: Empirical Studies*, edited by S. Sutcliffe, 3–18. Aldershot: Ashgate, 2004.

———. "Taking Stories Seriously: Vernacular Religion, Contemporary Spirituality and the Myth of Jesus in Glastonbury." *Temenos: Nordic Journal of Comparative Religion* 39–40 (2004): 125–42.

Bowman, Marion, and Ülo Valk, eds. *Vernacular Religion in Everyday Life: Expressions of Belief*. Sheffield: Equinox, 2012.

Branch, Michael. "Kalevala: from myth to symbol." *Books from Finland* 19, no. 1 (1985): 1–8.

Brown, Frances. *Joanna Southcott: The Woman Clothed with the Sun*. Cambridge: Lutterworth, 2002.

Bruce, Steve. "Pluralism and Religious Vitality." In *Religion and Modernization: Historians Debate the Secularization Thesis*, edited by Steve Bruce, 170–94. Oxford: Oxford University Press, 1992.

———. *Secularization: In Defence of an Unfashionable Theory*. Oxford: Oxford University Press, 2011.

Byrne, Georgina. *Modern Spiritualism and the Church of England 1850–1939*. Woodbridge: Boydell Press, 2010.

Candelaria, Michael P. *Popular Religion and Liberation: The Dilemma of Liberation Theology*. Albany: State University of New York Press, 1990.

Carroll, Anthony. *Protestant Modernity: Weber, Secularisation, and Protestantism*. Scranton: University of Scranton Press, 2007.

Conference of Bishops of the Anglican Communion: Holden at Lambeth Palace July 5 to August 7, 1920, Encyclical Letter from the Bishops with the Resolutions and Reports. London: Society for Promoting Christian Knowledge, 1920.

Cox, Harvey. *The Secular City: Secularization and Urbanization in Theological Perspective*. London: SCM Press, 1965.
Crystal, David. *A Dictionary of Linguistics and Phonetics*. Oxford: Basil Blackwell, 1989.
Currie, Robert, Alan Gilbert, and Lee Horsley. *Churches and Churchgoers: Patterns of Church Growth in the British Isles since 1700*. Oxford: Clarendon Press, 1977.
"Directory of Professional Services and Church Information." *Christian Science Journal* 132, no. 5 (May 2014): 52–127.
Dixon, Joy. *Divine Feminine: Theosophy and Feminism in England*. Baltimore: Johns Hopkins University Press, 2001.
Duke, James T., Barry L. Johnson, and James B. Duke. "The World Context of Religious Change in the Caribbean." *Social and Economic Studies* 44, nos. 2 and 3 (1995): 143–66.
Durkheim, Émile. *Elementary Forms of the Religious Life*. Translated by J. W. Swain. New York: Free Press, 1965.
———. *Les formes élémentaires de la vie religieuse: Le système totémique en Australie*. 1912. Reprint, Paris, 1960.
———. "L'individualisme et les intellectuels." *Revue bleue* 4, no. 10 (1898): 7–13.
Ellwood, Robert. "How New Is the New Age?" In *Perspectives on the New Age*, edited by James Lewis and J. Gordon Melton, 59–67. Albany: State University of New York Press, 1992.
Ervast, Pekka. *The Key to the Kalevala*. Translated by Tapio Joensuu. Edited by John M. Jenkins. Nevada City, CA: Blue Dolphin Publishing, 1999.
———. *Tietäjän Aarteisto*, edited by Martta Jalava. 3 vols. Tampere: Tempereen Paperinjalostustehdas ja Kivipaino Oy/Turku: Kirjapaino Polytypos, 1933–1956. http://www.pekkaervast.net/teokset/#T. Accessed June 2, 2017.
Field, Clive D. "Puzzled People Revisited: Religious Believing and Belonging in Wartime Britain, 1939–45." *Twentieth Century British History* 19, no. 4 (2008): 446–79.
Fogarty, R. S. *The Righteous Remnant: The House of David*. Kent, OH: Kent State University Press, 1981.
Frisk, Liselotte. "New Age Participants in Sweden: Background, Beliefs, Engagement and 'Conversion.'" In *New Religions in a Postmodern World*, edited by Mikael Rothstein and Reender Kranenborg, 241–55. Aarhus: Aarhus University Press, 2003.
Goldstein, Warren S. "Secularization Patterns in the Old Paradigm." *Sociology of Religion* 70, no. 2 (2009): 157–78.

Gorer, Geoffrey. *Exploring English Character*. London: Crescent Press, 1955.

Gorski, Philip S., and Ateş Altinordu. "After Secularization?" *Annual Review of Sociology* 34 (2008): 55–85.

Hanegraaff, Wouter J. "New Age Religion and Secularization." *Numen* 47, no. 3 (2000): 288–312.

———. *New Age Religion and Western Culture: Esotericism in the Mirror of Modern Thought*. Albany: State University of New York Press, 1998.

Harrison, J. F. C. *The Second Coming: Popular Millenarianism 1780–1850*. New Brunswick: Rutgers University Press, 1979.

Hedges, Ellie, and James A. Beckford. "Holism, Healing and the New Age." In *Beyond the New Age: Exploring Alternative Spirituality*, edited by Steven Sutcliffe and Marion Bowman, 169–87. Edinburgh: Edinburgh University Press, 2000.

Heelas, Paul, and Linda Woodhead. *The Spiritual Revolution: Why Religion Is Giving Way to Spirituality*. Malden: Blackwell, 2005.

Helve, Helena. "The Formation of Religious Attitudes and World Views: A Longitudinal Study of Young Finns." *Social Compass* 38, no. 4 (1991): 373–92.

Hickson J. M. *Heal the Sick*. London: Methuen, 1924.

Hirst, Julie. *Jane Leade: Biography of a Seventeenth-Century Mystic*. Aldershot: Ashgate, 2005.

Holm, Nils G. "Religion in Finland and the Scandinavian Model." *Social Compass* 38, no. 1 (1991): 9–15.

Hopkins, James K. *A Woman to Deliver Her People: Joanna Southcott and English Millenarianism in an Era of Revolution*. Austin: University of Texas Press, 1982.

Houtman, Dick, and Peter Mascini. "Why Do Churches Become Empty, While New Age Grows? Secularization and Religious Change in the Netherlands." *Journal for the Scientific Study of Religion* 41, no. 3 (2002): 455–73.

Hughes, Brian M. "Regional Patterns of Religious Affiliation and Availability of Complementary and Alternative Medicine." *Journal of Religion and Health* 45, no. 4 (2006): 549–57.

Jong, Jonathan, Jamin Halberstadt, and Matthias Bluemke. "Foxhole Atheism, Revisited: The Effects of Mortality Salience on Explicit and Implicit Religious Belief." *Journal of Experimental Social Psychology* 48 (2012): 983–89.

Jong, Jonathan, Matthias Bluemke, and Jamin Halberstadt. "Fear of Death and Supernatural Beliefs: Developing a New Supernatural Belief Scale to Test the Relationship." *European Journal of Personality* 27 (2013): 495–506.

Junnonaho, Martti, and Erik Gullman, "Ervast, Pekka (1875–1934)." In *Suomen Kansallisbiografia*, edited by Matti Klinge, 2:652–55. Helsinki: Suomalaisen Kirjallisuuden Seura, 2003.

Juster, Susan. *Doomsayers: Anglo-American Prophecy in the Age of Revolution*. Philadelphia: University of Pennsylvania Press, 2003.

Kääriäinen, Kimmo, Kati Niemelä, and Kimmo Ketola. *Religion in Finland: Decline, Change and Transformation of Finnish Religiosity*. Tampere: Church Research Institute, 2005.

The Kalevala: The Epic Poem of Finland into English. 2 vols. Translated by John Martin Crawford. New York: John B. Alden; London: G. P. Putnam's Sons, 1889.

Kaplan, Jeffrey. "Radical Religion in Finland?" *Nova Religio* 5, no. 1 (2001): 121–42.

Kay, Aaron C., Danielle Gaucher, Ian McGregor, and Kyle Nash. "Religious Belief as Compensatory Control." *Personality and Social Psychology Review* 14, no. 1 (2010): 37–48.

Kay, Aaron C., Daniella Gaucher, J. L. Napier, M. J. Callan, and K. Lautin. "God and the Government: Testing a Compensatory Control Mechanism for the Support of External Systems." *Journal of Personality and Social Psychology* 95 (2008): 18–35.

Kilvert, Francis. *Kilvert's Diary, 1870–1879: Selections from the Diary of the Rev. Francis Kilvert*, edited by William Plomer. London: Jonathan Cape, 1944.

Kollar, Rene. *Searching for Raymond: Anglicanism, Spiritualism, and Bereavement between the Two World Wars*. Lanham: Lexington Books, 2000.

Konadu, Kwasi. *The Akan Diaspora in the Americas*. Oxford: Oxford University Press, 2010.

The Lambeth Conference 1930: Encyclical Letter from the Bishops with Resolutions and Reports. London: Society for Promoting Christian Knowledge, 1930.

Lauha, Aila. "The Lutheran Church of Finland and Finnish Society in the 1920s and 1930s." In *Hungary and Finland in the 20th Century*, edited by Olli Vehviläinen and Attila Pók, 81–98. Studia Historica 68. Helsinki: Suomalaisen Kirjallisuuden Seura, 2002.

Leskelä-Kärki, Maarit. *Kirjoittaen maailmassa: Krohnin sisaret ja kirjallinen elämä*. Suomalaisen Kirjallisuuden Seuran toimituksia 1085. Helsinki: Suomalaisen Kirjallisuuden Seura, 2006.

Lewis, James R. "Approaches to the Study of the New Age Movement." In *Perspectives on the New Age*, edited by James R. Lewis and J. Gordon Melton, 1–14. Albany: State University of New York Press, 1992.

Lockhart, Alastair. "A Southcottian Healing Panacea, 1924–2012." In *The History of a Modern Millennial Movement: The Southcottians*, edited by J. Shaw and P. Lockley, 186–202. London: I.B. Tauris, 2017.

———. "Heterodox Healing and Alternative Religion in the 20th Century: An English Spiritual Healing Practice in Finland." *Suomen kirkkohistoriallisen seuran vuosikirja* (2013): 74–97.

———. "Religious and Spiritual Mobility in Britain: The Panacea Society and Other Movements in the Twentieth Century." *Contemporary British History* 29, no. 2 (2015): 155–78.

Lockhart, John. *Cosmo Gordon Lang*. London: Hodder & Stoughton, 1949.

Lockley, Philip J. "Jane Lead's Prophetic Afterlife in the Nineteenth-Century English Atlantic." In *Jane Lead and her Transnational Legacy*, edited by Ariel Hessayon, 241–66. London: Palgrave Macmillan.

———. "Millenarian Religion and Radical Politics in Britain 1815–1835: A Study of Southcottians after Southcott." PhD diss., University of Oxford, 2009.

———. "Southcottian Archives: A Global Guide." In *The History of a Modern Millennial Movement: The Southcottians*, edited by J. Shaw and P. Lockley, 203–21. London: I.B. Tauris, 2017.

———. "Southcottians in Britain, 1801–1851: Revealing a Popular Religion." In *The History of a Modern Millennial Movement: The Southcottians*, edited by J. Shaw and P. Lockley, 34–60. London: I.B. Tauris, 2017.

———. *Visionary Religion and Radicalism in Early Industrial England: From Southcott to Socialism*. Oxford: Oxford University Press, 2013.

Lodge, Oliver. "Christianity and Spiritualism." In *Life after Death According to Christianity & Spiritualism*, edited by J. Marchant, 156–76. London: Cassell, 1925.

Long, Joseph K. "Balm Jamaica Folk Medicine." PhD diss., University of North Carolina, 1973.

Luckmann, Thomas. *The Invisible Religion: The Problem of Religion in Modern Society*. New York: Macmillan, 1967.

———. "Secolarizzazione: un mito contemporaneo." *Cultura e Politica* 14 (1969): 175–82.

———. "Shrinking Transcendence, Expanding Religion?" *Sociological Analysis* 51, no. 2 (1990): 127–38.

Lukes, Steven. "Durkheim's 'Individualism and the Intellectuals.'" *Political Studies* 17, no. 1 (1969): 14–30.

Lyon, David. *Jesus in Disneyland: Religion in Postmodern Times*. Cambridge: Polity Press, 2000.

Madden, Deborah. "The Emergence of Southcottian Israelite Theology, 1815–1863." In *The History of a Modern Millennial Movement: The Southcottians*, edited by J. Shaw and P. Lockley, 78–94. London: I.B. Tauris, 2017.

———. "Israelites in America: The House of David and Mary's City of David, Benton Harbor." In *The History of a Modern Millennial Movement: The Southcottians*, edited by J. Shaw and P. Lockley, 140–63. London: I.B. Tauris, 2017.

———. "A Southcottian Methodist: The Prophetic Odyssey of George Turner." In *The History of a Modern Millennial Movement: The Southcottians*, edited by J. Shaw and P. Lockley, 61–77. London: I.B. Tauris, 2017.

Matthews, Ronald. *English Messiahs: Studies of Six English Religious Pretenders 1656–1927*. London: Methuen, 1936.

Mbiti, John S. *African Religions and Philosophy*. London: Heinemann, 1969.

McGuire, Meredith B. "Health and Spirituality as Contemporary Concerns." *Annals of the American Academy of Political and Social Science* 527 (1993): 144–54.

———. *Ritual Healing in Suburban America*. New Brunswick: Rutgers University Press, 1988.

McLeod, Hugh. *The Religious Crisis of the 1960s*. Oxford: Oxford University Press, 2007.

———. *Secularization in Western Europe 1848–1914*. Basingstoke: Macmillan, 2000.

Mews, Stuart. "Religion, 1900–1939." In *A Companion to Early Twentieth-Century Britain*, edited by C. Wrigley, 470–84. Malden: Blackwell, 2003.

———. "The Revival of Spiritual Healing in the Church of England 1920–1926." In *The Church and Healing*, edited by W. J. Sheils, 299–332. Oxford: Basil Blackwell / Ecclesiastical History Society, 1982.

The Ministry of Healing: Report of the Committee Appointed in Accordance with Resolution 63 of the Lambeth Conference, 1920. London: Society for Promoting Christian Knowledge, 1924.

Morris, Jeremy. "Secularization and Religious Experience: Arguments in the Historiography of Modern British Religion." *Historical Journal* 55, no. 1 (2012): 195–219.

Morrish, Ivor. *Obeah, Christ and Rastaman: Jamaica and Its Religion*. Cambridge: James Clarke, 1982.

Nelson, Geoffrey K. *Spiritualism and Society*. London: Routledge & Kegan Paul, 1969.

Nevett, T. R. *Advertising in Britain: A History*. London: William Heinemann / History of Advertising Trust, 1982.

Niblett, Matthew. "Joanna Southcott's Apocalyptic Theology, 1792–1814." In *The History of a Modern Millennial Movement: The Southcottians*, edited by J. Shaw and P. Lockley, 13–33. London: I.B. Tauris, 2017.

———. *Prophecy and the Politics of Salvation in Late Georgian England: The Theology and Apocalyptic Vision of Joanna Southcott*. London: I.B. Tauris, 2015.

Norenzayan, Ara, and Ian G. Hansen. "Belief in Supernatural Agents in the Face of Death." *Personality and Social Psychology Bulletin* 32, no. 2 (2006): 174–87.

Owen, Alex. *Place of Enchantment: British Occultism and the Culture of the Modern*. Chicago: University of Chicago Press, 2004.

Parker, Stephen. *Faith on the Home Front: Aspects of Church Life and Popular Religion in Birmingham, 1939–1945*. Bern: Peter Lang, 2005.

Partridge, Christopher. *The Re-enchantment of the West: Alternative Spiritualities, Sacralization, Popular Culture, and Occulture*. Vol. 1. London: T&T Clark, 2004.

———. *The Re-enchantment of the West: Alternative Spiritualities, Sacralization, Popular Culture, and Occulture*. Vol. 2. London: T&T Clark, 2005.

Phillippo, James M. *Jamaica: Its Past and Present State*. Westport: Negro University Press, 1970. [Originally published by John Snowdon: London, 1843.]

Primiano, Leonard Norman. "Afterword: Manifestations of the Religious Vernacular: Ambiguity, Power, and Creativity." In *Vernacular Religion in Everyday Life: Expressions of Belief*, edited by Marion Bowman and Ülo Valk, 382–94. Sheffield: Equinox, 2012.

———. "Vernacular Religion and the Search for Method in Religious Folklife." *Western Folklore* 54, no. 1 (1995): 37–56.

Puzzled People: A Study in Popular Attitudes to Religion, Ethics, Progress and Politics in a London Borough (Prepared for the Ethical Union). London: Victor Gollancz, 1947.

Ransom, Josephine. *A Short History of the Theosophical Society*. Adyar, India: Theosophical Publishing House, 1938.

Reijonen, Annikki. "Pekka Ervast, a Theosophist of the North," 1932. Accessed June 2, 2017, media.pekkaervast.net/penet/books_files/Pekka_Ervast_a_Theosophist_of_the_North.pdf.

Richards, Thomas. *The Commodity Culture of Victorian England: Advertising and Spectacle, 1851–1914*. London: Verso, 1990.

Roden, Fredrick S. "The Kiss of the Soul: The Mystical Theology of Christina Rossetti's Devotional Prose." In *Women's Theology in Nineteenth-Century*

Britain: Transfiguring the Faith of Their Fathers, edited by Julie Melnyk, 37–57. New York: Garland, 1998.

Ryan, Charles J. *H. P. Blavatsky and the Theosophical Movement: A Brief Historical Sketch*. Point Loma, CA: Theosophical University Press, 1937.

Santucci, James A. "Theosophical Society." In *Dictionary of Gnosis and Western Esotericism*, edited by Wouter J. Hanegraaff, 2:1114–23. Leiden: Brill, 2005.

———. "Theosophy." In *The Cambridge Companion to New Religious Movements*, edited by Olav Hammer and Mikael Rothstein, 231–46. Cambridge: Cambridge University Press, 2012.

Shaw, Jane. *Octavia: Daughter of God: The Story of a Female Messiah and Her Followers*. London: Jonathan Cape, 2011.

———. "Seymour, Alice (1857–1947)." In *Oxford Dictionary of National Biography*, edited by David Cannadine. Oxford: Oxford University Press, September 2012. Accessed May 15, 2017, oxforddnb.com/view/article/93403.

———. "Southcottians in the Early Twentieth Century: The Panacea Society." In *The History of a Modern Millennial Movement: The Southcottians*, edited by J. Shaw and P. Lockley, 164–85. London: I.B. Tauris, 2017.

Smith, Clifford P. *Historical Sketches from the Life of Mary Baker Eddy and the History of Christian Science*. Boston: Christian Science Publishing Society, 1969.

Smith, Mark, and Stephen Taylor, eds. *Evangelicalism in the Church of England c. 1790–1890: A Miscellany*. Woodbridge: Boydell Press, 2004.

Smith, Raymond T. Foreword to *Jamaica Genesis: Religion and the Politics of Moral Orders*, by Diane J. Austin-Broos, xiii–xix. Chicago: University of Chicago Press, 1997.

Snape, M. F., and S. G. Parker. "Keeping Faith and Coping: Belief, Popular Religiosity and the British People." In *The People's Experience*. Vol. 2 of *The Great World War, 1914–45*, edited by P. Liddle, J. Bourne and I. Whitehead, 397–420. London: HarperCollins, 2001.

Sohlberg, Jussi. "The Esoteric Milieu in Finland Today." In *Western Esotericism: Based on Papers Read at the Symposium on Western Esotericism Held at Åbo, Finland, on 15–17 August 2007*, edited by Tore Ahlbäck, 204–16. Åbo: Donner Institute for Research in Religious and Cultural History, 2008.

Southcott, Joanna. *The Answer of the Lord to the Powers of Darkness*. Marchant and Galabin, 1813. First published 1802.

———. *Answer to Mr. Brothers's Book, Published in Sept 1806, and Observations on His Former Writings*. Spa Fields: S. Rousseau, 1806.

———. *Full Assurance that the Kingdom of Christ is at Hand from the Signs of the Times*. London, 1806.

———. *The Long-Wished-For Revolution Announced to be at Hand in a Book Lately Published, by L. Mayer, When, as He Says, "God will cleanse the Earth by his Judgments, and when all Dominons shall serve the Most High," Explained by Joanna Southcott*. London: S. Rousseau, 1806.

———. *Strange Effects of Faith*. Exeter, 1801.

Stewart, Robert J. *Religion and Society in Post-Emancipation Jamaica*. Knoxville: University of Tennessee Press, 1992.

Stunt, Timothy C. F. "Brothers, Richard (1757–1824)." In *Oxford Dictionary of National Biography*, edited by David Cannadine. Oxford: Oxford University Press, 2004.

———. "Jezreel, James Jershom (1848x51–1885)." In *Oxford Dictionary of National Biography*, edited by David Cannadine. Oxford: Oxford University Press, 2004.

Sutcliffe, Steven, and Marion Bowman. "Introduction." In *Beyond the New Age: Exploring Alternative Spirituality*, edited by Steven Sutcliffe and Marion Bowman, 1–13. Edinburgh: Edinburgh University Press, 2000.

Sutton, Robert P. *Heartland Utopias*. DeKalb: Northern Illinois University Press, 2009.

Swatos, William H., and Kevin J. Christiano. "Secularization Theory: The Course of a Concept." *Sociology of Religion* 60, no. 3 (1999): 209–28.

Sykes, Richard. "Popular Religion in Decline: A Study from the Black Country." *Journal of Ecclesiastical History* 56, no. 2 (2005): 287–307.

Taylor, Anne. "Besant, Annie (1847–1933)." In *Oxford Dictionary of National Biography*, edited by David Cannadine. Oxford: Oxford University Press, January 2008.

Taylor, Claire Rachel. "British Churches and Jamaican Migration: A Study of Religion and Identities, 1948 to 1965." Vol. 1. PhD diss., Anglia Polytechnic University, 2002.

Temme, Willi. "From Jakob Böhme via Jane Leade to Eva von Buttlar: Transmigrations and Transformations of Religious Ideas." In *Pietism in Germany and North America 1680–1820*, edited by Jonathan Strom, Hartmut Lehman, and James van Horn Melton, 101–6. Farnham: Ashgate, 2009.

Thompson, E. P. *The Making of the English Working Class*. London: Penguin, 1991.

Thompson, Ken. *Emile Durkheim*. Rev. ed. London: Routledge, 2002.

Trzebiatowska, Marta, and Steve Bruce. *Why Are Women More Religious than Men?* Oxford: Oxford University Press, 2012.

Tschannen, Olivier. "The Secularization Paradigm: A Systematization." *Journal for the Scientific Study of Religion* 30 (1991): 395–415.
Vail, Kenneth E., III, Zachary K. Rothschild, Dave R. Weise, Sheldon Solomon, Tom Pyszczynski, and Jeff Greenberg. "A Terror Management Analysis of the Psychological Functions of Religion." *Personality and Social Psychology Review* 14, no. 1 (2010): 84–94.
Voas, David, and Mark Chaves. "Is the United States a Counterexample to the Secularization Thesis?" *American Journal of Sociology* 121, no. 5 (2016): 1517–56.
Warner, R. Stephen. "Work in Progress Toward a New Paradigm for the Sociological Study of Religion in the United States." *American Journal of Sociology* 98, no. 5 (1993): 1044–93.
Wickham, Edward. *Church and People in an Industrial City*. London: Lutterworth Press, 1957.
Willer, Robb. "No Atheists in Foxholes: Motivated Reasoning and Religious Belief." In *Social and Psychological Bases of Ideology and System Justification*, edited by John T. Jost, Aaron C. Kay, and Hulda Thorisdottir, 241–64. New York: Oxford University Press, 2009.
Williams, Ryan J., and Fraser N. Watts. "Attributions in a Spiritual Healing Context: An Archival Analysis of a 1920s Healing Movement." *Journal for the Scientific Study of Religion* 53, no. 1 (2014): 90–108.
Williams, S. C. *Religious Belief and Popular Culture in Southwark, c. 1880–1939*. Oxford: Oxford University Press, 1999.
Wilson, Andrew. *Betjeman*. London: Arrow Books, 2006.
Wilson, Bryan R. *Sects and Society: A Sociological Study of Three Religious Groups in Britain*. London: William Heinemann, 1961.
———. "Secularization and the Survival of the Sociology of Religion." *Journal of Oriental Studies* 26, no. 1 (1987): 5–10.
Windscheffel, Ruth Clayton. "The Jezreelites and Their World, 1875–1922." In *The History of a Modern Millennial Movement: The Southcottians*, edited by J. Shaw and P. Lockley, 116–39. London: I.B. Tauris, 2017.
Yoder, Don. "Toward a Definition of Folk Religion." *Western Folklore* 33, no. 1 (1974): 2–15.
York, Michael. *The Emerging Network: A Sociology of the New Age and Neo-Pagan Movements*. Lanham: Rowman & Littlefield, 1995.
———. "New Age and the Late Twentieth Century." *Journal of Contemporary Religion* 12, no. 3 (1997): 401–18.
Young, Allan. "The Anthropologies of Illness and Sickness." *Annual Review of Anthropology* 11 (1982): 257–85.

INDEX

Adkin, Clare E., 159n28
African religion, 71–77
Ahlbäck, Tore, 77
Allan, Gordon, 17–18
alternative spirituality, 23–25, 32–44, 47–49, 80–81, 121–25; Finland, 78–79, 80; Great Britain, 44, 47, 48, 53–9, 61–62, 86–92, 103; Jamaica, 70–77, 115–19; Netherlands, 13, 34; New Age movement, 24–25, 41, 48, 53, 121–25, 130–31, 153n75; United States, 66–70
Altinordu, Ateş, 32
Anglican Church. *See* Church of England
anxiety, 85–87, 94–95, 129–30
Asprem, Egil, 34
astrology, 67, 87
Austin-Broos, Diane J., 72, 73
automatic writing, 23, 52

balmyards, 73–74, 118
baptism, 73
Barltrop, Mabel, 4, 10, 15–16, 19, 21; death, 33, 85, 114; prophecies, 22–23, 149n92, 149n96, 149n100; and spiritualism, 23, 52; theology, 25–29, 54
Barrett, Leonard, 73–74
Beckford, James A., 123

Behmenists, 16–17
Berger, Peter L., 32, 36, 38–39, 96
Besant, Annie, 54
Besecke, Kelly, 41, 127
Blavatsky, Helena Petrovna, 53–54
Bluemke, Matthias, 96
Böhme, Jakob, 16, 25, 27
Bowman, Marion, 24, 42, 121, 127, 128
British Israelism, 19–21, 78
Brothers, Richard, 19–20
Bruce, Steve, 32, 48
Byrne, Georgina, 60

Caribbean culture, 70–77, 118–19
Carroll, Anthony, 32
Chaves, Mark, 35
children, 2–3, 8, 52
Christ (Jesus Christ), 59
Christian Science, 25, 53, 55–56, 57–58, 60, 61, 62, 66, 74, 92, 114, 129, 157n72
Christianity, 31–44, 59–62, 66, 87, 125–26, 128–29
Christiano, Kevin J., 96
Church Congress (1924), 11
Church of England, 4, 6, 22–23, 59–62
colonialism, 71–72, 112–13
consumerism, 37
Cox, Harvey, 34

curingyards (balmyards), 73–74, 118

data analysis: Finland, 65–66, 158n6; Great Britain, 51–53, 56–62, 88–92, 155n2–n7; Jamaica, 63–65, 89–90; metaphysical themes, 108–20; patterns of correspondence, 44–49, 88–90; religious language, 99–107, 109–10; United States, 63–64, 89–90, 92–93
death, fear of, 39, 85–87, 94–95, 129–30
Dewhirst, Harry, 68
Dixon, Joy, 53
Durkheim, Émile, 39–40, 41

Eddy, Mary Baker, 55
Elim Pentecostalism, 104
Ervast, Pekka, 66, 77–79, 81, 102
eschatology, 4–5, 18, 19, 21, 22–23, 92–97, 102, 103. *See also* feminine, in eschatology; masculine, in eschatology
evangelism, 72–73, 75, 115–19, 160n45
evil spirits, 75–77, 106
Exeter, Helen, 21

Faith on the Home Front (Parker), 87
Fall, The, 28–29
Father, aspect of godhead. *See* masculine, aspect of godhead
female, aspect of godhead. *See* feminine, aspect of godhead; feminine, in eschatology
feminine, aspect of godhead, 17, 21, 22, 28, 99; in eschatology, xx, 16–18, 21, 22, 28–29, 47–48
feminism, 23–25
feminist theology, 18

Field, Clive D., 87
folk religion. *See* vernacular religion
Fox, Rachel, 4, 21
Freemasonry, 24
Frisk, Liselotte, 48

Gaucher, Daniella, 96–97
George V, King of Great Britain, 5–6
God. *See* feminine, aspect of godhead; masculine, aspect of godhead
Goldstein, Warren, 36
Goodwin, Emily, 10–11, 28, 33, 85, 91
Gorski, Philip S., 32
Green, Jesse, 67, 158n12

Halberstadt, Jamin, 96
Hanegraaff, Wouter, 25, 35, 41, 53, 122, 123, 124, 126
Hansen, Ian G., 96
Harrison, J. F. C., 18, 20
Hedges, Ellie, 123
Heelas, Paul, 34, 48
Hickson, James Moore, 60
Hirst, Julie, 16
Hopkins, James K., 17
House of David community (Benton Harbor), 68–70, 79, 159n28
Houtman, Dick, 34
Hughes, Brian M., 122

imperialism, 112–13
individualism, 40
influenza epidemic (1918–1919), 10
Israelism, 19–21, 68–70, 78

Jesus Christ, 59
Jezreel, James, 21, 68
Jong, Jonathan, 96
Juster, Susan, 17

Kalevala, 78–79
Kaplan, Jeffrey, 33
Kay, Aaron C., 96–97
Klein, Ruth, 133–34
Kollar, Rene, 60
Krishnamurti, 57, 103

Lambeth Conference, of 1908, 60–61, 157n72; of 1920, 60, 61, 157n72; of 1930, 157n72
Lead, Jane, 16–17, 19, 159n20
Leskelä-Kärki, Maarit, 77
Lewis, James R., 53, 124
Lockhart, Alastair, 158n6
Lockley, Philip J., 159n20
Lodge, Oliver, 54–55
Luckmann, Thomas, 36, 37–38, 113, 125–26, 153n59
Lutheranism, 66, 162n94
Lyon, David, 32–33, 41

magic, 80, 84–85
male, aspect of godhead. *See* masculine, aspect of godhead; masculine, in eschatology
Mascini, Peter, 34
masculine, aspect of godhead, 17, 21, 28; in eschatology, 21, 28
McGregor, Ian, 96–97
McGuire, Meredith B., 40, 41, 48, 121, 122–23, 153n75
McLeod, Hugh, 31–32, 41, 126
Messiah, 47–48
metaphysics, 43–44, 108–20
Millenarianism, 17–18, 20–21, 22, 68–70, 85, 95–96
Mills, Michael, 70
missionaries, 72–73, 75, 115–19, 160n45
Morris, Jeremy, 35–36, 126–27

Mother, aspect of godhead. *See* feminine, aspect of godhead
Myalism, 73
mysticism, 16–17, 27, 33, 53, 61–62

Nash, Kyle, 96–97
nationalism, 78–79, 162n94
New Age spirituality, 24–25, 41, 48, 53, 121–25, 130–31, 153n75
Niblett, Matthew, 18
Norenzayan, Ara, 96

occultism, 23–25, 53–59, 66–68
Octavia (Mabel Barltrop). *See* Barltrop, Mabel
Octavia: Daughter of God (Shaw), 10–11
Owen, Alex, 23–24, 25

Panacea Society: advertising, 9–13, 83–86, 90, 164n37; archives, xv–xix, 13–14, 135–40, 141n2; history, 4–6, 133–34; patterns of correspondence, 44–49, 51–3, 88–90; theology, 25–29, 54, 71, 79–80, 85, 87, 124–25; Towers, xviii, 78, 117
Parker, Stephen, 87
Partridge, Christopher, 34, 53, 121–22
patent medicines, 84–85
Pentecostalism, 75, 104
personal religion, xvi–xvii, 32–44, 47–49, 121–25; occultism, 23–25, 53–59; transcendence, 37–38, 41–44, 113–15, 120, 125–31. *See also* alternative spirituality
pluralism, 40
positive thinking, 124
postmodernity, 32–33, 127

Primiano, Leonard Norman, 42–43, 127
prophets, 4, 15–25
Protestantism, 72, 75, 105–6
purification, 20–21
Purnell, Benjamin, 68, 159n28
Purnell, Mary, 68–70
Puzzled People (Mass Observation report), 87

religious change, xvi–xvii, 31–49; decline of mainstream beliefs, 31–44, 59–62, 66, 87, 125–26, 128–29; Finland, 33, 162n94; Great Britain, 33–34, 53–59; Jamaica, 33, 71–77; United States, 32–33, 35
religious language, 99–107, 109–10
resurrection, 21
Revelation, 18–19
Richards, Thomas, 84
Rosicrucianism, 24
Ruusu-Risti, 77–78

salvation, 21, 25–29, 59–60, 68, 87
secularization thesis, xvi–xvii, 31–44
Seymour, Alice, 4
shamanism, 78–79
Shaw, Jane, 10–11, 24, 33–34, 41–42, 53, 56, 60, 129
Shaw, William (d. 1822), 20
Shepstone, Helen. *See* Exeter, Helen
Shiloh, 18–19, 22, 28
sin, 75
skepticism, 81, 94, 102–7
slavery, 71–72
Social Reality of Religion (Berger), 39
South Africa, 13
Southcott, Joanna, 4, 11, 16, 17–19, 20, 22–23, 28, 79
spiritual healing, 1–9, 13–14, 63–81; of children, 2–3, 8, 52; Finland, 3–4, 8–9, 12, 44, 65–66, 77–79, 80; Great Britain, 12, 13, 44, 47, 48, 51–62, 88–92; India, 112–15; Jamaica, 2–3, 7–8, 12–13, 44, 47, 48, 63–65, 70–77, 79–80, 89–90, 145n82; Panacea Society method, xv–xvi, 1–4, 27–28, 142n10, 143n34, 144n71, 144n78; scepticism and discontent, 81, 94, 102–7; theology of, 25–29, 54, 73–77, 80, 87, 121–25; United States, 2, 7, 8, 12–13, 44–45, 55, 63–64, 66–70, 79, 89–90, 92–93
spiritualism, 7, 23–25, 27, 52–55, 59, 61, 62, 66–68, 92, 103, 104, 129
Stewart, Robert J., 72, 74–75
Strange Effects of Faith, The (Southcott), 17
superstition, 87, 102
Sutcliffe, Steven, 24
Swatos, William H., 96
syncretism, 73

Taylor, Claire Rachel, 33–34, 72
Temme, Willi, 17
theodicy, 119
theology, gendered, 16–18, 21, 22, 28–9, 42, 47–49
theosophy, 3, 10, 23, 25, 53–54, 56–59, 61, 62, 63, 66, 77, 80, 92, 114, 124, 129
Thompson, E. P., 17
Towers (Panacea Society regional agents), xviii, 78, 117
transcendence, 37–38, 41–44, 113–15, 120, 125–31
Trzebiatowska, Marta, 48
Tschannen, Olivier, 37
Turner, George (d. 1821), 20

urbanization, 34

Valk, Ülo, 42, 127, 128
vernacular religion, 42–43, 78–79, 127–31. *See also* alternative spirituality
Voas, David, 35

Warner, R. Stephen, 32, 36
water rituals, 73–75, 80
water-takers. *See* spiritual healing
Watts, Fraser N., 96
West African religion, influence on Jamaica, 71–77
White, James. *See* Jezreel, James
Wickham, Edward, 87
Willer, Robb, 86

Williams, Ryan J., 96
wisdom (Sophia), 17–18
women: alternative spirituality, 23–25, 47–49; and the Fall, 28–29; eschatological role of, 16–18, 21, 28–29; feminism, 23–25; as prophets, 4, 15–19, 21
Woodhead, Linda, 34, 48
World War I, 60
World War II, 5–6, 83–97
worldviews, 37
Wroe, John, 20–21s

Yoder, Don, 42, 127

www.ingramcontent.com/pod-product-compliance
Lightning Source LLC
Chambersburg PA
CBHW070805230426
43665CB00017B/2491